# POLITICS

*and*

# GRASS

*The Administration of Grazing*

*on the Public Domain*

———————————————

# POLITICS
## and GRASS

The Administration of Grazing
on the Public Domain

**BY PHILLIP O. FOSS**

UNIVERSITY OF WASHINGTON PRESS
SEATTLE • 1960

*Grass*

Next in importance to the divine profusion of water, light, and
air, those three physical facts which render existence possible,
may be reckoned the universal beneficence of grass. Lying in
the sunshine among the buttercups and dandelions of May, scarce-
ly higher in intelligence than those minute tenants of that mimic
wilderness, our earliest recollections are of grass, and when
the fitful fever is ended, and the foolish wrangle of the market
and the forum is closed, grass heals over the scar which our de-
scent into the bosom of the earth has made, and the carpet of the
infant becomes the blanket of the dead.

Grass is the forgiveness of nature—her constant benediction.
Fields trampled with battle, saturated with blood, torn with the
ruts of cannon, grow green again with grass, and carnage is for-
gotten. Streets abandoned by traffic become green grown, like
rural lanes, and are obliterated. Forests decay, harvests perish,
flowers vanish, but grass is immortal. Beleaguered by the sullen
hosts of winter it withdraws into the impregnable fortress of its
subterranean vitality and emerges upon the solicitation of spring.
Sown by winds, by wandering birds, propagated by the subtle
horticulture of the elements which are its ministers and serv-
ants, it softens the rude outlines of the world. It invades the
solitude of deserts, climbs the inaccessible slopes and pinnacles
of mountains, and modifies the history, character, and destiny
of nations. Unobtrusive and patient, it has immortal vigor and
aggression. Banished from the thoroughfares and fields, it bides
its time to return, and when the vigilance is relaxed or the dynasty
has perished it silently resumes the throne from which it has been
expelled but which it never abdicates. It bears no blazonry of
bloom to charm the senses with fragrance or splendor, but its
homely hue is more enchanting than the lily or the rose. It yields
no fruit in earth or air, yet should its harvest fail for a single
year famine would depopulate the world.

—Senator John J. Ingalls

# ACKNOWLEDGMENTS

I most gratefully acknowledge the assistance and cooperation of Bureau of Land Management personnel in district, state, area, and national offices. They were most helpful and considerate during the many weeks I used their offices, tied up their files, and sat in on their meetings. Neither the Bureau of Land Management nor any of its officials, however, is responsible for any particular selection or arrangement of data, or for any conclusions or implications that appear in this study.

Except for the published official reports and congressional documents, most of the data cited in chapters 3 through 8 do not appear in any collection or library. Consequently, the location of letters, memoranda, minutes of meetings, and the like, have not been specifically designated. Most such data was obtained from active "working" files in Bureau of Land Management offices at different levels, from personal files of advisory board members and from correspondence with past and present advisory board members and Bureau of Land Management personnel.

I am especially grateful for the information and advice received from Milo Deming and Ed Kavanaugh of the original Division of Grazing; from stockmen and advisory board members Sam Ross, Gerald Stanfield, David T. Jones, and Donald J. MacKay; from Representatives Sam Coon of Oregon and Lee Metcalf of Montana; from Senators Dworshak of Idaho and Neuberger of Oregon; and from former BLM Director Marion Clawson.

## Acknowledgments

F. R. Carpenter, first director of the Division of Grazing, was most helpful in supplying data on the early development of the federal grazing service.

Most of all, I acknowledge the encouragement and guidance of Professor E. S. Wengert during the preparation of the study.

Phillip O. Foss

# CONTENTS

# POLITICS

*and*

# GRASS

*The Administration of Grazing*

*on the Public Domain*

# 1. PROLOGUE

The "public domain" is the landed estate of the American people. Originally it included practically all the land within the boundaries of the first forty-eight states except Texas and the original thirteen colonies. With the passage of time most of this land was transferred to private owners by means of homestead acts, grants to railroads, and various other disposal methods. The government still retained, however, a vast residue of leftover lands in the deserts and high plateaus of the arid West. This land was generally too dry, rough, or rocky for agricultural purposes. Over much of the territory west of the one hundredth meridian land itself was worthless unless that land contained a creek, spring, or other source of water. Competition for water and the scant grass and browse of this free land was chiefly responsible for the range wars and the "romantic" legend of the guntoting cowboy.

Stockmen attempted to reserve grazing rights for themselves by homesteading waterholes, by acquiring land along creeks, by checkerboard patterns of ownership, and by various other devices. These schemes all had as their objective the free and exclusive use of parts of the public domain. This kind of finagling does not necessarily imply that the early stockmen were rogues or possessed of any particularly sinister or wicked intent. Most of the land so manipulated was of such low productivity that homestead tracts were too small to provide a reasonable living. Consequently, stockmen and farmers were forced to supplement their homestead with "free land" or go bankrupt.

3

In spite of the many ingenious methods used to "reserve" federal land for private use, there was considerable land which never became stabilized into this "reserved" status. This land belonged to everyone and to no one. It was "free land." It could be used by anyone who was strong enough to take it and hold it.

There were two general results of this "free land" situation. First, squabbles over range and water continued interminably and even the most powerful operators lived an uncertain economic existence. Second, the "free land" *had* to result in overgrazing. Cattlemen and sheepmen could not be expected to withhold stock from government range to prevent overgrazing when they knew that other stockmen would get the grass they left. Overgrazing permitted an accelerated rate of erosion by removing the forage that held moisture and soil. Erosion of soil led to still greater erosion with the result that the carrying capacity of the range decreased and floods and desert land increased.

Overgrazing caused millions of acres of grassland to become desert. Lands which produced native grasses "up to your stirrups" within the lifetime of persons now living became, and remain today, virtual deserts. The Department of Agriculture reported in 1936, "a range once capable of supporting 22.5 million animal units [an animal unit was one cow or horse or five sheep or goats] can now carry only 10.8 million." This meant that the forage capacity of the western range had been reduced by more than one half.

To remedy the evils of unrestricted competition for the range and consequent overgrazing and soil erosion, Congress passed the Taylor Grazing Act in 1934. By that year all of the most desirable land had become privately owned, but there still remained approximately 170,000,000 acres of government land. In 1934 this was still open range—the open range of cutthroat competition and extreme overgrazing.

The purposes of the Taylor Grazing Act as set forth in the act itself were "to preserve the land and its resources from destruction or unnecessary injury, to provide for the orderly use, improvement and development of the range." To carry out these broad purposes the act authorized the Secretary of Interior to establish grazing districts and to make provisions for the protection, administration, regulation, and improvement of such districts.

This study outlines the history of the public domain and goes on to a more detailed examination of the formation and administration of public policy for the control and regulation of the federal range under the Taylor Grazing Act. Formation and administration of policy are not, of course, separate functions or processes. The mode of policy administration determines the meaning and effect of past policy decisions and influences future decisions. Public policy is understood to mean a decision, or series of decisions, which determine the intensity, course, and direction of governmental activity. The formation of public policy is primarily concerned with *what* will or will not be done. Administration has traditionally been concerned with *how* things are done—with the methods and techniques for the execution of policy. However, if the execution of policy is itself a part of the policy-forming process, then administration must also be involved in policy development. Within the purview of this study, the term "politics" is defined as the process of forming public policy. In those areas where administration is involved in policy determinations it therefore becomes engaged in politics.

A list of the factors which might conceivably effect the formation of public policy would be endless. Some of the factors which are commonly influential in policy development may be categorized as: the physical environment (topography, climate, vegetation, and so forth); the social environment of decision-makers (class, status, wealth, traditions, and the like); the level of available technical knowledge and the status of technicians; and the institutions organized for the purpose of developing and formalizing public policy (political parties, interest groups, legislative bodies, courts, and the bureaucracy).

Some of the implications of the preceding four categories for the development of grazing policy are summarized below.

*Physical environment* is not a constant. Within limits, man changes his physical environment to suit his needs and desires. In the past, most of these changes have occurred on an *ad hoc* basis without any long-range, coordinated planning. Large-scale changes in man's physical environment have ordinarily been accompanied by a public policy (developed through a political process) which encouraged or allowed the change to take place.

*The social environment* of decision-makers has of course conditioned the political process and the policies developed from it. The social environment of political elites not only has helped shape policies and institutions, but has acted to reshape existing institutions and to adapt legally formalized policies to fit the demands of the most influential publics.

*The level of technical data* or scientific knowledge determines in large part the recognition of dangers and opportunities in the physical and social environment and the facilities and methods available to apply to these previously recognized situations. Not only is the level of scientific knowledge important but the degree to which that knowledge is accepted may in a given situation be more significant than the level of the knowledge itself. The degree of acceptance, and indeed the level of knowledge, is likely to be determined by an existing public policy.

When technological conflicts arise or when technical data are suspect or inadequate, the problem is ordinarily resolved through a political process. When the status of "science" is high, values and belief systems may be rationalized and defended on the basis of "scientific fact." In these instances value conflicts may appear as technological conflicts—which may again be resolved through a political process.

In our society we ordinarily think of legally constituted legislative bodies as the *policy-forming institutions*. Certainly legislatures perform this function, but they do so along with and in relation to other institutions. In many instances policy may have actually been developed in the courts, by interest groups, by an administrative agency, or by a combination thereof. In these instances, legislatures act primarily as enunciators of policies already developed. The formal pronouncements of legislative bodies are, in the words of Norman Wengert, likely to be like icebergs: "more of the real substance lies hidden beneath the surface than is immediately evident in the language of the law."[1]

Because of the diversity of American society, the nature of

the legislative committee system, and the phenomenon of weak political parties and strong interest groups, we have developed a multiplicity of specialized policy-making subsystems. Each of these subsystems operates within the broad confines of the generally accepted mores of the society, but within these limits it tends to be self-governing. The principal policy-makers in such a subsystem ordinarily include some members of the congressional committees most directly involved, leaders of the interest groups affected and senior officers of the administering agency. One such subsystem is concerned with the grazing activity on the federal range. By examining the methods used by this group in the formation and execution of grazing policy on the public range we are enabled to consider, in a realistic continuum, the factors which shape a public policy.

This study is an extended case history of the development of public policy for the administration of grazing on the public lands of the United States. These lands have little economic value at present, but they will become increasingly important as agricultural technology develops and as population pressure increases. The methods and techniques used in the formation of grazing administration policy are not at all unique. They may, in fact, be fairly typical of the mode of public policy formation in the United States.

# 2. THE PUBLIC DOMAIN

The total extent of public domain acquired by the United States within the boundaries of the first forty-eight states was approximately 1, 400, 000, 000 acres of land. This chapter is concerned with the methods by which this land was acquired, the policies under which most of it was transferred to private ownership, and the effects of these policies on the people and lands of the arid West.

## Acquisition

The public domain originally included all the land that was at any time owned by the government of the United States and that was available for sale, grant, or other disposition. National parks, Indian reservations, national forests, and the like were the property of the federal government, but they were not considered to be public domain because they had been set aside, or "reserved, " for a particular purpose and were withdrawn (at least temporarily) from the possibility of transfer of ownership from the federal government. In brief, the public domain was a commons awaiting transfer to a more specific owner or to a specific federal purpose.

The first land to become public domain was an area west of the Appalachian Mountains which was "ceded" to the infant government of the United States by seven of the original thirteen colonies.[1] This area included the present-day states of Ohio, Indiana, Illinois, Michigan, Wisconsin, Alabama, Mis-

sissippi, Tennessee, and parts of Pennsylvania and Minnesota.[2]

Beginning as early as the Revolutionary War period, six
states with clearly defined boundaries,[3] had protested the
claims of the larger states to this territory because it would
restrict them to their definite boundary lines, while the larger
states could become larger still by expanding to the west.
Maryland maintained in the Continental Congress, in 1779,
that if these lands should be taken from the British by the
"common blood and treasure of the thirteen states" they should
then be parceled out into "free, convenient, and independent
governments, in such manner and at such times" as the Congress should decide.[4] Maryland further declared that she would
not become a signatory to the Articles of Confederation until
the states claiming western lands had relinquished such claims
to the federal government.

By 1780 New York had relinquished her claims to western
lands. Virginia followed suit in 1784 and by 1802 the remaining five states had ceded their western lands.

The United States in 1803 purchased French claims to the
Mississippi and its western drainage system. By this purchase
almost one third of the present land area of the United States
was acquired. This area, nearly one million square miles, vir-
tually doubled the size of the United States. The Louisiana Purchase contained all or parts of the present states of Louisiana,
Arkansas, Missouri, Iowa, Minnesota, North Dakota, South
Dakota, Nebraska, Kansas, Oklahoma, Colorado, Wyoming,
and Montana. The total cost to the United States, $27,000,000
was about five cents per acre.

Spain had held what is now the state of Florida from the days
of the early explorers and had unsuccessfully attempted colonization. Fearful of the growing power of the United States,
and discouraged by her unsuccessful attempts at colonization,
Spain sold its Florida territory to the United States in 1819
for about $6,500,000. The Florida territory added another
72,000 square miles to the United States at a cost of about
fifteen cents per acre.

After the prosecution of a successful military campaign
against Mexico, that country, in 1848, ceded to the United
States a vast area in the Pacific Southwest which included the

present states of California, Nevada, and Utah and parts of New Mexico, Arizona, Colorado, and Wyoming. Ultimately Mexico received about $16, 000, 000 for this territory or approximately five cents per acre.

Texas had also been Mexican territory but had been settled by Americans. These Americans successfully revolted against Mexico, and in 1836, Texas declared itself an independent state. Texas was admitted into the Union in 1845, but since she had been an independent republic rather than a dependent territory she had a stronger bargaining position than states admitted from a territorial status. As a consequence, the new state of Texas was able to retain title to the public lands within her boundaries. No part of the state of Texas, therefore, has ever been public domain as we have defined it. Texas also claimed lands which were outside the present boundaries of the state. To satisfy these claims, the United States in 1850 purchased from Texas an area of approximately 123, 270 square miles. Included were southwestern Kansas, central Colorado, eastern New Mexico, part of Wyoming, and the panhandle of Oklahoma. Texas received about $16, 000, 000, or approximately nineteen cents per acre, for this territory.

The last big acquisition of territory in what became the first forty-eight states was the addition of the present states of Washington, Idaho, and Oregon. By agreement with Great Britain the boundary between Canada and the United States was set at the forty-ninth parallel in 1846. Further territorial disagreements in this area were finally resolved in 1872 through the mediation of the German Emperor.

Finally, the United States purchased an area of about 30, 000 square miles in southern Arizona and southern New Mexico from Mexico. Mexico received $10, 000, 000 or about fifty-three cents per acre.

By these acquisitions the original thirteen colonies expanded to the present dimensions of the first forty-eight states. Inadvertently omitted by these various purchases and treaties were three pieces of "No Man's Land, " which lay outside the boundaries of any purchases and cessions. These patches were "pieced in" by treaty with Great Britain in 1818, with Spain in 1819, and with the Ute Indians in 1868.[5]

The total extent of public domain acquired by the government within the forty-eight states was approximately 1, 400, 000, 000 acres of land (Table 1). The cost in money payment was about

TABLE 1

ACQUISITION OF THE PUBLIC DOMAIN

| How Acquired | Acres | Cost of Acquisition |
|---|---|---|
| State cessions (1781-1802) | 233, 415, 680 | $ 6, 200, 000 |
| Louisiana Purchase (1803) | 523, 446, 400 | 23, 213, 568 |
| Red River Basin | 29, 066, 880 | - |
| Cession from Spain (1819) | 43, 342, 720 | 6, 674, 057 |
| Oregon Compromise (1846) | 180, 644, 480 | - |
| Mexican Cession (1848) | 334, 479, 360 | 16, 295, 149 |
| Purchase from Texas (1850) | 78, 842, 880 | 15, 496, 448 |
| Gadsden Purchase (1853) | 18, 961, 920 | 10, 000, 000 |
| TOTAL | 1, 442, 200, 320 | $77, 879, 222 |

Source: Marion Clawson, *The Public Domain in 1953*, Department of the Interior, Bureau of Land Management, p. 2.

$78, 000, 000, or about five and one half cents per acre. The United States acquired title to this domain subject to the occupancy rights of the Indians. The story of how the white man wrested these lands from the Indians has been told and retold and need not concern us here.

The states formed from the various acquisitions were given no title to the public lands within their borders, and they had no voice in their administration. Until disposed of, the public lands belonged to the nation, with Congress alone responsible for their administration or disposal.[6] Stated in another way, the public land states had never owned any part of the public domain and waived any claims they might have had to such public lands when they were admitted to statehood.

### Disposal of the Public Domain

During the nineteenth century most of the original public domain was transferred to private ownership. The details of this transfer cannot be considered here, but a brief review of the major lands disposal policies seems necessary and appropriate.

*Land Sales*

The infant nation, still under the Articles of Confederation, was in desperate need of revenue. One possible source was in the sale of public lands.

The Northwest Ordinance of 1785 provided for sale of land in fee simple—that is, the buyer got complete control of the land and could dispose of it as he wished. The lands were to be sold at auction to the highest bidder. Half the lands were to be sold in units of 640 acres (a section or one mile square) and one half in units of 23, 040 acres (a township or six miles square). The minimum price acceptable was set at one dollar per acre. [7]

While these minimum quantities and minimum prices may not seem unreasonable today, they were unreasonable at that time if the purpose was to encourage settlement and provide an opportunity for farmers to acquire land at low cost. It appears, therefore, that the ordinance was drafted to provide revenue and to encourage land speculation. The need for revenue and the greed and influence of land speculators combined to form a federal land disposal policy of settlement through land speculators. In fact the Congress of the Confederation did not even adhere to the provisions of the ordinance, but contracted to sell several million acres at prices of eight to nine cents per acre to land speculators—some of whom were members of the Congress.

In 1790-91 Alexander Hamilton published an analysis of the nation's resources and economic prospects. Hamilton was especially interested in finding means for providing revenue for the federal government. He believed that the success of the new nation depended upon the development of an industrial economy, as opposed to the agrarian democracy envisioned by Jefferson. [8] Hamilton therefore contended that the sale of public lands, rather than free land grants, would provide some revenue and at the same time would act to discourage people from moving away from industrial areas and thus reduce the supply of cheap labor needed for infant industries.

Opposed to this policy was a group, usually identified with

Jefferson, who wished to promote an agricultural economy by providing for the easy acquisition of land by prospective farmer-settlers.

Possibly because of the poor financial condition of the government, the Hamiltonian contingent won out in the passage of another land disposal act in 1796. This act raised the minimum price to two dollars per acre and again set the minimum sales unit at 640 acres. Purchasers were allowed one year's time in which to complete payment. Certainly this last was not much of an inducement. During the four-year life of the act only 49, 000 acres of land were sold.[9]

Although settlers were not buying land in any quantity during this period there was a large number of squatters who simply went out and found uninhabited land which suited them and "settled" upon it. These people intended to stay on the land and, in the words of Governor St. Clair of the Northwest Territory, "very considerable difficulty" might attend any attempt to remove them.[10]

In 1800 a greatly liberalized land bill was enacted. The new law retained the minimum two dollars per acre price but it reduced the minimum unit of sale to 320 acres and extended payment over a four-year period. Provisions were also included for the establishment of land offices near the frontier. In 1804 the minimum unit of sale was lowered to 160 acres.[11]

In 1812 the General Land Office was established, as a unit in the Treasury Department, to administer land surveys and sales. It remained in the Treasury Department until 1849, when it became a unit of the newly established Department of Interior. It remained a separate organization, however, until 1946, when it was consolidated with the Grazing Service to form the present Bureau of Land Management.[12]

The credit system of land sales continued until 1820 but was considered to be generally unsatisfactory because of the difficulty in collecting balances due and the high percentage of lands that were allowed to revert back to the government.

Following the panic year of 1819, the Land Act of 1820 abolished the credit system, reduced the minimum unit of sale to eighty acres, and reduced the minimum price to $1.25 per acre.

Higher minimum prices were later established for certain

classes of land and in 1854 a system of graduation of the minimum statutory price was established. Under this act some
lands that had remained unsold for a long period were valued
at prices as low as twelve and one half cents per acre. About
25, 000, 000 acres were sold under the Price Graduation Act
until its repeal in 1862.

Supposedly these land sale acts were established to provide
revenue for the federal treasury. In this purpose they had only
limited success. During the whole twenty-four-year period
from 1796 to 1820 the federal government collected only
$27, 900, 379 from the sale of public lands. This was the period
when revenues were most urgently needed. In the forty-six-
year period from 1796 to 1842 total receipts amounted to only
$122, 172, 013. From 1842 to 1862 total receipts from land
sales amounted to $64, 125, 589.[13]

It seems evident that the earlier land sale acts were designed primarily as aids to land speculators, as methods to
prevent the movement of cheap labor out of industrial areas,
and as a method for supporting the prices of eastern lands.
Later modifications of these acts came as a result of the increased political pressures which western states and territories were able to exert. Certainly there existed no real plan
for the orderly settlement of the western frontier.

*Land Grants*

As we have seen, during the early days of the republic the
government was short on cash and long on land. At the same
time that lands were being sold, substantial amounts were
given away in the form of grants for military service, for
education, and for internal improvements.

Military bounties were first used in the Revolutionary War
to induce soldiers to desert from the British army. Later,
land bounties were granted to induce Americans to enlist in
the Continental Army. Colonels were promised five hundred
acres with lesser amounts being offered according to rank.
Other bounty acts were passed for the War of 1812 and the
Mexican War. Beginning in 1850 a series of acts liberalized
military bounties to include grants to any soldier or his heirs
who had been on active duty for a period of fourteen days or
more in any war in which the United States had been engaged.

An act of 1852 made these "warrants" assignable and they became the subject of much speculative exchange. For some
years "warrants were quoted in the stock exchange reports
along with stocks and bonds."[14] The total acreage disposed
of by the military bounty acts was about 68,000,000 acres.[15]

If the purpose of these military bounty acts was to provide
farms for ex-soldiers, they were unsuccessful.

> The Commissioner of the General Land Office . . . wrote . . .
> "The files and records of this office show that not one in five hundred
> of the land warrants issued and placed in the hands of the soldiers or
> their heirs have been located by them, or for their use and benefit
> . . . the most part having been used by persons to acquire title to the
> public lands for speculation purposes."[16]

The states' rights issue, real or rationalized, has been with
us since colonial days. So too with states' rights to public lands.
Beginning with the ordinances of 1785 and 1787 the states received land grants to help support schools. Ordinarily these
grants were made to new states upon admittance to the Union.
The first such grants gave the states one section in each township. This was later increased to two and eventually to four
sections per township. The states also received a large va-
riety of grants for higher education and other state-supported
institutions. "Directly and indirectly the government gave over
a hundred million acres of land for educational purposes."[17]

Beginning in 1823, grants to states for internal improvements
became a common practice. The first of this series was grants
for wagon road purposes. From 1828 to 1869 over 3,000,000
acres were transferred to the states for this purpose. The
wagon road lands were granted to the states to defray the cost
of road construction. In some instances the states simply
transferred the lands to construction companies as payment
for building the roads.

The same principles and general methods were used in making grants to states for canal construction and river improvement. The distribution and extent of canal and river grants
are shown on the following page.[18]

A more general plan of grants to states for internal improvements was embodied in an act of 1841. This act provided
for grants of 500,000 acres each to public land states. Eighteen
states received grants under this plan.[19]

*Canal Grants*

|           | *Acres*        |
|-----------|----------------|
| Indiana   | 1, 480, 408. 87 |
| Ohio      | 1, 204, 113. 89 |
| Michigan  | 1, 251, 235. 85 |
| Wisconsin | 338, 626. 97   |
| Illinois  | 324, 282. 74   |
| Total     | 4, 598, 668. 32 |

*River Improvement Grants*

|           | *Acres*        |
|-----------|----------------|
| Alabama   | 400, 016. 19   |
| Wisconsin | 683, 722. 43   |
| Iowa      | 1, 161, 513. 69 |
| Total     | 2, 245, 252. 31 |

These acts established a precedent for granting lands for railroad construction. However, grants of lands to states for roads, canals, and river improvements was not the same thing as granting lands to private railroad companies. Naturally, proposals for railroad grants met with considerable opposition.

One of the arguments advanced by proponents of the scheme was that the government would increase the value of its remaining holdings by reason of the proximity of a railroad. Thus John C. Calhoun, in 1846, reasoned that by granting alternate sections to a railroad, the government would more than double the value of the remaining sections and also would be able to sell them more quickly.

By 1850 congressional views on grants to railroads had softened enough to enable Senator Stephen A. Douglas of Illinois and others to carry through to enactment the first railroad grant to the Illinois Central Railroad.

Other railroad grants followed. About 15, 000, 000 acres were donated to railroads in 1856 and about 5, 000, 000 acres in 1857. The big grants, however, came after the secession of the South, when grants for the transcontinental railroads

were approved. These grants were considerably more gen-
erous than those previously donated—twenty sections per mile
on both sides of the track was common in the territories.
Grants to states for railroad purposes totaled 37, 789, 169
acres. Direct grants to private railway companies totaled
91, 239, 389 acres.[20] In addition to the federal grants cited
above, the state of Texas also donated 32, 153, 878 acres for
railway construction.[21] By the time of passage of the Taylor
Grazing Act (1934) the railroads had disposed of about five
sixths of their original holdings.[22]

As they relate to range resources, the railroad grants had
three significant effects: the coming of the railroad encouraged
the sale or homesteading and plowing up of much range land
that was unsuitable for farming; large holdings by railroad
companies encouraged land sales in larger blocks than would
otherwise have been feasible; and checkerboard patterns of
railroad landownership encouraged such land patterns by
ranchers. In the West Calhoun's predictions did not always
work out. The rancher bought the checkerboard railroad sections and grazed his cattle without charge on the alternate
sections of public domain, usually making them worthless to
anyone else.

The state of Louisiana had spent several million dollars con-
structing levees along the Mississippi. As a consequence some
3, 000, 000 acres of federal land had been reclaimed and sold
with the proceeds going into the federal treasury. Louisiana
contemplated additional work of this nature and applied to
Congress for financial assistance. Congress obliged with the
Swamp Land Act of 1849, which granted to Louisiana "the
whole of those swamps or overflowed lands, which may be or
are, found unfit for cultivation."[23] With Louisiana grants as
a precedent the measure was soon expanded to include all the
public land states. Very little land reclamation resulted from
these grants. Much of the land transferred to the states was
not "swampy" or in need of reclaiming in the first place. The
states, in turn, conveyed large amounts of land to railroads
and other companies for only token efforts at drainage or other
reclamation. Fraudulent collusion with state officials was commonplace in the disposal of the 64, 000, 000 acres of land transferred under the swamp land grants.[24]

Desert land grants to states were next on the list of land donations. The Carey Act of 1894 provided that quantities of land be donated to certain states on condition that it be irrigated, settled, and in part cultivated.[25] About 14,000,000 acres were made available for state reclamation purposes. Altogether the federal government has donated over 200,000,000 acres to the states, 168,000,000 acres in military bounties, and 91,000,000 acres to railroads.

Arizona, New Mexico, South Dakota, and Washington still retain most of their original grants. On the other hand, California, Kansas, Nevada, Oklahoma, and Oregon have disposed of most of the lands granted to them. In the western range states, with which we are primarily concerned, state land grants were usually scattered in small blocks. The usual practice was to designate sections 16 and 36 of each township as school land. In Arizona, New Mexico, and Utah, sections 2 and 32 were also so designated.[26]

While this system may have had advantages in the humid East, it acted to prevent sound range management practices in the arid West. According to Lyle F. Watts:

> The handling of State range land has been based almost wholly on a desire to secure the maximum current revenue. Sale of the maximum acreage has been encouraged without regard for the fitness of the land for private ownership. Leasing has usually been with a view to securing the greatest possible price. No provision has been made for the protection of the range and watershed resources through wise management.[27]

## Pre-emption

> ". . . they will settle the lands in spite of everybody."—Jefferson, 1776.[28]

We have previously noted that frontiersmen frequently appropriated desirable pieces of public land and lived on them as if they were their own property. These "squatters," throughout the years, had pressed for legislation which would legalize or confirm their "rights." Often they were squatters only because of the slowness of Congress in appropriating money for land surveys which often lagged far behind settlement.[29] The first act to acknowledge the claims of the squatters was the Pre-emption Act of 1830.

The term "pre-emption" meant an arrangement by which the person who occupied public land was given a preference or option to purchase that land over other potential purchasers. The 1830 act was temporary and applied only to settlers who had cultivated public domain land in 1829. Such persons could enter up to 160 acres of such land at the minimum price of $1.25 per acre. With this act as a precedent, similar bills were passed in 1832, 1835, 1838, and again in 1840.

By this time pre-emption had become a national issue. After a stormy session, the Pre-emption Act of 1841 was finally passed. The basic provision of the act was that henceforth an individual could legally go out on the public domain and stake out a claim to the exclusion of others. The maximum amount of land allowed was again 160 acres to be paid for at the minimum price of $1.25 per acre.

The pre-emption acts marked the beginning of the end of the old policy of land disposal for revenue. They encouraged the transfer of land to actual settlers rather than to speculators and in small amounts so as to extend the landowning privilege to a maximum number of people. Finally, the pre-emption acts laid the groundwork for the homestead acts that were to follow.

## Homesteads

"Whenever there are in any country uncultivated lands and un-employed poor, it is clear that the laws of property have been so far extended as to violate natural rights."—Jefferson[30]

The Hamiltonian notion that the principal function of the public domain should be to provide revenue had persisted throughout the history of public land policies even though there had been large amounts of land donated by the government prior to the passage of the Homestead Act of 1862. This measure reversed the trend, although it continues to some extent today.

The Homestead Act was the culmination of a long struggle for free land which began in colonial times. As early as 1797 settlers on the Ohio had asked for four hundred acres for each family. [31]

By 1825 Senator Thomas Benton of Missouri moved to instruct the Committee on Public Lands to make inquiry into "the

expediency of donating land to settlers." According to Benton,
"no country under the sun was ever paid for in gold and sil-
ver before it could be settled and cultivated."[32] Senator Benton pulled out all the stops in the following burst of oratory:

> I say give without price to those who are not able to pay; and that
> which is so given I consider as sold for the best of prices; for a price
> above gold and silver; a price which cannot be carried away by de-
> linquent officers, nor lost in failing banks, nor stolen by thieves, nor
> squandered by an improvident and extravagent administration. It brings
> a price above rubies—a race of virtuous and independent farmers, the
> true supporters of their country, and the stock from which its best
> defenders must be drawn.[33]

Representative Orlando B. Ficklin of Illinois also became
lyrical in his support of a homestead act:

> Unless the government shall grant head rights, or donations of
> some kind, these prairies, with their gorgeous growth of flowers,
> their green carpeting, their lovely lawns and gentle slopes, will for
> centuries continue to be the home of the wild deer and wolf; their
> stillness will be undisturbed by the jocund song of the farmer, and
> their deep and fertile soil unbroken by the ploughshare. Something
> must be done to remedy this evil.[34]

By 1848 a Free Soil Party had been organized in support of
"free [land] grants to actual settlers."[35]

In the 1851-52 session of Congress, Andrew Johnson of Tennessee introduced a homestead bill which passed the House
but was defeated in the Senate. This was the first time a homestead act had come to a vote in Congress. The vote in the
Senate showed the beginnings of southern opposition which was
to stymie passage of a homestead act until after the secession
of the South. By this time the plantation system of the South
appeared to have reached its economic limits. Any further
expansion, and especially expansion by immigrants from northern Europe who settled mainly in the North, would redound to
the benefit of the antislave states. Therefore, as time went on,
the homestead bills came to be considered "abolition" bills
by southern congressmen.

In each session of Congress from 1851 to 1862 homestead
bills were introduced and defeated. A bill was finally passed
in 1860 but was vetoed by President Buchanan.

While Buchanan's veto placated the South, it raised a storm of protest among Democrats in the West and provided the best possible campaign material for the young and growing Republican party. The *Dubuque* (Iowa) *Herald* commented:

Last Saturday the old reprobate, who now sits in the Presidential chair at Washington vetoed the Homestead Bill. This act fills up the measure of James Buchanan's recreancy to Democratic principles—it is one of the most infamous of his infamous administration. The slave propagandists demanded that the Bill should be vetoed, and their pliant tool was swift to obey them. Let the pimps and hirelings of the old sinner defend this last act of his, if they dare—Let them come before the masses of the people with "Old Buck's" veto of the Homestead Bill on their banner, and ask the people to vote for his and the nigger traders' candidate for President. They dare not do it. [36]

The main issue in the election of 1860 was the slavery issue, but in the West especially, homesteading was a question of paramount importance. We have noticed that the political connection between homesteading and abolition was such that one could not be considered without the other. To westerners, however, homesteading was a vital issue in itself apart from the slavery question. Consequently the Republican platform of 1860 carried a strong homestead provision which undoubtedly won many western voters for the party.

With the election of Lincoln, southern secession, and the absence of the southern delegation from Congress, the next homestead bill encountered little opposition. It passed the House by a vote of 105 to 18 and the Senate by a vote of 33 to 7, the negatives coming from the border states. [37] On May 20, 1862, President Lincoln signed the bill.

In brief, the original Homestead Act provided that any citizen, or any person who had officially filed notice of intention to become a citizen, and who was twenty-one years of age (or younger if the head of a family), could acquire title to 160 acres of surveyed public land by paying a small filing fee, making certain improvements and maintaining his residence on the property for five years. [38]

This was the first law to provide free land with settlement as the main requirement for obtaining title. As such it was

probably the most significant land policy measure enacted in
the United States. Altogether almost 1,500,000 homesteaders
acquired over 200,000,000 acres of land under this act. These
figures indicate only the homesteads that were finally "proved-
up." Many original entries never went to patent. People became ill, discouraged, or for other reasons relinquished their
claims. Quite often, in the range region, the person who filed
on a homestead had no intention of making any improvements.
He would retain control of the property as long as possible
and then repeat the process on a different tract. In the meantime his friends or relatives could file on the old homestead. [39]
In 1865 original homestead entries totaled 1,160,500 acres. [40]
Five years later, when they would have become eligible for
transfer of title, only 519,727 acres went to patent. [41]

According to Clawson, "About 150 million acres were entered upon in the 1880's, but apparently only 30 to 40 million
acres of this were patented. The wave of homesteading after
1900 resulted in about half of the land so entered upon going
to final patent." [42]

A commutation clause in the act gave the homesteader the
right to buy his homestead from the government, after establishing residence, at the regular $1.25 or $2.50 per acre
pre-emption price. Prior to June 30, 1880, not over 4 per
cent of the homestead entries were so terminated, but from
1881 to 1904 about 23 per cent were commuted. [43] The land
was commuted by persons who wished to harvest the timber
on it; by those who had originally filed with the intention of
commuting and reselling; and by those who had tried to make
a living on 160 acres of arid land, failed, and commuted and
resold to salvage what they could from what had been a bad
bargain in the beginning.

By 1881 the wave of settlement had passed the hundredth
meridian and, to a large extent, the 160-acre homestead law
was no longer practical. In fact, the 160-acre limit may have
been out of date at the time of passage of the act. In the words
of Hibbard:

The great weakness of the Homestead Act was, and is, its utter
inadaptibility to the parts of the country for which it was not designed.

The idea of the farm small in acres within the semi-arid regions was tenacious, but untenable. It was even vicious in its operation. [44]

Although the homestead law was not nullified until the passage of the Taylor Grazing Act, several attempts were made to devise more realistic methods for disposing of the public domain in the arid West.

### The Timber Culture Act

The first of these modifications was the Timber Culture Act of 1873. This law provided that any person who would plant forty acres of timber with trees not more than twelve feet apart and keep them in a healthy growing condition for ten years would receive title to the quarter-section of which the forty acres was a part. Only one quarter in any section was to be obtained in this manner. [45]

While a plan to cover the plains with trees may seem impractical today, it probably seemed reasonable enough to congressmen from the states of the humid East who comprised most of the Congress in 1873. It soon became evident, however, that the law was impractical and an invitation to fraud. Nine years after its passage the act was repealed—but not before 9,856,264 acres had been transferred to private ownership and an additional 1,010,624 acres commuted. It is significant that, of the 10,000,000 acres transferred under the Timber Culture Act, almost 8,000,000 acres went to final entry in the treeless states of Kansas, Nebraska, North and South Dakota. [46] In the words of Hibbard, "It was one of the most complete failures, so far as accomplishing what Congress had in mind is concerned, to be recorded in the long list of unfortunate public land acts. "[47]

### The Desert Land Act

By 1877 some congressmen realized that large areas in the West were unsuited to cultivation because of lack of water. They used essentially the same method in attempting to solve this problem as they had done in the problem of the treeless plains. In the latter instance they had simply offered free land to persons who agreed to plant trees. With regard to the desert lands, the problem seemed equally simple: offer desert land to

persons who would irrigate it. Consequently Congress passed
the Desert Land Act, which provided that a settler might purchase one section (640 acres) of land provided he would irrigate it within three years after filing.

The Desert Land Act was the first of the land laws to recognize that an acre of land in the arid West would not produce as
much as an acre in the humid East. Apparently recognizing this
fact, Congress increased the acreage to 640 acres. But it added
the stipulation that the land must be irrigated. The efficient irrigation of 640 acres by one man is impractical today with all
the most modern machinery at his disposal. It was a fantastic
requirement in 1877. Furthermore, the settler was unlikely to
have the capital necessary to install such an irrigation system.
Even if he had the capital there was usually no source of water.
Consequently, over great areas, the act became a farce and
one other way of acquiring public land by going through a sense-
less ritual. According to the Commissioner of the General
Land Office, some cattle companies contracted with themselves
to build irrigation ditches from points where no water existed
to other points where the topography would have prevented irrigation even if there had been any water in the ditches.[48]

It should be noted that the Desert Land Act was not a homestead act but a conditional sale act. At the same time that the
government was giving away land that theoretically could produce crops, it also offered for sale land that supposedly could
not produce crops for $1.25 per acre. As a result many peo-
ple paid the twenty-five cents per acre entry fee and held it for
three years before relinquishing it to some friend or partner
who went through the same process—so much of the land on
which entries were made never was transferred under the act.
The figures bear out this statement: a total of 32,464,599
acres were originally entered but of this total only 8,380,652
acres were purchased.[49] It seems safe to assume that these
8,000,000 acres were either key tracts for range purposes
or were tillable (not desert) lands. On the whole the law was
almost a complete failure because of unavailability of water.[50]

## The Kincaid Act
Probably the first congressional act to consider disposal
of public land for grazing purposes was the Kincaid Act of

1904. This was limited and special legislation in that it applied only to about 8,000,000 acres in northwestern Nebraska. The terms of the act were similar to the Homestead Act of 1862, except that the amount of land was increased to 640 acres in recognition of the fact that this territory had been open for settlement for a quarter of a century or more and had been passed over by homesteaders because it was unsuited for cultivation. The few homesteaders who had filed in the area were allowed to add three quarter-sections more to the quarter-section they already had. The 640-acre unit was a sort of "guesstimate" of the amount of land needed in that particular area for a successful operation. Within ten years after the passage of the act all but a quarter million acres of this land was entered.[51] Apparently this act was successful.

*The Enlarged Homestead Act*

Partly under the impetus of the successful Kincaid Act a similar law was enacted in 1909 to apply to nine public land states and territories. In this act, however, the amount of land was reduced to 320 acres. This was only half the amount allowed under the Kincaid Act, but it was twice the amount allowed under the old Homestead Act; Congress probably felt it was making a radical departure from established policy.

In the meantime a system of dry farming had become popular. Various systems of dry farming had, of course, been practiced for hundreds of years, but no such methods had been used extensively in the United States until after the turn of the century. About 1900 the summer-fallow system was popularized and publicized. The system consists, briefly, of alternating patches of land each year between cropping and fallow. This method makes it possible to conserve enough moisture so that some lands too dry to produce crops every year are enabled to do so in alternate years. Secretary of the Interior Franklin K. Lane described this dry-farming method as "the most valuable discovery made in recent years as affecting the public domain."[52]

As a consequence of the success of the dry-farming method thousands of homesteads were entered on land that had been passed over by earlier homesteaders. Some of these new dry-farming homesteads were successful, but most were failures.

Hundreds of square miles of range land were plowed up and later abandoned. Thousands of deserted shacks and rusty windmills dotted the plains and symbolized the blasted hopes and wasted years of homesteaders who had tried to make range land into crop land. The human cost was high and the destruction of the range was a tremendous loss, not only to the stockmen of that day but to the succeeding stockmen for years to come. This range destruction hurt the stockmen directly, and it also removed the moisture-retaining grass cover and resulted in accelerated erosion.

Because of the constant complaints from homesteaders and the high percentage of relinquishments of homesteads before final proof, Congress amended the act in 1912 reducing from five to three years the time required to perfect an entry.[53]

According to Webb, this reduction in time was an improvement over the old law:

> This act seemed to grow out of the realization that on the remaining land the average family could not hold out for five years. The point of starvation was reached short of that, and consequently it would be humane to shorten the required time of residence to three years.[54]

The logic of this assertion and of the Congress which passed the law is questionable. Neither the 160-acre homestead nor the enlarged homestead was impractical in the West because of the length of the residence period. Both were impractical because the acreage involved in them was too small to support a grazing operation, and the land was generally unfit for anything else. Reducing the period of residence did not cause the rain to fall or crops to grow. About all it could do would be to transfer title to the homesteader sooner so he could sell and get out.

### Grazing Homesteads

The high casualty rate among homesteaders did not deter other millions of innocents from filing new homestead claims. As the years passed the western range was being steadily fenced off and pushed back. During this same period stockmen had sponsored bills to allow leasing of federal lands and prevent or minimize homesteading.[55] But Congressmen still clung to a sort of sentimental belief in homesteading and to suspicion of the western cattle "barons" who had used the range so long.

At the same time Congress finally realized that the existing homestead acts were no longer practical—if they ever had been. Consequently, the size of homesteads was increased to 640 acres in the Stockraising Homestead Act of 1916.

Once again, Congress had acted too late with too little. The enlarged homestead (320 acres) would have been a practical acreage at one period in the settlement of the West but by the time of passage that period had passed, and the acreage was inadequate. Later on a 640-acre homestead might have been practical but when the act was finally passed it was again too late. In 1916 the remaining public land was generally of such low productivity that 640 acres was inadequate to support a family.

The act is particularly significant, however, because it was the first act of Congress to deal specifically with the land problems of people who earned their living by grazing livestock. Prior to this time the stockman had been regarded as a "trespasser on the public domain, an obstacle to settlement, and at best but a crude forerunner of civilization of which the farmer was the advance guard and the hoe the symbol."[56]

Even so the act did not in reality apply to western stockmen as a whole. It lured into the desert a group of farmers to whom 640 acres sounded like a lot of land. Their entry on the range usually meant that the old stockman was fenced off while the homesteader overgrazed his homestead section in an attempt to make a living or until he abandoned his claim, sold out to a stockman, or was able to add sufficient territory to his homestead to enable him to stay in business. In an attempt to control strategic points on the range, stockmen or their employes also entered claims to grazing homesteads.

The Grazing Homestead Act continued in force until the passage of the Taylor Grazing Act, which had the effect of superseding and nullifying it. The former was the last of major public-land disposal methods. It concluded a long series of congressional land acts which, from our vantage point in time, appear to have been inept and impractical.

We have noted in passing some of the social costs of unsuitable land policies. We turn now to a consideration of the effects of these policies on western landownership patterns, on the western livestock industry, and on the land itself.

## Results of Land Policies on Ownership Patterns

The system of rectangular land surveys, in conjunction with the homesteads, sales, and grants, resulted initially in landownership patterns scattered out into little squares of 160 or 640 acres. These surveyor's squares were, of course, superimposed upon the landscape without regard to topography. We have lived with this system of land surveying so long that it may seem to be the natural and logical method. Possibly it was the most logical method in the eastern part of the United States. In the West, however, this method of surveying lands created problems of land disposal, landownership, and land use. Major John W. Powell, in his *Report on the Lands of the Arid Region of the United States,* recognized the difficulties for the West inherent in the rectangular survey system:

> Many a brook which runs but a short distance will afford sufficient water for a number of pasturage farms; but if the lands are surveyed in regular tracts as square miles or townships, all the water sufficient for a number of pasturage farms may fall entirely within one district. If the lands are thus surveyed, only the divisions having water will be taken, and the farmer obtaining title to such a division or farm could practically occupy all the country adjacent by owning the water necessary to its use. For this reason divisional surveys should conform to the topography, and be so made as to give the greatest number of water fronts. [57]

As could be expected, the watering places were the first to be transferred to private ownership. According to Clawson:

> As the range became crowded with range livestock, but generally before the intrusion of farmers, some ranchers began to protect themselves by acquisition of "key tracts." The key tract often contained the only available stock water for some distance. By preventing trespass on the land he owned, the rancher could obtain exclusive use of all the grazing land that could be used by livestock watering on his land. This process was usually effective. [58]

When an individual owned a "key" tract it meant not only that he had free use of the adjoining public lands but also that ordinarily those lands would not be desired by anyone else. As a consequence, much more public land remained in the hands of the government than would have been the case if the lands had been surveyed and distributed according to topographical features.

As pressure for grazing land increased, stockmen began to buy blocks of railroad lands. It will be recalled that the railroads were granted lands by alternate sections, so that their ownership pattern resembled a checkerboard. By purchasing a block of these checkerboarded lands the stockman also acquired the free use of the alternate sections of public domain. In effect, he got two for the price of one.[59]

East of the Mississippi, where land enclosures were generally small, lands were ordinarily fenced with stone, rails, or dense hedges. In the West these methods were impractical because of the large areas involved and the lack of wood for rail fences. In 1874, however, J. F. Glidden of DeKalb, Illinois, patented a successful barbed wire fence and a machine for making it. By 1880 barbed wire factories were turning out 40,000 tons of this cheap fencing material; by 1890 this output had been tripled.[60] Western stockmen were quick to take advantage of this new method of controlling the public range. Two Colorado cattle companies were reported to have fenced off a million acres each of government land. Three million acres were fenced off in two New Mexico counties. Smaller, but still considerable, amounts of fenced government lands were reported in other range states.[61]

By 1885 fencing of public lands had become so prevalent and complaints so numerous that Congress passed a law making illegal the erection of any obstacle to free passage on the public domain.[62] The next year President Cleveland ordered the removal of all fences, and the Secretary of Interior moved to carry out his orders.[63] By 1891 the Commissioner of the General Land Office was able to state that only thirteen cases of illegal enclosure of public lands had been reported during the previous year and that these cases had involved only 34,358 acres.[64]

The illegal fences had some stabilizing influence on the range. Stockmen made some attempt to manage fenced public domain lands. With the passage and enforcement of the act of 1885, however, the range once more became wide open to the first comer. By mutual agreements stockmen were sometimes able to keep out of each other's way, but sooner or later someone would slip over the boundaries and range wars would result. Nomadic sheep operators generally ignored local agreements and grazed wherever they were strong enough to stay. When they were forced off one range they moved to another and repeated the process.

After the first years of enforcement of the law of 1885, stockmen gradually began fencing off the public domain again. When complaints of illegal fencing became serious enough the government caused the fences to be removed but when the pressure was off they were usually built up again. When the Taylor Grazing Act was passed, these privately owned fences on the public range were considered evidence of prior use of the lands and thus gave the owner preference in obtaining "range rights" for his livestock.

Many of the homesteaders who were able to stay on their claims long enough to gain title later gave up and moved off the land but retained title to it. During the big cattle boom many eastern and foreign companies, as well as western stockmen, acquired large tracts and later went into bankruptcy, with the lands passing into the hands of their creditors. We have already noted the grants of land to states and railroads. Part of these lands are retained by their original owners. All these factors have contributed to a situation in the West where much of the land is held by absentee owners in parcels of various sizes and is rented, leased, or used without charge by local stockmen. Such leased or vacant land is ordinarily overgrazed and has deteriorated considerably.

## Results of Land Policies on Stockmen's Tenure and Methods

The old lawless West of range wars and conflicts between homesteaders and stockmen, and between cattlemen and sheepmen, was lawless not because it was populated by a peculiar breed of hyperaggressive and unscrupulous people, but because of political acts which resulted in land policies that were not suited to the region and that had the effect of encouraging conflict, insecurity, and disrespect for law.

Congress offered the homesteader a piece of land so small

that he was forced to use public land that did not belong to him. When he used public land he came into conflict with others who desired to use the same land and whose legal (or illegal) rights were as good as his. Since this was an illegal or extra-legal matter, there existed no means of arbitrating or settling disputes except by mutual agreement or conflict.

When stockmen were able to agree on a division of the public range, they found their plans thwarted by the homesteader who had a legal right which they did not possess. But the home-steader enjoyed a legal right only on his claim, and this was usually insufficient to provide a livelihood. So he did the same thing the old stockman did: he ran his cattle on the public domain. In so doing he had not only deprived the pioneer stockman of the area within his homestead but also competed with the stockman for the public domain. If and when he became estab-lished, he resented the intrusion of succeeding homesteaders as much as did the oldtime cattleman. As long as Congress persisted in thinking of the West as potential farmland, and of the stockman as a temporary first wave of settlement, this source of conflict would continue.

Economic and personal security were constantly threatened by conflicts between cattlemen and between cattlemen and homesteaders—and then came the sheep. Sheepmen have prob-ably been in trouble intermittently since herding first began. According to the Book of Genesis, "every shepherd is an abom-ination to the Egyptians."[65]

In hearings on the Taylor bill, Congressman Taylor said:

During the last few years, large sheep owners have been coming in there, roaming over the public domain, up and down those little creeks. They come in there where farmers are living along the creeks, where they have milk cows, work horses, or little herds of cattle. They have been grazing on those lands around the farms. Those big nonresident sheep owners have been bringing their flocks in there. I might say that Senator Stanfield, from [Oregon,] has been grazing 15,000 sheep in my district. For 2 or 3 years they have been coming in there, paying no attention to the little people at all. They do not have to pay any attention to them, because it is open commons. It is a part of the public domain. They can go in there with their sheep and have them to eat out the range right up to a man's gate, and he has nothing to say about it. He has no recourse at all.[66]

In the same hearing Taylor, in forceful terms, summed up the effects of unsuitable land policy on personal and economic security:

> At this time, there are large areas where it is a free-for-all and general grab-and-hold-if-you-can policy with roving herds using the range. There is no security or safety to honest stock business. We have had many sheep and cattle wars. For many years there has been more or less a kind of guerrilla warfare going on between and among the sheepmen and cattlemen with bitterness, strife, ill-will, and more or less litigation, and some sad killings. [67]

## Results of Land Policies on the Range

What was the range like before the white man came? To Fremont it was "rich prairie . . . covered with a luxuriant growth of grass . . . a region of great pastoral promise."[68] Lewis and Clark found it "a beatifull level plain . . . covered with grass from 9 inches to 2 feet high."[69] Pedro de Castaneda of Coronado's expedition wrote:

> Who could believe that 1,000 horses and 500 of our cows and more than 5,000 rams and ewes and more than 1,500 friendly Indians and servants in traveling over these plains would leave no more trace where they had passed than if nothing had been there—nothing—so that it was necessary to make piles of bones and cow dung now and then so that the rear guard could follow the army. [70]

But a letter from Coronada to Antonio de Mendoza reads in part

> . . . we found no grass during the first days, but a worse way through mountains and more dangerous passages than we had experienced previously. The horses were so tired that they were not equal to it, so that in this last desert we lost more horses than before. [71]

According to Francis Parkman in *The Oregon Trail*:

> No living thing was moving throughout the vast landscape, except the lizards that darted over the sand and through the rank grass and prickly pears at our feet. . . . Before and behind us, the level monotony of the plain was unbroken as far as the eye could reach. Sometimes it glared in the sun, an expanse of hot, bare sand; sometimes it was veiled by long coarse grass. Skulls and whitening bones of buffalo were scattered everywhere . . . [72]

The impressions of the traveler varied with the kind of country he passed over, the season of the year, the particular year, and the imagination of the traveler. Certainly the whole of the western part of the United States was not a waving sea of grass so high it polished the cowboy's boots as he rode. But neither was it all "hot, bare sand" littered with bleached bones of buffalo.

The Forest Service has conducted the most intensive study of range trends to date. This was a scientifically conducted study and did not depend upon the romanticized impressions of passing travelers and tellers of tall tales. The area covered by this report consisted roughly of a square piece of territory running west from the hundredth meridian to the Sierra Nevada and Cascade ranges and from the Canadian boundary to the California-Mexico line. Because this report is the most authoritive of any study to date, some of the findings are quoted below:

> The existing range area has been depleted no less than 52 percent from its virgin condition, using depletion in the sense of reduction in grazing capacity for domestic livestock. Practically this means that a range once capable of supporting 22.5 million animal units can now carry only 10.8 million.
>
> The depletion consists of the disappearance largely or altogether from many parts of the range of such valuable forage plants as the bluebunch wheatgrass, the giant wild-rye, ricegrass, dropseed, sacation, and California oatgrass. It consists of the replacement of palatable and nutritious plants such as prairie beardgrass and sandgrass by the unpalatable sand sagebrush and yucca, wild-rye by greasewood, winterfat by shadscale and rabbitbrush. It consists also of the replacement of perennial grasses by much less nutritious annual grasses and weeds. It consists of the invasion of foreign plants, such as the worthless star thistle in California, the nearly worthless Russian thistle now found everywhere, the poisonous Klamath weed, and only a few of limited value, such as cheatgrass for only a few weeks each year, and the alfileria of southern Arizona and California, for a few weeks in wet years.
>
> Still further, depletion consists of marked reduction in density of the better forage plants, with the perennial gramas and fescues as an example. The ordinarily desirable thickening of forests by reproduction and the expansion of brush areas has to some extent also reduced the space for forage plants.[73]

The Forest Service report also stated that the percentage of range depletion varied from a low of 30 per cent in national forests to a high of 67 per cent on the public domain.[74]

The livestock industry retaliated with two reports entitled, "If and When it Rains" and "Erosion—Then and Now." These reports attempted to prove that the depleted condition of the range, as found by the Forest Service, was the result of drought—and not overgrazing. They produced statements of persons who spoke of the range country as a desert, some of which we have noted, and attempted to prove that the range area passed through years of drought, when the range appeared to be depleted, and other wet years when the range produced heavy forage. The implication was that lands that the stockman was forced to overgraze in dry years would "come back" when the rains came.

There is undoubtedly an element of truth in these contentions. But any stockman knows that lands which have gone to sagebrush owing to heavy grazing during dry years will not automatically come back to normal with a year or two of favorable precipitation. This does not mean that the depleted range can never come back, but that water alone will have only minimal effects unless supplemented by brush eradication and reseeding. There can be no doubt, the stockmen's associations notwithstanding, that the western range area has been tremendously depleted by overgrazing.

The fact that the range has deteriorated through overgrazing is no condemnation of the stockman. Part of the overgrazing was caused by his inability to adjust to the dry years. It is impossible to guess what weather conditions will exist a year or two in advance. As a consequence stockmen have frequently been "caught" and forced to overgraze the range in dry years because it was physically or economically impossible to tailor their herds to meet the condition of the range.

In addition to this factor, however, public land policies *forced* overgrazing upon the stockman and homesteader. The homesteader, as we have seen, was given a plot of land too small to support a family. He overgrazed his homestead first. Then he turned his cattle loose on the public domain to compete with the older stockman for the range. They, in turn, competed with the sheepmen, and all were forced to overgraze. This concept was aptly stated in the hearings on the Taylor Grazing Act:

Mr. Sherman. The difficulty on the public lands is that nobody has control. The only way a stockman can get grass for his stock on the public lands is to get there ahead of anyone else and have his stock eat it up. . . . The rule has been to take it all as you go. If you do not, somebody else will take it, and you have only invited the intrusion of other stock.[75]

We have thus far considered the effects of an unrealistic land policy which invited overgrazing and range depletion. But another result of these land policies was possibly even more serious—the destruction of the range by plowing. As we have seen, the homestead laws were drafted and passed by a Congress which considered stockraising to be only the advance guard of farming. The homesteaders themselves were also generally farmers, or if not, they were forced to break up the sod in an effort to make it produce enough to maintain themselves. The exaggerated hopes for the dry-farming method aided and abetted the movement to plow up the range.

F. R. Carpenter, first Director of Grazing, tells a story of an Indian who sat on his pony and watched, with amazement and disbelief, an early homesteader plowing up the sod. Finally the Indian shook his head in bewilderment and rode away muttering, "Ugh, wrong side up." This epitomizes the history of millions of acres of land that was not suited to agriculture and was turned "wrong side up" and destroyed as range. By 1936 about 25,000,000 acres of western range had been plowed up and later abandoned. It is estimated that approximately 50,000,000 acres of relatively good range land has become submarginal crop land.[76]

Federal land policies encouraged the removal of the plant cover of the range by plowing and overgrazing. The results of the removal of this protective cover was an acceleration in the rate of erosion. Erosion, of course, is not a modern phenomenon. The prophet Ezekiel admonished the shepherds of Israel by saying, "Seemeth it a small thing unto you to have eaten up the good pasture, but ye tread down with your feet the residue of your pastures?"[77] Erosion has always been present, but not at the accelerated rate which has prevailed during the last half century. In the words of Arthur Sampson:

Through the ages, rain, running water, waves, moving ice, and wind have been at work making great valleys, plains, drainage channels, and deltas. Even so, during the epoch of primitive man, the topsoil over much of the earth's surface was formed faster than the forces of erosion carried it away.

But during the relatively short span of time that civilized man has exploited the earth—his livestock thinning the pasture vegetation and his plow breaking the sod—soil has been removed at a much faster rate than it was built up.

On parts of all continents erosion has exacted a heavy economic toil. Man-made deserts, and ruined cities amid barren wastes, attest to the devastating power of uncontrolled erosion. The 728 million acres of grazing land in the western states do not provide forage for half the animal units that they did 50 years ago.[78]

This accelerated rate of erosion is not caused *primarily* by the action of natural forces. Wind and water existed on the range prior to the time of the white man and did not then produce the same undesirably high rate of erosion. One is forced to conclude that accelerated erosion on the western ranges was the result of the public policies adopted for the disposal of the public domain.

In summary, the federal government acquired the lands that comprise the United States, aside from the thirteen original colonies, by cessions from states, by treaties with foreign countries and/or Indian tribes, and by purchase. The lands of Texas were acquired when Texas became a state. Transfer of land to private ownership passed through three general stages: sales for revenue; grants to states and corporations for internal improvements, and to individuals for services to the government; and alienation through the various homestead acts. Most of the western range region which passed into private ownership was transferred via the homestead laws and state and railroad grants.

Altogether the government has transferred over a billion acres to private ownership. About one third of this total was sold, and the balance was given away in the form of grants and homesteads. About one fourth of the original public domain still remains in the hands of the government. In the eleven western states—the range region—the government owns about half of the total acreage. Of the total acreage remaining in the hands of the government, about 142,000,000 acres are administered by the Bureau of Land Management as grazing districts. Other categories of federal lands include national forests, Indian reservations, parks and monuments, wildlife refuges, military and other reservations and grazing lands administered by the BLM under a leasing system (section 15 lands).

The land disposal policies of the federal government were not the results of any long-range program of settlement, distribution, or land utilization. Lands were first offered for sale to provide revenue and to discourage movement of people from the industrial centers of the east. Lands were granted to states and corporations for internal improvements. In the first instance the need for additional revenue was the motivating force; in the second, the improvements and the investment opportunities were the important factor. In neither case was the land itself or the mode of settlement considered in making the political decision.

The pre-emption acts and the homestead acts were the results of political pressures from the West and from northern abolitionists. The Homestead Act was opposed by the South because of a fear that it would give a preponderance of power to the antislave North.

In the election of 1860 the Democratic party split, not only over the slavery question, but also over the homestead issue. Some results of the party split were the election of Lincoln and the Republican party, and the passage of the 160-acre Homestead Act.

Generally speaking, the Homestead Act of 1862 and its succeeding modifications came too late to fit the area remaining open to homesteading. The result was unnecessary human hardship and failure, deterioration of the range, and accelerated erosion. "Too little and too late," best summarizes the homestead acts.

The rectangular survey system, coupled with the grant and homestead systems, resulted in crazy-quilt landownership patterns in uneconomic units, which encouraged and invited conflict and economic instability, overgrazing, and attempted cultivation of submarginal lands. These, in turn, resulted in an accelerated rate of erosion, increased siltage, and floods.

This incalculable waste of land and human resources was the result of policies developed and carried out through a political process. This same political process, however, can be used to correct the mistakes of the past. It not only can rectify past mistakes but can cause the range to produce more than it ever did in its pristine state.

The elements of nature are not given, static, unchangeable quantities. They can be modified by men. Large-scale modifications must ordinarily depend upon political action. Such action can be either generally harmful or beneficial. This chapter has outlined a series of political acts which from our vantage point in time we have judged to be generally harmful to the people and lands of the range region. The next chapter describes a political action designed to rectify some past mistakes and provide a basis for improving the western range.

# 3. THE TAYLOR GRAZING ACT

Probably the first official admission of the unsuitability of the homestead laws to the western range region is contained in the annual report of the commissioner of the General Land Office in 1875. According to the commissioner:

In all that section lying between the one hundredth meridian on the east, and the Cascade Range and the Sierra Nevada Mountains on the west, and, within these limits, from the Mexican line on the south to the international boundary on the north, a totally different set of conditions, geographical, physical, and climatic, are found to exist. Within this vast area agriculture, as understood and pursued in the valley of the Mississippi and to the eastward, has no existence . . . it may be safely affirmed that, except in the immediate valleys of the mountain streams, where by dint of individual effort water may be diverted for irrigating purposes, title to the public lands cannot be honestly acquired under the homestead laws. [1]

Following a visit to the range region in the fall of 1875, President Grant, in his annual message to Congress the following December, said:

In territory where cultivation of the soil can only be followed by irrigation, and where irrigation is not practicable, the lands can only be used as pasturage, and this only where stock can reach water . . . and cannot be governed by the laws as to entries as lands every acre of which is an independent estate by itself.

Land must be held in large quantities to justify the expense of conducting water upon it to make it fruitful or to justify using it as a pasturage. [2]

One year later in his message to Congress newly-elected
President Hayes said:

These lands [west of the hundredth meridian] are practically un-
saleable under existing laws, and the suggestion is worthy of consideration that a system of leasehold tenure would make them a source
of profit to the United States, while at the same time legalizing the
business of cattle raising which is at present carried on upon them.[3]

Following the most extensive survey of western resources
that had been made to that date, Major John W. Powell, in
his *Report on the Lands of the Arid Region of the United States,*
suggested that:

The grasses of the pasturage lands are scant, and the lands are of
value only in large quantities.
The farm unit should not be less than 2,560 acres.
Pasturage farms need small tracts of irrigable land; hence the
small streams of the general drainage system and the lone springs
and streams should be reserved for such pasturage farms.
The division of these lands should be controlled by topographic features in such manner as to give the greatest number of water fronts
to the pasturage farms.
Residences of the pasturage farms should be grouped, in order to
secure the benefits of local social organizations, and cooperation in
public improvements.
The pasturage lands will not usually be fenced, and hence herds
must roam in common.
As the pasturage lands should have water fronts and irrigable tracts,
and as the residences should be grouped, and as the lands cannot be
economically fenced and must be kept in common, local communal
regulations or cooperation is necessary.[4]

Powell then proposed a bill "to authorize the organization
of pasturage districts by homestead settlements on the public
lands which are of value for pasturage purposes only." The
bill provided for the establishment of pasturage districts to
be operated by associations of nine or more persons. Members of the association were to be allowed to homestead 2,560
acres, of which no more than twenty acres could be irrigable
land. The act provided further that no person be entitled to
more water than was necessary to irrigate twenty acres. The
rectangular survey system was to be abandoned and the lands
were to be parceled out by the association. Water rights were

to be transferred with the title in all subsequent conveyances.[5]

Powell's bill was too much of a break with prevailing lais-sez-faire philosophy and did not receive serious considera-tion. Powell pointed out that unless some such legislation was quickly enacted a few persons would monopolize the water and render the public domain worthless to anyone else. This, of course, is precisely what happened.

Powell's observations are significant not only because of the accuracy of his prophecies but also because a modification of his "pasturage districts" became the grazing districts of the Taylor Grazing Act—fifty-nine years after his original proposals. The president of the National Livestock Associa-tion, in his annual address in 1901, endorsed Powell's sug-gestions by recommending grazing homesteads of 2, 560 acres.[6]

Probably the first leasing bill was introduced by Senator Foster of Washington in 1899. This was a bill "to provide for the leasing of the public lands for grazing purposes and to produce revenue for agricultural development."[7]

The American Cattle Growers endorsed a bill (S. 33 11) submitted to the Fifty-seventh Congress (1901-2) which pro-vided for the leasing of all public lands at a uniform rate of two cents per acre. Preference was to be given to owners of cultivated land bordering on public domain, to stockmen who were also landowners, and to "stock growers who were in ac-tual use and occupancy" of the public domain in 1900.[8] The bill seemed to favor the large stockman too much to receive favorable consideration. However, certain features of Powell's bill combined with the cattlemen's bill of 1901 formed the ba-sis for the Taylor Grazing Act as finally passed in 1934.

In response to pressure from both the stockmen and con-servationists, President Theodore Roosevelt appointed a Public Land Commission in 1903, to study the western range and make recommendations particularly with regard to grazing on the public domain. After two years of study, the commission sub-mitted a plan which included:

Classification of the grazing lands and setting them aside in grazing districts. Lands having agricultural possibilities would be grazed un-der permits granted for each year or season only, and should be sub-ject to homestead entry. Lands considered to be valuable for grazing only should be occupied under permit for periods extending up to ten years, with a reclassification at the end of each period. While such a permit remained in force, no entry or settlement was to be allowed. [9]

The stockmen themselves, particularly the cattlemen, had by this time become aware of the unsuitability of the land laws affecting the public domain. The Public Land Commission had sent out questionnaires to a representative sample of the stockmen of the West. Of the 1, 400 stockmen who replied, 1, 090 favored some form of government control. [10]

On April 3, 1906 (59th Congress, 1st Session), Senator Burkett of Nebraska introduced a bill (S. 5511) which would authorize the President, with the consent of the governor of the state concerned, to establish grazing districts on the public domain. Such districts were to be administered by the Secretary of Agriculture who was to "charge and collect reasonable fees for grazing permits."

In the next session of Congress Senator Burkett resubmitted his bill (S. 7618) with the section requiring the governor's approval deleted. At the hearings on the bill, the American National Livestock Association submitted a resolution, unanimously adopted at its annual convention of January 23, 1907, which endorsed and approved the intent and purpose of the Burkett bill. [11] The committee made no recommendation on the bill.

By 1907 the commissioner of the General Land Office, in a statement vindicating Powell's predictions, said:

Much of the remaining public lands are semi-arid or desert in character and cannot be artifically irrigated. For these lands we have no law regulating their use or disposition. This condition has delivered the public range over to those who are powerful enough to appropriate and hold it against the weaker claimants, but mere physical force in holding the range is the least of the abuses. Monopolization of the pools, springs and streams to which the grazing herds and flocks must resort for water, and the acquisition of strips of patented lands to which title was acquired obviously to prevent access by others to the adjacent public range, is the greatest public wrong. These abuses are so universal and so far removed from decent respect for common rights that I most earnestly recommend the enactment of a comprehensive range law. [12]

In a message to Congress on February 13, 1907, President Theodore Roosevelt said:

Let me also again urge that legislation be passed to provide for Government control of the public pasture lands of the West. . . . The local control of the range should be in the hands of western men familiar with stock raising, and there should be full local participation in the management of the range; for cooperation between the stockmen and the Government officers is absolutely essential. The grazing fee should be small and at first almost nominal . . . such control would not be taken hurriedly, but gradually, as grazing districts can be organized.

The opposition to the [proposed] measure comes primarily from those who do not make their homes on the land, but who own wandering bands of sheep . . . and also from the men who have already obtained control of great areas of the public land largely through the ownership or leasing of water at what might be called the strategic points of the range. [13]

Following the President's lead, Senator Curtis of Kansas introduced a grazing bill on February 18, 1908, (S. 5431) which provided for a committee composed of users of the range, which was to issue permits, decide disputes on range rights, and so forth. This was probably the first bill to propose a kind of advisory board system. Senator Curtis reintroduced his bill, now S. 6345, in the next session but neither bill got to the floor of the Senate. In the meantime Senator Burkett had unsuccessfully reintroduced his bill a third and fourth time.

Several similar bills were introduced by Senator LaFollette (S. 3462 in 1911), Representative Stephans (H.R. 23582 in 1912), Representative Kent (H.R. 10539 in 1913), Senator King (S. 1516 in 1919), Representative Sinnott (H.R. 7908 in 1921), Senator Smoot (S. 3236 in 1922), and Senator Phipps (S. 2325 in 1924). Several of these bills were reintroduced in succeeding sessions of Congress. None was reported out of committee. Congressman Sinnott's bill (H.R. 7908) appears to be the first grazing bill which specified administration of the public lands by the Department of Interior; previous bills had all specified Agriculture. This bill had been originally drafted in the Department of Interior and had the blessing of Secretary Fall. Another unusual feature of Sinnott's bill was that fees were to be levied according to the amount of rainfall.

Most of these grazing bills were introduced by congressmen from the range states. Supposedly they spoke for a considerable number of constituents. At the same time, however, other

western congressmen were still committed to the homestead
idea. Congressman Ferguson of New Mexico, for instance,
was one of the principal supporters of the 640-acre grazing
homestead. The homestead supporters, of course, opposed
the leasing or permit bills. Probably the most common charge
against them was that they were designed to aid the "big interests" and "cattle barons." The numerous, well-publicized
cases of fraud and illegal fencing in which western stockmen
had been involved also worked to create an unsympathetic attitude toward the stockmen and the grazing bills.

Generally speaking, the grazing bills were favored by the
cattlemen and opposed by the sheepmen. Possibly because of
the nomadic nature of many sheep operators in the early part
of the century, the sheepmen had opposed any regulation of
the federal range. Instead they had favored the homestead
principle. In 1909 the annual convention of the National Woolgrowers Association approved a resolution which stated in
part: "We reiterate our opposition to any change in the laws
governing the public lands of the United States save that only
which shall promote the interest and welfare of the bona fide
homesteader."[14]

When the Enlarged Homestead Act was passed in 1909 and
the new influx of homesteaders began to fence off the range,
the sheepmen changed their minds. They were violently opposed to the Grazing Homestead Act of 1916 and consequently
the Woolgrowers Association in that year voted conditional
support of a federal grazing bill.[15] After the passage of the
Grazing Homestead Act, however, the association reverted
to its former stand. According to the president of the association in 1917, the woolgrowers should strive to bring about
the "final disposition of the public domain."[16] The president
went on to say, "it is perhaps a waste of effort to look for
help or encouragement or even justice from a government
which is run on political rather than scientific or economic
principles."[17] It would appear that the National Woolgrowers
Association wanted neither homesteads nor grazing regulation.

There were, of course, some individuals who were opposed
to government "meddling" of any sort and, as always, a group
of "states' righters" who held out for state control. We might

also note in passing that it was difficult to arouse public interest in the conservation of grass as compared with conservation of trees and wildlife. People do not ordinarily write poems and grow lyrical about grass. To most people grass is simply something that grows everywhere and oftentimes is something of a nuisance. Grass and weeds are almost synonymous. It is not at all surprising, therefore, that even during the Roosevelt-Pinchot era, a period of intense interest in the conservation of natural resources, the conservation of grass received little attention.

One other factor that tended to prevent favorable consideration of the grazing bills was the jurisdictional dispute between the departments of Interior and Agriculture. The Department of Interior believed that national forests should be administered by Interior. The Department of Agriculture not only believed it was best qualified to administer the national forests, but also considered itself best qualified to administer any regulation of grazing activities on the public domain. In a speech at Salt Lake City in July, 1919, Secretary of Agriculture Houston summarized the case for the Department of Agriculture in these words:

> The Department of Agriculture could apply a similar system for the Department of the Interior that it now applies on the national forests, or it could be charged directly with the duty. The fact that the Interior Department has title and will retain title to the public domain makes no difference. Grazing is an agricultural problem. [18]

When Henry C. Wallace became Secretary of Agriculture and Hubert Work Secretary of Interior, the interdepartmental dispute showed some signs of cooling off. In a letter to Congressman Sinnott, chairman of the House Public Lands Committee, Wallace said:

> I feel that here is an important public service urgently needed, that action should be promptly taken to restore these lands and to cooperate with the livestock industry in bringing about their better use. As to the matter of jurisdiction, I am not so much concerned about who does the work as I am that it be done, done promptly, and done well. [19]

By 1926 E. A. Sherman of the Forest Service (Agriculture) and E. C. Finney of the Department of Interior were able to draft a bill which was approved by both departments. This bill provided for the creation of grazing districts under the super-

vision of the Department of Interior. But by the time the bill
was introduced by Senator Phipps in 1927, the western stockmen were so aroused over a dispute with the Forest Service
on grazing fees that the Phipps bill (S. 4076) died in committee.[20]

While none of the bills outlined above ever got out of committee, they do indicate some trend in the thinking of persons
interested in the control of the ranges of the public domain.
There was, first of all, a recognition of the unsuitability of
the homestead laws. The idea of grazing districts under federal control was first introduced. The placement of the seat
of this proposed federal control shifted from the Department
of Agriculture to the Department of Interior. The cattlemen,
at least, came to support some kind of regulation. The idea
of some sort of advisory board of local stockmen was developed. The issue of states' rights, which continues to plague
the administration, was first raised as applied to grazing
lands on the public domain.

During the years the Forest Service had been issuing grazing permits for the national forests, the fees had been increased several times, but still remained somewhat lower
than commercial rates for comparable range. About 1920 Congress began to search for additional revenues to pay off the
huge national debt incurred during World War I. Congressional
committees, and in particular the House committees on Agriculture and Forestry, began to apply pressure to the Department of Agriculture for an increase in grazing fees on national
forests. The Forest Service apparently stalled for time as
best it could with "studies" and other delaying tactics. These
activities alerted and annoyed the western stockmen. Among
these stockmen were powerful interests who had opposed the
Forest Service grazing fee system since its inception. This
group took advantage of the controversy over grazing fees to
make things as uncomfortable for the Forest Service as possible. On March 4, 1925, Senator Cameron of Arizona introduced a resolution to investigate "all matters relating to national forests and the public domain and their administration."[21]

The Senate, with Senator R. N. Stanfield of Oregon as chairman of the investigating subcommittee, approved the resolu-

tion. The subcommittee held hearings both in Washington and throughout the West during the summer and fall of 1925.[22] It would appear that the subcommittee conducted no real investigation but used the hearings procedure primarily as a method for giving persons dissatisfied with the Forest Service an opportunity to air their views. The Forest Service was caught between a Congress which pressed for increased grazing fees and a Congress which used increased fees as a weapon against it. Twenty years later congressional committees used precisely the same method to hamstring the Grazing Service.

One result of the Stanfield committee hearings was an outburst of antagonism against the Forest Service in the West. A second result was the introduction of the Stanfield Bill, as approved by the aroused stockmen, for the administration of national forests and the public domain. A third result was stimulation of the opposition of the American Forestry Association, the Society of American Foresters, and other conservation groups, and ultimately the defeat of the bill. The net effect of the investigation appears to have been a weakening of the position of the Forest Service and a postponement of much-needed regulation of grazing on the public domain. As a result of the Forest Service fee controversy western stockmen were more distrustful than ever of federal regulation. The same fee controversy convinced eastern conservationists that the stockmen were out to loot the public domain and that no legislation should be enacted which would in any way accrue to their benefit. And the range continued to deteriorate.

The election of Herbert Hoover as President in 1928 and the appointment of Ray Lyman Wilbur as Secretary of Interior gave impetus to the states' rights concept, further confused the grazing issue, and delayed action on control and regulation of the public domain. Secretary Wilbur proposed in a speech at Boise, Idaho, on July 9, 1929, that the public lands be transferred to the states in which they were located.[23]

President Hoover followed up this proposal in a letter to the conference of public land states' governors at Salt Lake City, August 26-27, 1929. The President's letter read in part:

It may be stated at once that our Western States have long since passed from their swaddling clothes and are today more competent to manage much of these affairs [public lands and reclamation] than

is the Federal Government. Moreover, we must seek every opportunity to retard the expansion of Federal bureaucracy and to place
our communities in control of their own destinies. [24]

In accordance with the President's suggestion, a commission
was formed to study the sentiments of the parties involved.
The commission submitted a report to the President in January, 1931, which contained substantially the same proposals
as he had originally suggested. The commission had encountered considerable opposition, not only from conservationists, but also from some of the western states, which were
disinclined to assume the burden of public land administration.
In the words of Governor Dern of Utah: "The States already
own, in their school-land grants, millions of acres of this
same kind of land, which they can neither sell nor lease, and
which is yielding no income. Why should they want more of
this precious heritage of desert?"[25]

Nevertheless the commission's recommendations were embodied in a bill and introduced (by request) by Senator Gerald
Nye and Congressman John M. Evans. The bill provided for
a grant of the vacant public lands to the states in which they
were located—provided the state legislature voted to accept
them. The federal government was to retain the mineral rights.
The lands were to be held in trust by the states for the support of education. After extensive hearings clearly indicated
almost universal disapproval, the bill was dropped.

In the meantime (1928) Congress had approved a bill[26] to
allow the Secretary of Interior to enter into agreements with
the state of Montana and various private owners in the area
between Mizpah and Pumpkin creeks in southeastern Montana
to bring these lands together for the purpose of joint leases
to stockmen. The Mizpah-Pumpkin Creek area lies south of
Miles City, Montana, in Custer County. Part of this area had
been homesteaded but most of the homesteads had been abandoned and had "gone back" to the federal government or belonged to banks, mortgage and loan companies, and other absentee owners. The drought of 1919 and the hard winter of
1919-20 had accelerated the homesteader exodus. By 1926
most of the homesteaders had gone, leaving the usual monuments to an unsound land policy: dilapidated shacks, rusty
windmills, patches of plowed ground, and scattered quarter-

sections and half-sections of fenced-in property. The fences gradually fell down, probably with some help from local stockmen, and the whole area became a grazing commons. This included both publicly and privately owned lands. Following the pattern we have previously observed, the area soon became overstocked and overgrazed.

Stockmen were not inclined to lease these lands, first, because they were using them anyway without cost, and second, the public and private lands were so interspersed that the fencing off of privately owned lands into a range large enough to support a reasonable herd would necessitate the illegal fencing of public domain.

Absentee landowners continued to pay taxes on lands which produced no revenue or allowed the property to become tax delinquent and revert to the country for nonpayment of taxes.

At this juncture (1926), Nick Monte, stockman and later regional grazier for the federal Grazing Service, Evan W. Hall, agricultural development agent for the Milwaukee Railroad, and Paul Lewis, Custer County extension agent, discussed the possibility of forming some kind of cooperative association to regulate the use of this area and at the same time make it produce some revenues. This group formulated a plan by which an association would lease or otherwise gain control of the lands in question and reapportion grazing on a permit system. Interested stockmen were consulted and generally approved the idea. Senator Thomas J. Walsh and Representative Scott Leavitt, both of Montana, were approached and became interested in the project.

The outcome of these preliminary efforts was the passage of a bill in 1928 which provided for the control of this range area (108, 804 acres) through a stockman's association under the direction of the Department of Interior. The district was to be conducted on an experimental basis for a period of ten years.

The association traded state lands in the area for federal lands of equal value outside the district, thereby eliminating the need for leasing state lands. Federal lands were leased by the association for twenty dollars per section. The association offered to pay the taxes on private lands for the privilege of using them. This may not appear to be much of an inducement, but at that time the owner was losing money on his investment. This arrangement made it possible for him to break even—with the promise of improvement of his properties. The association also purchased 2, 600 acres which had already reverted to Custer County.

The association started with an executive board of seven members, which was later reduced to three. Members paid $1.25 for running a cow and calf on the range for eight months, plus an additional fifteen cents per head to pay for the purchase of county lands. The carrying capacity of the range was determined as accurately as possible and permits were issued to members by a board of three directors. Originally each permittee was required to develop one watering place for each hundred head of cattle for which he had a permit.

The experiment proved to be a success. According to Harold Ickes:

> The result after three years is that there is twice as much grass on the Mizpah as before, although the carrying capacity has been increased from 3000 to 5000 head.
> The success of the Mizpah River-Pumpkin Creek experiment has brought numerous requests from different parts of the West for permission to form similar associations. . . . I feel, however, that rather than deal with the matter piecemeal, it would be wiser to deal at one swoop with the whole public domain by giving this department authority to regulate grazing on it, which . . . should have been done many years ago. [27]

A bill had been introduced to deal with the whole public domain in "one swoop" in the Seventy-second Congress the preceding year. This was the Colton Bill (H.R. 11816). According to chief forester R. Y. Stuart:

> This bill is the outgrowth of a joint and several study by representatives of this department, in cooperation with representatives of the Department of the Interior, covering the various proposals which have been made at this and previous sessions of Congress for regulating the use of the public-domain land chiefly valuable for grazing. [28]

Secretary of Agriculture Arthur M. Hyde, in a letter to the chairman of the Committee on Public Lands, said:

> I can not too strongly urge that comprehensive legislation of this character receive your prompt and favorable consideration. The re-

maining public unreserved lands are too great a potential agricultural
asset for the Nation to longer neglect and ignore.[29]

Secretary of Interior Wilbur was also favorably impressed:

H.R. 11816 has received very careful consideration in this department and it is believed to be a workable and desirable piece of legislation. Its benefits will not be local, but State and Nation wide.
I recommend early and favorable action.[30]

The committee reported:

The Committee on the Public Lands, to whom was referred the bill
(H.R. 11816) to stop injury to the public grazing lands by preventing
over grazing and soil deterioration, to provide for their orderly use,
improvement, and development, to stabilize the livestock industry
dependent upon the public range, and for other purposes, having considered same, report favorably thereon with the recommendation that
the bill do pass.[31]

The Colton Bill passed the House but died in committee in
the Senate. Even so, it was the first grazing bill ever to pass
either house. Congressman Edward T. Taylor of Colorado,
reintroduced the Colton Bill in the first session of the Seventy-third Congress. Taylor had been in Congress since 1909
and had worked for the passage of the Grazing Homestead Act
of 1916.[32] With the passage of the years, however, he had
come to realize that federal control of the public range could
no longer be avoided. Apparently Taylor was a strong states'
rights man, but he realized the futility and impracticality of
attempting to transfer the public range land to the states.

The original bill, however, had included one section designed to pacify the states' righters. Section 13 of the bill
stated in part:

That this act shall not become effective in any State until sixty days
after the approval by the legislature of such State; and each such approving State, in its discretion, may designate and authorize one or
more representatives or officials of said State with whom the Secretary of the Interior is hereby authorized to make and enter into suitable agreement for the cooperative administration of public grazing
upon said public lands of the United States.[33]

In a letter to the chairman of the Committee on Public Lands,
Secretary Ickes recommended "the bill be enacted into law
provided Section 13 thereof is eliminated."[34] Secretary Wal-

lace wrote: "the total elimination of section 13 from the bill is recommended."[35] But the states' rights people still had strong supporters, in this instance from the western states. According to Representative Ayres of Montana:

> Every State has its local conditions, including elevation, climatic conditions, water, feed, shelter, the winter elements, the summer range, and the proper use at all times of the year. Every State has a different condition and different problems to settle and can do it best themselves *[sic]*. [36]

In attempting to clarify his position Ayres offered an illustration and encountered some opposition from **F. R. Carpenter**, a Colorado cattleman and witness before the committee:[37]

> Mr. Ayres. Do you not suppose that the condition of bringing in the herds over these lands that are brought from foreign States could be handled better and more successfully if these open public lands were turned over to the respective States where they could make laws among themselves and to affect each other, and prohibit, if necessary, the importation over the State line?
> Mr. Carpenter. I think it is possible, but not very probable.
> Mr. Ayres. You do not think it is probable?
> Mr. Carpenter. No; I do not.
> Mr. Ayres. Why is it not probable?
> Mr. Carpenter. Due to the fact that the administration of State lands is different in each State, and it is administered under different State land boards, and different interests control in the different States. You will find the sheep men control in some States, and that the cattlemen control in others, and the coppermen control in others, and you would get widely divergent interests in lands combatting each other. If you are going to work under systematized control you have got to make it national control. [38]

Senator Dennis Chavez of New Mexico questioned Secretary Ickes' objection to Section 13 in the following interchange:

> Mr. Chavez. I know that the Secretary is in absolute good faith. . . . But if it is a good thing to do this as is provided for in the bill, what reasonable objection can there be to a State like New Mexico, or a State like Colorado, cooperating with the Government?
> Secretary Ickes. Would you give somebody else the veto power over the way you control your property?[39]

Representative Taylor, in commenting on President Hoover's proposal to transfer the land to the states, said:

The States were not willing to take limited title to the surface, and they are not willing to do that now. They are not willing to do that now, and they never will be. The Federal Government, on the other hand, is not willing to give them all the sub-surface rights. Therefore, we are at a dead standstill on that, and there is no use in talking about it. That is a closed incident.[40]

Taylor then summarily disposed of the whole idea in these words:

When it comes to conveying the 173,000,000 acres of public domain that Uncle Sam owns, from the blue sky to the center of earth, to the States, I know and all the old members know that Congress will not vote for that kind of a bill. . . . It is a very much larger and more complicated subject than some of you may realize. President Hoover's large Public Lands Commission, which held meetings and hearings for some 2 years, recommended that the surface only of the public lands be conveyed to the States. However, no State would be willing to accept that kind of a title. Therefore, there is an absolutely impassable barrier to anything of that kind; and it is a waste of time to discuss it.[41]

Section 13 was eventually deleted and both surface and mineral rights were reserved to the federal government in the bill that finally passed.

When the bill reached the floor of the Senate, Huey Long scored one final blow for states' rights to the public domain:

The State of Louisiana has borne most of the expense of creating these public lands. Contrary to what the public generally thinks, the domain in these public territories was derived almost wholly from contributions made through the State of Louisiana, particularly the Louisiana Purchase. . . . I have always believed that whenever land transfers were made back to the States, as an act of popular recognition, the citizens of Louisiana should be allowed to have some preemptory right of homestead in them. However, we will not contend for that.[42]

Charges of attempts at dictatorial bureaucracy also were voiced in the hearings on the bill. Ayres complained that:

The trials and tribulations of the western people are only a magazine story to these bureaucrats. They have never had the experience of the log cabins or the dug-outs of the Dakotas, Montana or Wyoming.

They have never operated a sheep camp, have never lived in sheep wagons, nor have they ever followed a round-up. Neither have they been compelled to quench their thirst, day in and day out, month in and month out, with nothing but alkali water. They are trying now to administer those lands down here in swivel chairs, two or three thousand miles away.

Now Mr. Chairman, I say to you, the West does not need additional parasites, and particularly not at the rate of $2,000,000,000 per year, at the expense of the livestock men. And that is the class of parasites that you cannot clear out; once they are hooked on, they are there forever.[43]

### Representative Carter of Wyoming was most distressed:

This bill will give the Secretary practically dictatorship over our livestock industry of the West and can be compared to the dictatorship of Russia. It gives him power that rightfully belongs to the States. As sovereign States surely we have some right to the lands within our boundaries just as the Southern and Eastern States had.[44]

Since the act would practically eliminate further homesteading, there was much opposition from those who clung to the old homestead idea for both sentimental and practical reasons. Representative White of Idaho said:

We have definitely set up a plan for acquiring these lands and building up communities, and we have followed that plan and made America what it is. Now today we are going to turn it over into the hands of the big organized cattle industry.[45]

And Representative Carter of Wyoming was no less vehement in his objections:

The title should read: "A bill to take away from the livestock industry of the West the free use of 173,000,000 acres of public domain, abolish the 640-acre homestead and desert entry laws, and retard the political and economic growth of the West."[46]

Again Representative Taylor brought these gentlemen back to earth:

The praises and eulogies upon the American homesteader will continue as long as our Republic survives. The West was built, and its present proud development rests more largely upon the courage, privations, and frightfully hard work of the pioneer homesteaders. . . .

But my dear sirs, if those hardy pioneers had had to go onto the kind of land that is contemplated within this bill, the West would still be a barren wilderness.[47]

There were also the usual charges that the bill was the hand-iwork of the cattle barons. Representative White of Idaho charged:

> I tell you, gentlemen, the big sheep and cattle interests are putting forth that argument here, and I want to say to you that these depart-ments here see something to seize upon; they want to finish up Amer-ica; they want to close the door to it. I have seen one door after an-other slammed in the face of the individual and the country gradually safeguarded for the big interests, and this is just another move in that direction, to close up the door. [48]

But Congressman Pierce of Oregon had a different impres-sion of whose faces "doors had been slammed upon":

> It is a mistake to year after year pass this by and allow the hogs, the men who want to tramp the grass in the ground as they do in the very early spring, to the ruin of the native grasses, to do that, and that drift over from Mr. White's district from the Idaho country and across the line into the beautiful Jordon Valley, with sheep moving there right now herd after herd. [49]

F. R. Carpenter maintained the law was needed to protect the small stockmen against the big interests:

> . . . homestead filings . . . are not homestead claims in any sense of the word, but they are simply to control strategic points on the range, and used largely as a subterfuge by the large interests to reg-ulate this large area . . . the small man in my country . . . has come to the belief that there is a process of elimination and dissemina-tion. We believe that the Federal control over this area should be ex-tended. That is the only chance against being completely wiped out of existence as far as the cow industry is concerned, and that is to have this range controlled by the Federal authorities. [50]

There were probably some congressmen who generally fa-vored the bill but who sincerely believed it could be best ad-ministered by the Forest Service; others used this jurisdic-tional question to hold up the proceedings and if possible start the old jurisdictional feud again in the hope of killing the bill altogether. To these congressmen, Sherman, associate for-ester, replied:

> . . . during the 50-year period the carrying capacity has, instead of where 3 cows could graze formerly, gone down to where 1 can graze now, and if you continue the quarrel for the next 50 years as to the division of that range, it will be a goat instead of a cow when action is finally taken. [51]

The bill met with mixed reactions from the organized stockmen. Congresswoman Greenway of Arizona and Congressman
Englebright of California both introduced statements into the
hearings from the organized cattlemen of their respective
states opposing the Taylor bill.[52] On the other hand, both the
New Mexico Woolgrowers Association and the New Mexico Cat-
tlegrowers Association endorsed the bill.[53] Probably Dan H.
Hughes, who represented the Colorado Woolgrowers Association, most candidly and accurately summed up the attitude of
western stockmen when he testified that:

> We are vitally concerned with the question of the control of the re-
> maining public domain. We believe that it should be done, and done
> immediately. . . .
>
> The livestock industry of the West concedes the need of regulating
> the remaining public domain for grazing purposes. Our experience
> teaches us that the main value of that land, or probably the only value
> of large parts of it, is the grazing value. We are using it for that
> purpose, and we have built up our institutions on that basis. For that
> reason, we ask that we be protected as preferred users of that public
> domain. We recognize that the courts have said that we have no es-
> tablished rights there, and that we simply use it in common with oth-
> ers, but certainly, when we have gone there and put this land to a ben-
> eficial use, we are entitled to protection in that use.[54]

Opponents of the Taylor Bill were fighting a losing battle.
By 1934, the nation was in the midst of a depression. Old
values were being questioned or discredited. Old ways of doing,
or not doing, things were being jettisoned or revamped. The
old shibboleths had lost—temporarily at least—much of their
effectiveness. It was a time of change, and people were generally ready for changes if for no other reason than the feel-
ing that things could not be worse and that any change might
be an improvement.

In the midst of depression, dust storms were dramatizing
the effects of improper use of land.

The departments of Agriculture and Interior were headed
by two aggressive individuals, Henry A. Wallace and Harold
Ickes. Both were firmly convinced of the need for federal
regulation of the western ranges. Henry Wallace wrote:

> There now is widespread recognition of the fact that the uncontrolled
> use of these lands during the past half century has gravely impaired
> their social and economic value. Unseasonal and excessive grazing

has caused a progressive deterioration in the vegetative cover over much of the land so that both in density and palatability it is markedly inferior to what it was during earlier stages of occupancy and use.[55]

Harold Ickes supported the bill in no uncertain terms:

> As the result of continued delay in the enactment of such an act as that now pending evidences have accumulated of the deterioration of the land resulting in a lessening value and use through lack of proper administration; erosion; the killing of plant life and soil cover and a growing damage from lack of flood control and watershed protection.
>
> Given proper legislative authority, I am confident that this long-continued damage to one of the valuable natural assets of the Nation could be stopped, and the tide could be turned toward improvement, not only in the value of the lands involved, but in benefits to the great livestock industry and the innumerable persons dependent upon that industry. . . .
>
> The Government is asking permission from the Congress to exercise the same prudence and care in maintaining and protecting this great national asset that a private individual would use with respect to his own property. It fortunately happens that the upbuilding of the public range coincides with the best interests of the States in which that range is located and of the stockmen whose herds and flocks are dependent upon the range.[56]

But Ickes went further than a mere expression of support. On March 31, 1933, Congress passed the Emergency Conservation Work Act creating the Civilian Conservation Corps. This organization provided badly needed jobs for young men and used them primarily in conservation work on federally owned lands. Naturally, there was a scramble among western states to secure as many of these camps as possible. But Ickes withheld them from the public domain on the grounds that "it would be unsound, economically, to include such work in the conservation program in the absence of a satisfactory future control of the lands benefited and the permanency and continued maintenance of such projects."[57]

At the same time he dangled before the eyes of western congressmen the promise of immediate assignment of C.C.C. camps to the public domain as soon as a suitable grazing control bill could be enacted. He reminded the stockmen who used the federal lands that C.C.C. labor could be used to construct fences, waterholes, and stock driveways.[58] Secretary Wallace added:

The initiation of those activities [grazing control] will at the same time afford a wide field for constructive and creative work by the members of the Emergency Conservation Corps created by the act of March 31, 1933, and will afford many opportunities for profitable employment by members of the corps within their home or adjoining States. These reasons in themselves would seem to warrant early and favorable consideration of the measure. [59]

When Congress dragged its feet and did not pass the bill during the first session of the Seventy-third Congress, Ickes solicited legal advice and found he had authority to withdraw all the public lands if he chose to do so. This would mean that the unreserved public lands would become a federal reservation and could be administered by the Department of Interior without further legislation. Ickes threatened to withdraw the whole public domain if Congress did not quickly pass a suitable grazing control bill. By this time Congress was well enough acquainted with Ickes to know that he was entirely capable of such drastic action, especially when he had the support of the President. On February 21, 1934 the President had written:

My dear Mr. Secretary:
   I have discussed with you and the Secretary of Agriculture, Congressman Taylor's bill, H.R. 6462, to give to the Secretary of the Interior the power of regulating grazing on the public domain.
   I favor the principle of this bill; and you and the Secretary of Agriculture are authorized to say so to the House Committee on the Public Lands.
   Very Sincerely,
                                           Franklin D. Roosevelt[60]

The Taylor Grazing Act passed the House of Representatives on April 11, 1934. During the next two months the nation experienced some of the worst dust storms in its history. "The dust storms of May 11 carried sands from western deserts to the sidewalks of New York and sifted them down around the dome of the Capitol in Washington. According to Senator Gore of Oklahoma they were 'the most tragic, the most impressive lobbyists, that have ever come to this Capital.'"[61] The Senate passed the bill on June 12, 1934[62] and the President signed it June 28, 1934.[63]

In commenting on the act in retrospect, Congressman Taylor said:

I fought for the conservation of the public domain under Federal leadership because the citizens were unable to cope with the situation under existing trends and circumstances. The job was too big and interwoven for even the States to handle with satisfactory coordination. On the western slope of Colorado and in neaṛby States I saw waste, competition, overuse, and abuse of valuable range lands and watersheds eating into the very heart of western economy. . . . The livestock industry, through circumstances beyond its control, was headed for self-strangulation. Moreover, the States and the counties were suffering by reduced property values and decreasing revenues. [64]

On November 26, 1934, the President signed an executive order withdrawing for classification all public lands in the states of Arizona, California, Colorado, Idaho, Montana, New Mexico, Nevada, North Dakota, Oregon, South Dakota, Utah, and Wyoming.[65] This action made possible the classification of public lands for their highest use and also prevented a rush of homestead applications before the provisions of the act could become effective.

The purposes of the act, as set forth in the preamble, are: "To stop injury to the public grazing lands by preventing overgrazing and soil deterioration, to provide for their orderly use, improvement, and development, to stabilize the livestock industry dependent upon the public range, and for other purposes." To accomplish these purposes the Secretary of Interior was authorized to establish grazing districts, not exceeding 142,000,000 acres[66] in area, on lands which were, in his opinion, valuable chiefly for grazing.[67]

The Secretary is authorized to

Make rules and regulations . . . enter into such cooperative agreements, and do any and all things necessary to accomplish the purposes of this Act and to insure the objects of such grazing districts, namely to regulate their occupancy and use, to preserve the land and its resources from destruction or unnecessary injury, to provide for the orderly use, improvement, and development of the range. [68]

The act allows the Secretary considerable discretion in exchanging federal lands for state and private lands to consolidate land holdings within a district.[69]

The Secretary is also instructed to provide "for cooperation

with local associations of stockmen, State land officials and
official State agencies engaged in conservation . . . of wild
life." He may also accept gifts of land or money donations to
assist in the maintenance or improvement of the district. Provisions were also to be instituted for appeals from decisions
of the district administrative officers. [70]

Section 14 authorizes sale at public auction of "any isolated
or disconnected tract" which does not exceed 1,520 acres
provided that owners of contiguous property are given thirty
days in which they may elect to match the high bid and purchase the property. Any mountainous area, up to 760 acres,
not necessarily isolated or disconnected, may also be sold
upon the application of a person who owns contiguous lands. [71]

Lands which are situated so that they cannot be practically
included in a grazing district (known as section 15 lands) may
be leased. Again, contiguous property owners have preference. [72]

Originally 50 per cent of the fees were to be returned to the
state in which the district was located, 25 per cent were to
be used for range improvement purposes, and 25 per cent
were to remain in the United States Treasury. Probably this
clause was included to placate some of the state governments.
At any rate, in 1947, the amount of fees accruing to the states
was reduced to $12\frac{1}{2}$ per cent. [73]

An amendment of June 26, 1936, increased the area which
might be included in grazing districts from 80,000,000 to
142,000,000 acres, created the position of director of grazing, placed other employees under civil service and ordered
the Civil Service Commission to "give consideration to the
practical range experience in public-land states of persons
found eligible for appointment." The amendment also stipulated
that "no Director of Grazing, Assistant Director, or grazier
shall be appointed who at the time of appointment or selection
has not been for one year a bona-fide citizen or resident of the
State or of one of the States in which such Director, Assistant
Director, or grazier is to serve." Obviously these last two
sections of the amendment were written in an attempt to pop-
ulate the grazing service with western stockmen.

The Pierce Act of 1938 gave the Secretary authority to lease
state, county, or privately owned lands to round out the opera-

tion of a grazing district.[74] This authority was used considerably when cattle prices were low but at present very little land is so leased. State, county, and private landowners have been able to obtain greater revenue by sale or lease to other parties than the federal government and have consequently terminated most of the Pierce Act leases.

Section 9 of the original act provided for "cooperation with local associations of stockmen." F. R. Carpenter, first director of grazing, used this clause as his authority for creating a system of stockmen advisory boards. These advisory boards were given legal recognition and permanent status by an amendment of 1939 which provided for the membership and authority of advisory boards in the districts.[75]

In 1940 these advisory boards were organized into a National Advisory Council to "consider and make recommendations on grazing administration and problems of a national scope. Shortly thereafter state advisory boards were formed in several of the states. An amendment to the Federal Range Code for Grazing Districts in 1949 officially provided for state advisory boards and the National Advisory Board Council."[76]

The act authorized the Secretary to classify any lands which are "more valuable or suitable for the production of agricultural crops than for the production of native grasses . . . or more valuable . . . for any other use . . . and to open such lands to entry, selection, or location for disposal."[77] Homestead entries on such reclassified lands may not exceed 320 acres. No lands may be disposed of in any fashion until they have been reclassified. In effect, this section repealed the Grazing Homestead Law.

### Range "Rights"

The avowed purposes of the Taylor Grazing Act were to "stop injury to the public grazing lands by preventing overgrazing" and to "stabilize the livestock industry dependent upon the public range." To carry out these purposes it was first necessary to determine the grazing capacity of the district—that is, the maximum number of livestock that could be grazed without injury to the range. After this figure had been decided upon, it was next necessary to work out a system to allocate this grazing capacity to the various claimants according to some orderly and consistent criterion—to stabilize the use of the range.

The first director and his staff knew they were dealing with an extremely difficult problem and proceeded as cautiously as time permitted. Stockmen who had been fighting over the right to use these lands for fifty years or more could not be expected to submit passively to indifferent regulation. No efforts at regulation of grazing numbers or seasons of use were imposed the first year. During this period meetings were held, and stockmen were informed of the policies which would later be followed. This gave them some time to become accustomed to the idea and possibly to make some adjustments in their method of operations.

The act furnished a clue to the method of allocating grazing privileges. "Preference," said the statute, "shall be given in the issuance of grazing permits to those within or near a district who are landowners engaged in the livestock business . . . or owners of water or water rights, as may be necessary to permit the proper use of lands, water, or water rights owned, occupied, or leased by them."[78] This clause restricted grazing rights to landowners or owners of water or water rights; the propertyless nomad was thereby eliminated from consideration. The clause, "as may be necessary to permit the proper use of lands" was interpreted to mean that the applicant must have private holdings sufficient to sustain his livestock when they were off the district, and conversely, that the district lands should complement his private holdings.[79] The words "in or near a district" caused considerable dispute at first because some operators had customarily trucked cattle in or had driven stock for long distances. But after these requirements of the statute had been satisfied, there was still "three times as much private land devoted to supporting livestock which was 'in or near a district,' as there was range to complement such private lands and give them a 'proper use,'"[80] so some additional restrictive device was necessary. The director, after meetings with the stockmen, decided upon an additional system of preferences based on customary past use of the federal lands. This modified "squatter's right" idea was based on the old western common law of "first in time is first in right."[81] The director found legal justification for this concept in the language of the statute which stated "grazing privileges recognized and acknowledged shall be adequately safeguarded."[82]

Since it was impractical and impossible to determine who was originally "first in time" on the range a "priority period" was established as the five years immediately prior to passage of the act. A stockman who had made substantial use of the public range in connection with his private properties for two consecutive years or any three years during this priority period had priority "rights."

In summary, preference in obtaining grazing privileges was accorded to owners of land or water who could support their livestock during the seasons when they were off the grazing district, who required the federal lands in conjunction with their own to form an economic ranching unit, and who had used the range during the priority period.

Further interpretation of the statute makes it possible for the various applicants to decide by mutual agreement the extent of their individual grazing privileges. Such agreements must be in writing, signed by all parties concerned, and approved by the advisory board and the district range manager (DRM). The total animal unit months (A.U.M.'s) authorized under such a cooperative agreement must not exceed the carrying capacity of the range and the provisions of the agreement must be in accordance with the Federal Range Code.[83] This arrangement makes it possible to bypass the rigidities inherent in the priority-period requirement.

Preference for grazing privileges, then, was given to lands and not to people. F. R. Carpenter expressed it this way:

The Taylor Act says preference rights shall be given "FOR THE PROPER USE OF LANDS." Not of the people; not the proper use of the livestock, but of the LANDS . . . these rights will be given to you not as individuals, nor as owners of livestock—we do not care how many cattle or sheep you have or how much experience or lack of experience you have in the livestock business. We care only for your lands. We want to build up your lands and give them stability and value. In doing that we wish to give them the adjunctive pasture rights which naturally belong to them, and in proportion to their carrying capacity, fertility and crop yield.[84]

Since range "rights" are tied to lands it is only logical that they should be transferable with the lands. However, a permittee may transfer his privileges to other lands he owns or to lands owned by other persons provided the lands to which the privilege is transferred meet commensurability requirements. [85]

Naturally the range "rights" materially enhance the value of base properties, especially since the grazing fees have been consistently low. Some ranchers will therefore attempt to obtain a permit for the maximum number of A.U.M.'s so they can quote these favorable figures to prospective ranch buyers, even though they do not need or use all the "rights" to which they may be entitled. Other operators will apply and pay for the maximum A.U.M.'s to which they are entitled simply to keep out other stock and to act as a cushion in the event they need the maximum amount in some particular year. These practices do not damage the range in the short run. Unless frequent utilization checks are accomplished, however, such practices may result in an overcommitted range. Estimates or measurement of the forage, in these circumstances, may show that it is not being sufficiently utilized and the "book" carrying capacity may be increased.

The process involved in weighting and evaluating these various preferential "rights" need not concern us here except that we should note that they are tremendously complicated and time-consuming for the grazing district staff, and are subject to varying interpretations which may in turn lead to disputes and litigation.

The original carrying capacity of the districts was usually established by estimates of the advisory boards, since funds and personnel were not initially available to make scientific range surveys. Probably most of the boards tended to overrate the capacity of the range, but some limits had to be set, and this was probably the quickest and best method available under the circumstances. If scientific surveys later disagreed with the board's original estimate, a new carrying capacity was established and the number of animals licensed on each permit was adjusted accordingly. If the adjustment was upward there were probably few objections. If the adjustment was downward, however, the permittees sometimes protested and questioned the validity of the range survey. The following comment of

Rad Hall of the American National Livestock Association is typical of the complaints against range surveys which reduced range "rights":

> The question is whether to take the judgment of an experienced livestock man who grew up in the business and, in many cases, has spent a lifetime in one area or the judgment of a young college graduate with his magnifying glass which he uses to count the spears of grass in order to make learned deductions therefrom. [86]

The real question, of course, is whether estimating is more accurate than measuring. But admittedly it is difficult to accept the validity of a measure if it is likely to reduce one's income.

Persons who believe they are entitled to a grazing permit submit an application to the district office. The DRM investigates land titles involved, productive capacity of the base property, use during the priority period, and such other data as may be required to determine the applicant's eligibility. The application and the accompanying data are then submitted to the advisory board, which recommends whether or not the application shall be approved, the number of A.U.M.'s authorized, season of use, and area of use. The advisory board recommendation is a recommendation only in the sense that it may be overruled by the DRM. Applications of advisory board members are acted upon by the DRM. Any adverse action taken on a permit must be explained to the applicant, and he must be given an opportunity to appear before the DRM and the advisory board and present his case. [87] Ordinarily the advisory board holds a "protest" meeting at which any dissatisfied applicants may appear. If the applicant is still dissatisfied, he may appeal the decision, in turn, to the hearing examiner, the director of the Bureau of Land Management, and finally the Secretary of Interior. He does not have recourse to the courts unless action is initiated by the DRM to carry out the decision being appealed. Ordinarily the DRM suspends action until he has the support of a favorable decision by the examiner. If the DRM is certain of his grounds, however, he may pronounce the decision in full force and effect immediately. [88] This, of course, happens very rarely because the DRM runs the risk of being sued for the loss involved if the decision goes against him on appeal.

Cases which are appealed from the protest meeting are referred to a hearings examiner, who serves according to the provisions of the Administrative Procedures Act of 1946, which provides that

> . . . there shall be appointed by and for each agency as many qualified and competent examiners as may be necessary . . . who shall be assigned to cases in rotation so far as practicable and shall perform no duties inconsistent with their duties and responsibilities as examiners. Examiners shall be removable by the agency in which they are employed only for good cause established and determined by the Civil Service Commission . . . examiners shall receive compensation prescribed by the Commission independently of agency recommendations or ratings. [89]

The hearing officer conducts hearings in the various grazing districts. These administrative tribunals are conducted in courtroom fashion and take on much of the atmosphere of a court of law. Appellants may be represented by counsel and the DRM is ordinarily represented by an attorney from the solicitor's office. The present hearing officers decisions are apparently quite convincing. The only case directly involving the adjudication of grazing privileges to be filed in the courts during the period from 1951-55 was dismissed. [90]

For several years the hearing examiner has had one to three years' backlog of cases pending. According to a bureau study team report:

> Approximately 50 appeals are disposed of each year. The present backlog of appeals represents nearly a 3-year work load. As range adjudication is intensified it is obvious that many additional appeals will be filed. A single appeal can prevent the final adjudication of any administrative unit in a district for an indefinite period (3 years or more). [91]

Table 2 shows that the hearing examiner has been getting farther behind each year. [92]

This time lag may encourage some operators to appeal, even though they may know they do not have a case, simply to gain the use of the range for an additional three years. This undesirable situation is not new in the BLM. In 1949, Gordon Griswold, chairman of the National Advisory Board Council (NABC) said, "Some operators, depending upon the long duration of an appeal, often appeal purposely to take advantage of a favorable market situation."[93]

### TABLE 2

#### GRAZING ADJUDICATION APPEALS 1951-55

| Fiscal Year Ending | Appeals Filed During Year | Cases Concluded by Hearing, Dismissal, or Withdrawal | Cases Pending at End of Fiscal Year |
|---|---|---|---|
| 6-30-51 | 64 | 74 | 52 |
| 6-30-52 | 68 | 61 | 59 |
| 6-30-53 | 104 | 53 | 110 |
| 6-30-54 | 64 | 61 | 113 |
| 6-30-55 | 84 | 54 | 143 |

While these delaying tactics on the part of individual operators create injustices, the important objection is that the
district from which the appeal originates is left in an unset-
tled condition until the appeal is finally heard. Not only is the
DRM handicapped and final adjudication of the range postponed,
but the other users may be unable to plan long-term operations. Certain procedural changes have been instituted in the
most recent revision of the Federal Range Code which are
designed to expedite the hearing process. [94] Whether these
changes will be sufficient to reduce the present backlog to
reasonable proportions is doubtful.

The simple and obvious solution to this important problem
would be to appoint another hearing examiner. But according
to Dent Dalby, "The inadequacy of funds in our appropriation
for such purposes as well as the shortage of qualified personnel are some of the negative considerations."[95]

Grazing permits are issued on a year-to-year basis until
such time as the grazing capacity of the range is established,
the character and amount of base property substantiated, and
livestock operations become generally stabilized. Once these
objectives have been accomplished, term permits may be
issued for periods up to ten years.

Individual, partnership, or group allotments of specific
parts of the range may be accomplished by mutual agreement
when approved by the DRM. [96] The operators, as would be expected, generally prefer allotments because they can manage
their livestock more easily and more cheaply. The allotment
also relieves the operator from competition for that part of
the range, so that he may voluntarily reduce his use, knowing

that if he leaves forage no one else will take it. He is encouraged to improve the grazing capacity of his allotment by the
granting of preference for any increases allowed. The BLM
has encouraged the assignment of such allotments because it
facilitates inspection and management of the range, encourages permittees to construct range improvements (when used
with term permits) and generally aids in both rehabilitating
the range and stabilizing the operations of permittees. These, of
course, are the principal objectives of the Taylor Grazing Act.

Grazing permits may be canceled or reduced if the permittee (1) loses ownership or control of his base properties, (2)
ceases to use his base properties as part of a livestock operation, (3) fails to make substantial use of his grazing privileges, (4) fails to pay the grazing fee or charges levied by a
local cooperative grazing association, or (5) fails to comply
with the terms of agreements for the construction of range
improvements. In the event of range depletion resulting from
drought or other causes, or the diminution of lands within the
district because of withdrawal or reclassification, grazing
privileges may be reduced proportionately.[97]

When the Taylor Grazing Act was in process of passage,
Senator McCarran of Nevada proposed an amendment which
was incorporated in the act. The amendment read:

. . . except that no permittee complying with the rules and regulations
laid down by the Secretary of the Interior shall be denied the renewal
of such permit, if such denial will impair the value of the grazing
unit of the permittee, when such unit is pledged as security for any
bona fide loan.[98]

This clause may have the effect of affording some protection to lending agencies and may also be of some assistance
to the rancher in originally securing a loan. But it might also
seriously handicap the administrator because obviously almost any rancher can secure a "bona fide loan" which will prevent cancellation of his permit unless the administration can
also show that he has violated the act or the Federal Range
Code. The effects of this clause are conjectural. In a recent
congressional hearing Director Woozley testified that the provision had not caused any adverse effects since he became director.[99] It is doubtful if the director could know definitely
the number of cases in which this provision had been a factor

in a decision as to whether or not a permit should be renewed. If this clause has not caused any "adverse effects" to date, it is a potential source of trouble and should be eliminated from the statute. However, it is not likely the statute will be so amended because the general public is not likely to become agitated over the undesirable potentialities of this obscure clause.

The system of allocating grazing privileges appears to have been a limited success if the stated objectives of the act are accepted as the standard for judgment. It will be recalled that the purposes of the act were "to stop injury to the public lands by overgrazing" and to "stabilize the livestock industry dependent upon the public range." The permit system probably has reduced overgrazing over much of the public range.[100] If overgrazing has not been eliminated, it is not the fault of the permit system or the grazing officials but rather of those who have opposed appropriations sufficient to provide the necessary controls.

The permit system has certainly acted to "stabilize the livestock industry dependent on the public range." It may have forced some operators into bankruptcy who were denied the use of the range but it did "stabilize" the operations of the preferred applicants. It stopped the range wars and it stopped deterioration of the range by unregulated, competitive grazing.

Whether or not the permit system is equitable and economically sound is less certain. It seems likely that the permit system, coupled with low grazing fees, may have acted to perpetuate some uneconomic ranching units and some inefficient operators.

The matter of equity is, as always, a difficult question. The practice of allocating permits to lands, rather than persons, makes impersonal and uniform decisions more easily attainable. But it automatically excludes the nonlandowner from participating in the benefits which nearby landowners may derive from public property. It also excludes landowners who are not "in or near" a grazing district. This arrangement may not be altogether equitable but it does make for increased stability; it is more easily administered than would be a system which gave all ranchers equal "rights"; it probably encourages range development and conservation practices because ranchers can look forward to using the same range for long periods; and it protects those stockmen who developed a ranching unit in expectation of continued use of the federal range.

The provision which requires that the permittee have sufficient base property to maintain his livestock when they are off the range also acts to prevent much undue hardship and many bankrupt stockmen. The passage of the Taylor Grazing Act marked the end of an era in which the government invited overly optimistic and ignorant people to waste their lives and savings in farming or ranching operations which were predestined to failure.

Probably most of the criticism of the permit system is lodged at the preference given to those ranchers who could prove they had customarily used the range during the priority period. The use of some "priority period" for establishing preferential rights to the use, or ownership, of lands is well established in English and American history. In early England the user of the commons had a right to continue in that use subject to the base fee in the King. In negotiating treaties with the Indian tribes we proceeded on the presumption that the Indian had some "rights" to the land simply because he was there first and had customarily used it. Squatter rights were recognized by the various pre-emption acts. The homestead acts conveyed title to the individual primarily because he lived upon and used the land. We have mentioned the old western common law of "first in time is first in right" in mining claims. Although a long and consistent precedent does not establish the justice or efficacy of a particular procedure, it does establish a presumption of equity and justice. The burden of proof then falls on those who would question the established precedent. Certainly the granting of preference to customary users of the range involves less personal and economic dislocation than some other system.

The selection of the "priority period" (1919-34) has been frequently questioned because these were years of drought and low prices and consequently many customary users of the range were forced out of business or forced materially to reduce their herds and flocks. The selection of this particular base period was a matter of administrative expediency. Obviously one could not seek to establish original customary use because such usage often extended back fifty years or more. The period of customary prior use had to be recent to be of any significance or value. The longer the period, the more difficult would become the establishment of reliable data. No matter what period was used some inequities would result.

Finally, it is charged that the act and the permit system acted to perpetuate an inequitable and uneconomic landownership and land use system. This charge is generally true, although the creation of grazing districts and the "swapping" of lands did much to improve landownership patterns and land use. This last was a very considerable improvement over the old system—or lack of system. But the charge remains essentially correct. The old system, as we saw in chapter 2, was the result of a series of political decisions over a period of many years. Probably the only practical way of correcting this situation in 1934 would have been for the federal government to purchase all, or most, of the private land holdings in the range area and redivide them according to a system similar to that advanced by Major Powell. While this would have been theoretically possible, it would have been politically impossible. Political decision makers in 1934 may have liked to speculate on what might have been but they were faced with a reality which demanded immediate attention. Any proposal to remedy this undesirable factual situation had to be politically acceptable or nothing at all would have been accomplished.

In summary, by the beginning of the twentieth century it became increasingly apparent that the homestead acts were no longer practical. Stockmen also began to realize that unrestricted competition for the free range was destroying the forage and was responsible for range wars and the instability of the western livestock industry dependent on the public lands. It became increasingly clear that some kind of regulation or control was imperative.

Beginning with Senator Foster's leasing bill in 1899, almost every succeeding Congress saw the introduction of bills to provide for the regulation of use of the public grazing lands. These bills were opposed by persons who were committed to the homestead idea, by those who feared such bills were disguised land-grabbing schemes and by those who simply resented governmental "meddling" of any kind. When it became apparent that some sort of regulatory act would eventually pass, the opponents of such regulation unsuccessfully proposed state ownership and control of the public lands.

Finally a range regulatory bill, the Taylor Grazing Act, was passed in 1934. The avowed purposes of the act were to stop further injury to the public lands, to provide for their orderly use and development, and to stabilize the livestock industry dependent on them. The Secretary of Interior was authorized to carry out these objectives by the establishment of grazing districts and the issuance of grazing permits to qualified applicants for a "reasonable" fee.

Preference in awarding grazing permits was given to those stockmen who lived "in or near" a grazing district, who owned private lands capable of supporting their livestock when they were off the district (commensurate properties), and who had a history of use of the public range during the five years immediately prior to the passage of the act.

The permit system automatically disqualified nomadic stockmen, those who did not own commensurate properties "in or near" a grazing district and those who had not used the range during the priority period.

The provisions of the permit system worked a hardship on many stockmen and undoubtedly were inequitable in many instances. However, no system could have been devised which would not have produced some inequities. The system has without doubt accomplished one of the major objectives of the Taylor Grazing Act: the stabilization of the livestock industry dependent on the public range.

# 4. THE FEDERAL GRAZING SERVICE

The preceding chapters have described a series of situations which resulted in the adoption by the Congress of the United States of a policy of federal regulation and control of grazing on the public lands. We have previously noted, however, that the policy-forming process does not stop with a formal declaration of the policy and that the methods used to carry out the expressed policy continue to shape that policy. Such methods are determined to a considerable degree by organizational structure. In turn, the physical environment is decidedly influential in shaping the structure of the organization.

The study of administrative organization has traditionally been concerned with organization to maximize efficiency and economy. Reorganization moves and particular theories of organization, e.g., decentralization, are ordinarily explained, defended, or rationalized as providing "greater integration and coordination," or "better service," or "a more efficient organizational structure." These may be, in fact, the real reasons for the reorganization and it may be successful in accomplishing these objectives. However, all reorganizations are not carried out for these reasons, although they are practically always the rationale set forth. Reorganization may be effectuated simply to eliminate or render impotent certain personnel and increase the influence of others. It may be accomplished at the behest of an interest group to enable it to exercise more influence over the agency. It may be done to

73

divide organizations or territory in such a way as to facil-
itate the policies of the administrator. In a word, the reorganization device may be effectively used as a political instru-
ment to change the power structure of the organization and
often that outside the organization.

An administrative reorganization may also be considered
an attempt to restore an equilibrium which appears to be out
of balance as a result of ecological or ideological changes.
The reorganization may thus be attempted by new power-holders or it may be an attempt by the incumbents to maintain
their power by realigning the structure of the institution.[1]

This chapter describes the physical environment in which
the federal grazing activity functions, the development of the
original organizational structure, and subsequent modifications
of that structure. While the proponents of most of these reorganizations paid homage to the goals of "economy and efficiency" and stressed the democratic aspects of decentralized administration, it will become evident that other considerations were also involved in the determination of structural changes.

Originally the Taylor Grazing Act stipulated a limit of
80,000,000 acres for inclusion in grazing districts. Shortly
after the law was enacted, statewide meetings were held in
the range states and committees were designated by the stockmen to recommend areas which should be included within grazing districts. The areas recommended by these committees
far exceeded the original 80,000,000-acre limitation. Consequently, the limit was raised to 142,000,000 acres by an
amendment of 1936.[2]

An area of 142,000,000 acres is 221,875 square miles. This
is 9,000 square miles larger than the republic of France. It
is almost twice the area of Japan. Naturally, in such a large
area there exist wide diversities in topography, climate,
soils, and vegetation. Probably the most uniform feature of
these lands is the low precipitation rate. According to F. R.
Carpenter, 95 per cent of the public lands are within a zone
of less than fifteen inches of annual rainfall.[3] The grazing districts are scattered throughout all the western states except
Washington. Table 3 shows the acreage administered by the

## TABLE 3

### AREA OF GRAZING-DISTRICT LANDS, 1955

| State | Number of Districts | Federal Lands* (acres) | Nonfederal Lands† (acres) |
|-------|---------------------|------------------------|----------------------------|
| Arizona | 4 | 12,814,086 | -- |
| California | 2 | 4,308,958 | 1,118 |
| Colorado | 8 | 7,941,312 | 52,447 |
| Idaho | 5 | 12,853,537 | 208,627 |
| Montana | 6 | 5,945,557 | 25,341 |
| Nevada | 6 | 47,177,464 | 346,401 |
| New Mexico | 6 | 14,434,263 | -- |
| Oregon | 6 | 12,609,890 | 687,708 |
| Utah | 11 | 25,010,996 | 582,710 |
| Wyoming | 5 | 14,343,358 | 3,825 |
| TOTAL | 59 | 157,439,421 | 1,908,177 |

*Includes reserved lands administered by agreement.
†Includes private lands administered by agreement and lands leased pursuant to the Pierce Act of June 23, 1938 (52 Stat. 1033).

Bureau of Land Management, by states, as of June 30, 1955.[4]

Since the area administered under the Taylor Grazing Act covers such a wide expanse of territory any generalizations about it are difficult. However, some description of this region seems necessary. For purposes of simplification we may divide it into three general zones—the eastern plains, the southwest, and the intermountain region—and attempt some summary description of each.

The plains region includes eastern Montana, Wyoming, Colorado, and New Mexico. Over most of this area annual precipitation varies between twelve and twenty inches. Most of the moisture falls during the spring and summer. The rate of evaporation is less in the northern plains than in the southern plains area. The average wind velocity is higher than in any part of the United States. The landscape is generally a flat, treeless prairie. On the eastern edges there still remain some of the tall grasses such as little bluestem and big bluestem. Most of the grass cover is the shortgrass type of which blue grama and buffalo grass are the chief species.

These grasses are short but highly nutritious. Ranges that appear bare to a visitor from the tall grass country may be supporting fat cattle. The short grasses tend to be supplanted by desert grass in New Mexico. Cattle predominate in this area, with most animals moving to eastern markets. In the southern part of this region cattle graze all year round. In northern section both hay feeding and winter range are used.

The southwest region includes southern California, southern Nevada, and Arizona. Much of this area is desert or semi-desert, with rainfall averaging less than ten inches annually over much of the territory. Over most of this region the forage consists of desert shrubs with pockets of short grass and curly mesquite. Both cattle and sheep are produced, with cattle predominating. Stock graze all year round and are ordinarily sold as feeders to California feed lots.

The intermountain region includes eastern Oregon, southern Idaho, northeastern California, most of Nevada and Utah, western Montana, western Wyoming, and western Colorado. Most of the grazing district lands are located in this region. Probably desert shrubs are the most common forage with some bunch grass and desert grasses. Part of this area is forested, but in the open forest sections considerable forage is available. Cattle and sheep are about equal in importance; that is, there are about five times as many sheep as cattle. Because of variations in elevation, it is often possible to graze the high ranges during the summer and the lowland desert during the winter months. Most cattle go to Pacific Coast markets and lambs to eastern markets.

Another method of classifying range may be according to a "snow line" which differentiates the area into two broad categories of ranch operating methods. F. R. Carpenter describes the distinction thus:

The range as a whole is divided into two sections that vary widely in their manner of use; the division line is the snow line running east and west through southern Nevada, Utah and Colorado. North of that snow line sufficient moisture stays on the ground in winter to make it usable by livestock during the winter months. As a result, all of it is necessarily connected in a year-round operation with other private lands furnishing pasturage or feed for the balance of the year. Below or south of the snow line no seasonal water for stock is available and the use of the desert depends solely on developed watering places, such as wells, tanks, reservoirs and taps. Arizona and New Mexico come in this category. Between the great land-controlled areas in Oregon, Idaho, Montana, Wyoming, Colorado and the northern part of California, Nevada, and Utah on the one hand, and the southern areas where water controls on the other, comes the twilight zone of southern Nevada, California, and Utah where both land and water holes play a basic part in the use of the desert. [5]

In 1955, 18,937 permittees grazed a total of 2,418,183 cattle, 52,929 horses, 6,281,913 sheep and 21,014 goats on federal grazing districts. [6] Nevada used the federal range more than any other state with 3,147,530 A.U.M.'s used by 1,152 operators. Utah was next with 2,471,856 A.U.M.'s used by 3,099 operators. [7]

In 1955 it was also estimated that about 119,000 antelope, 769,000 deer, 17,000 elk, 500 moose, and 5,000 mountain sheep subsisted on grazing district lands. [8]

While this study is primarily concerned with the administration of grazing on the federal range it should be noted that these lands have other values. Some areas produce saleable timber in considerable quantities, large areas have recreational values which are difficult to calculate, and the watershed values of part of this domain are worth many times their value for grazing. Some sections of the range have also been withdrawn for military purposes. All these competing users have a clientele which seeks to accomplish its purposes through political action.

The demands of these different users and potential users are not entirely irreconcilable. Game animals generally prefer a different type of forage than do domestic animals, so that competition between the two is not likely to be serious unless the range becomes overcrowded. The recreational values of this area are not ordinarily spoiled by the presence of sheep or cattle unless, again, the range is overcrowded. On the other hand, the presence of hunters, fishermen, campers, and the like, does not detract from the value of the forage, if these sportsmen conduct themselves in a civilized manner. Occasionally, however, the sportsmen have been guilty of leaving gates open, cutting fences, and killing livestock instead of game. There is no incompatibility between timber and grazing interests unless the range is so overgrazed as to injure young growth. Proper range stocking will not impair watershed values.

Maximum utilization of the federal range can be obtained only by a management that considers all these values. It seems obvious that such management is not likely if one group dominates the administration, nor is it likely that such management could be successful if the lands were privately owned. However, most of these other uses for the range depend upon the control of grazing. Consequently the Taylor Grazing Act emphasized the grazing aspect of land use. The early administrators also were most interested in the grazing function or sought primarily to accomplish other objectives through the control of grazing. E. N. Kavanaugh, who developed many of the original policies of the grazing service, states,

> Primary but not the only consideration was given to the development of policies and procedures that would serve to protect and stabilize the use of the public range and that portion of the livestock industry dependent thereon. [9]

Since grazing was the overriding and controlling factor, and since stockmen were most immediately affected, it is only natural that they were most prominent in the organization of the original Division of Grazing in the Department of the Interior.

The first director of grazing, Farrington R. Carpenter of Hayden, Colorado, was appointed on September 7, 1934. Carpenter was a stockman and a lawyer with wide experience in problems of the range area. In his own words,

> I have lived my life between 2 great National Forests (The Routt and the White River). I saw it first withdrawn and put under control in 1906. I witnessed the attempt of the big cow outfits to outmaneuver the local officials. I was here when the cow men fell on their faces in 1922 and could neither stock their allotments nor pay their fees. I saw the big sheepmen of Wyoming and later of Utah "take over" and almost monopolize the Forest ranges, eliminating most small local outfits and adding nothing to the County's assessment rolls. As county attorney for 8 years I sued them for unpaid taxes. I saw the big sheepmen buy out ranches and destroy all improvements and even abandon irrigation ditches to decrease their assessed valuation. [10]

Carpenter was also a constituent of Congressman Taylor and testified in favor of the act during the hearings. The story of Carpenter's appointment and his actions in establishing an organization to administer the federal range are best told in his own words.

He [Ickes] wanted a combination lawyer and stockman to administer the Act and in reading over the proceedings ran into my testimony and asked Oscar Chapman [Assistant Secretary of Interior] about me as he was also from Colorado. As a result I was appointed after an interview with Ickes in which I told him of three reasons why I should not be appointed:

1. I was a Republican;
2. I was a cowman who was identified as being anti-sheep;
3. I was not interested in building up a Federal Reserve.

There was no appropriation to administer the Act, so I was loaned 17 men from the Geological Survey and the General Land Office. Without consulting Ickes, I went to Rex Tugwell, Acting Secretary of Agriculture, and asked for the loan of his two best Forestry Service men who knew the grazing problem. I then got advice on them and asked for Ed Kavanaugh of Oregon and Ernest Winkler of Utah and they were assigned to me.

There were no maps of the Domain, believe it or not. The status changed every hour as entries were made and the only records were in District Land Offices scattered around in politically helpful locations. Each township was a separate sheet of record and bore the imprint of various Registers. The only people who knew where the remaining public lands were and what they were, were the stockmen who used them and they had first hand and accurate knowledge. A few of them, very few, had some idea of the way the Public Lands were being devastated, but all of them had had a taste of Federal bureaucracy in the "Papa knows best" philosophy which then guided the Forest Service. None of the stockmen wanted to be regulated and many didn't want to pay a fee for pasture, though most of them knew that there were some pirates who should be kicked off. The two Forest Service men were very able and fine graziers and initiated me into the doctrine of "commensurate rights" and preference by 'priority of use." [11]

Among the personnel transferred to the new Division of Grazing were Depue Falck, E. R. Greenslet, G. M. Kerr, and J. A. Peterson from the Classification Branch of the Geological Survey, and Archie Ryan and Joe Leech from the Division of Field Investigations. Hugh Bryan and Milo Deming were employed as technicians. [12] With this small group of borrowed personnel, Carpenter set out to administer a vast range empire which to that time had defied any control or regulation.

Carpenter needed first to find out where lands were located which might be practically included in grazing districts. As he has indicated, up-to-date maps were not available. Even if they had been available, reference to a map alone could not have indicated the proper boundaries and the knowledge necessary for the organization of grazing districts. Accordingly a series of statewide organizational meetings were held during December, 1934, and January, 1935, in strategically placed cities in the range area. In Carpenter's words,

At these meetings State Committees, composed of representative stockmen, were elected to recommend boundaries for such grazing districts.

Following the series of Statewide hearings the committees elected at such hearings considered the range problems of their respective States and recommended the establishment of 50 districts involving an aggregate area of approximately 142,000,000 acres of vacant, unreserved, unappropriated public land. The action of these committees was taken without reference to the provision in the existing law limiting the creation of such districts to 80,000,000 acres of vacant, unappropriated, unreserved public land. Accordingly, in the absence of further authority from the Congress, only 32 of the districts proposed could be established. [13]

In the state organizational meeting at Vale, Oregon, on December 15, 1934, Carpenter said:

We will have the election of a state committee. Its duties will be to assist the Government land classifiers in drawing the lines of the districts. We ask for ten cattlemen and ten sheepmen. I think we will arrange for the caucus after we come back from the noon recess. I will ask that the leaders in your wool growers and livestock associations take charge of the meeting for the purpose of holding a caucus for the selection of the state committee. [14]

Once having determined the boundaries of the grazing districts, Carpenter attempted to formulate regulations regarding range administration, to gather as much data as possible on the districts to be administered and, at the same time, to put the program into effect.

This was a most ambitious undertaking. As E. N. Kavanaugh points out, [15] if these lands had been vacant the problem would have been comparatively simple. But the lands were vacant only in the sense that no private individual held title to them. They had been used for many years by stockmen who depended on continued use for the maintenance of their ranching operation.

Carpenter was faced with the necessity of acquiring a tremendous amount of information in the shortest possible time and of making policy decisions which required access to this information. The law itself was couched in very general terms and was actually in the nature of a general policy statement. According to Carpenter, "Advisory boards looked like the answer." These boards could provide much of the information necessary and at the same time assist in the decision making process both on detail matters and major policy items. The use of these boards would also help secure local compliance and support and "lessen the costs of change." They would also act as an information agency for the administration. Carpenter explains his policies in these words:

When I undertook to interpret and put into regulations a statute as loose and general as the Taylor Act . . . I was determined:

1. Not to have the range ruled by a case-hardened bureaucracy.

2. To let carefully filtered local advice have great weight, but not to ever let the boards "get the bit in their teeth."

3. To keep the General Land Office from centralizing it all with the attendant absurd delays.

4. To give the permittees a democratically constructed machine and warn them that "eternal vigilance" and attendance at the polls was the price of retention.

5. To tie the permit to the land and not allow its transfer without the land or other equal commensurate real estate. In the permits below the snow line, "water" was substituted for "land."

6. To allow economic forces to work out "sizes" of permits and transfers.

7. To give stability to the value of permits both for the owner and the mortgager.

8. To keep the service civil and cooperative but with a firm hold on all final decisions and an eye to the long range policy. [16]

It should be noted that these advisory boards were not appointed by the administration nor by the stockmen's associations. They were elected by the permittees. This was the system that Congressman Taylor called "home rule on the range."

The first regulation published by the administration concerned the use of advisory boards. Circular 1 provided for a special election of local stockmen who were to take the regular oath of office of a federal official. "By this means the practical local viewpoint will be available at all times in the administration of the law."[17] But the boards were to do more than supply the "practical local viewpoint." According to Carpenter, they were to be "the local governing agency as to all matters of a range regulatory nature concerning their particular district. The Interior Department will exercise necessary supervision and provide basic technical criteria."[18]

Circular 2 provided that during the organization period range permits would be issued to "established stockmen . . . upon the basis of their operations prior to the time the administration of the public range was inaugurated."[19]

Using these methods, the Grazing Division organized thirty-two grazing districts during its first year of operation. The thirty-two districts encompassed 178,000,000 acres, of which 75,000,000 was federal land.

When the districts were first organized, the principal duties of Grazing Division personnel were the issuance of grazing permits and the construction of range improvements. Grazing fee notices were prepared by grazing district personnel, but all collections and accounting was handled by the General Land Office. In 1939 collection and accounting functions were transferred to the Grazing Division.

The range improvement program was primarily dependent on the use of the Civilian Conservation Corps. In the first year of its operation, the Division of Grazing was assigned sixty C.C.C. camps, with about 12,000 men, to carry out range improvements on the public domain.[20] Use of the C.C.C. was continued until 1943, when the corps was discontinued. At one time as many as one hundred camps were assigned to the Division of Grazing.[21] Very likely most of the range improvements constructed since the inception of the act were accomplished by the C.C.C. The availability of C.C.C. labor was a most fortunate circumstance for the infant Division of Grazing.

During the second year of its operation the Grazing Division established a field headquarters in Salt Lake City and nine regional offices throughout the range states. Personnel increased from a total of thirty-five to sixty. Five additional districts were added for a total of thirty-seven districts. These districts included a gross area of 198,000,000 acres of which 80,000,000 were federal lands. The director's report notes that, "The organization of the Division of Grazing has been developed on the principle of decentralizing administration."[22]

In January, 1936, representatives from all the district advisory boards and the administration met in Salt Lake City and worked out a new set of regulations to replace the temporary circulars issued the year before. Probably the most important decisions of this meeting were the establishment of range fees and the criterion for issuing grazing permits. The grazing fees were set at five cents per month for each head of cattle or horse and one cent per month for sheep and goats.[23] Grazing permits were to be issued according to the following order of preference:

1. Qualified applicants with dependent commensurate property with priority of use.
2. Qualified applicants with dependent commensurate property but without priority of use.
3. Qualified applicants who have priority of use but not commensurate property.
4. Other qualified applicants.[24]

During the first year of administration the constitutionality of the act was challenged by two Oregon sheepmen, Joe Odiago and Cleto Achabal, who charged that it was an unconstitutional delegation of legislative powers. We have previously noted that provisions of the act were somewhat vague and that the Secretary was authorized to do "any and all things necessary" to carry out its provisions. However, federal judge John H. McNary of the United States District Court for Oregon overruled demurrers filed in behalf of the defendants in an opinion which stated in part:

The provision of the act authorizing the Secretary of the Interior to establish grazing districts and make such rules and regulations as shall be necessary to accomplish the purposes of the law, does not constitute a delegation of legislative power but creates administrative duties. Obviously the fixing of boundaries of grazing districts so as to prevent overgrazing and soil deterioration is a matter of detail, and a necessary subject of inquiry and determination by an administrative officer.[25]

In August, 1939, the old Division of Grazing was reorganized into a new Grazing Service with R. H. Rutledge as the director. The new organizational plan provided for a functional division with four major categories—operations, range management, range improvement and maintenance, and land acquisition and control.[26] Each of these divisions was headed by a branch chief located in Washington.

Carpenter had stressed decentralization and organization by area but this reorganization moved toward greater central- ization of control in Washington. The new director appeared to be satisfied with his handiwork. According to him, "This plan proved advantageous from standpoints of public service, ef- ficiency, and economy. Definite progress was made in orienta- tion of personnel on lines of authority, responsibility, and accountability." He also said, "The new set-up functioned smoothly during the first year of its complete service and with further training, especially in the field, the whole organiza- tion will be in a better position to perform the jobs assigned to it."[27]

By this time (June 30, 1940) the staff had grown to 205 peo- ple who now administered 258,000,000 acres of range land in fifty-three districts, on which grazed 12,000,000 head of live- stock. During the first six years of its existence the Grazing Service had expended $2,668,000 and had collected $3,069,200 in grazing fees.[28]

In August, 1941, the Grazing Service was "decentralized" by moving the headquarters from Washington, D.C., to Salt Lake City. According to Director Rutledge, "Spokes radiate from this hub to the 10 regional offices, none of which is more than 500 miles from the Director's desk in the Walker Bank Building."[29]

By 1945 a new director of grazing, C. L. Forsling, was attempting to promote a rather extensive program of range rehabilitation. Forsling estimated this program would require the services of 20,000 men for three and one-half years at a cost of $191,000,000.[30] By this time sixty grazing districts were in operation encompassing a gross area of 265,000,000 acres.[31] Not only did Director Forsling's optimistic program fail of acceptance, but the existing organization was drasti- cally curtailed.

During 1946 Senator McCarran and others were able to re- duce the Grazing Service to a "paper" organization. This story will be told in some detail in a later chapter. At this point we need only note that the Grazing Service was abolished as a

separate organization on July 16, 1946, and consolidated with
the old General Land Office to form the present Bureau of
Land Management.[32] By this time Harold Ickes had been replaced by Julius A. Krug as Secretary of Interior, and C. L.
Forsling had resigned. Total personnel were reduced by 79 per
cent. Some of the people discharged had over twenty years of
government service. Four regional offices and many field offices were closed.[33]

According to the new director, Fred W. Johnson, the reorganization program was effectuated to "integrate the program for management of the 778,000,000 acres of public domain." The director also characterized the reorganization
plan as a "modern administrative structure for more efficient
handling of problems involving the Nation's public land."[34]

The new organization was headed by a director, an associate
director, and an assistant director. The work of the central
office was divided into six categories or staff sections: adjudication, land planning, range management, forestry, engineering and construction, and administration. Seven regional
field offices were established with the regional administrator
reporting directly to the director. The seven regional administrators, in turn, were responsible for the operation of twenty-five district land offices, ten forestry offices, sixty district grazing offices, and one experiment station.[35] According to Marion Clawson:

> The Bureau of Land Management maintains only one level of dis-
> trict offices below the regional office, but these are specialized: dis-
> trict land offices, where applications for leasing or otherwise obtain-
> ing land are filed; district grazing offices, where range lands are
> administered; public survey offices, which are concerned with cadas-
> tral surveys; and forestry offices in some areas.[36]

Probably the only "integration" that Director Johnson spoke
so fondly of, occurred in the director's office and in the regional administrator's office—if it occurred there.

The new "modern administrative structure," as we have
noted, practically wiped out the Grazing Service. If the grazing districts had been forced to rely on congressional appropriations entirely, the Taylor Grazing Act would have been
almost completely ineffective. But the advisory boards came
to the rescue of the administration and allotted about $200,000

of range improvement funds to help pay salaries of employees in the fiscal year 1947. [37] At this time, 50 per cent of the total grazing fees collected were transferred from the Treasury to the state governments in which the grazing districts were located in lieu of taxes. Most of the states then transferred these monies to the district advisory boards to be used for range improvements. These were the funds which the advisory boards used to pay salaries of employees. Even with this contribution the grazing service operated as a skeleton force.

This contribution by the advisory boards was particularly significant because it indicated their general acceptance of the program and because it had the effect of placing local administrators under the supervision of the advisory board. Possibly one could expect the advisory boards to support the grazing district program because it was a program which they had probably been most instrumental in shaping. [38] But the payment of employees' salaries by advisory boards is probably unique in administrative history. In effect, the regulators were being supervised by those who were to be regulated.

Senator McCarran of Nevada, leaders of the livestock associations, and advisory board members wanted to keep grazing fees as low as possible but they did not want the Taylor Grazing Act repealed. They apparently wanted enough federal supervision of the range to keep out nomadic stockmen and those who did not own land or water rights "in or near a grazing district." In other words, they hoped to retain the status quo and at as low a cost as possible.

With these objectives in mind they hit upon that happy administrative device "the study" as a way to solve their problems. Rex Nicholson, a California cattleman, was appointed by Secretary Krug to make a study of grazing fees, organization and personnel for the grazing activity. [39]

One of Nicholson's first moves was to meet with the American National Livestock Association and the National Woolgrowers Association at Salt Lake City on September 16-17, 1946. Nicholson was introduced to the stockmen by Senator McCarran, who declared: "He is going to reorganize the Grazing Service, and if he gets a free hand you will benefit 100 per cent." [40]

At the same meeting Nicholson met with the National Ad-

visory Board Council and received their recommendations.[41]
He also sent out a questionnaire to district advisory board
members. Nicholson's completed study actually appears to
have been little more than a consolidation of the ideas of advisory board members. Nicholson's proposal side-stepped any
consideration of fees based on the value of the forage or any
other criterion. It assumed that grazing fees should cover
only the cost of administering the program. The problem then
became one of determining how extensive the program should
be and what part of the cost of that program accrued to the
direct benefit of the stockmen who used the federal range. The
primary problem, with this approach, was no longer one of
grazing fees. It now became a problem of how extensive the
administration should be and what portion of that administration directly benefited the stockmen.

We have previously noted that the users did not want to jet-
tison the whole program—they wanted just enough administration to protect them from nomadic stockmen and others who
were not qualified under the act. Therefore they wanted a small
organization both because it would cost less and because it
would not be able to regulate them to any considerable degree.
To satisfy these objectives Nicholson proposed an organization not to exceed 242 persons.

The Secretary of Interior then obtained an estimate from the
Bureau of Agricultural Economics to the effect that only 70
per cent of the costs of range administration accrued to the
benefit of the users of the range while the other 30 per cent
benefited the public generally.

From this point on it became simply a matter of calculating
70 per cent to the cost of employing 242 persons plus other
costs incidental to the program. This was the figure that was
then to be raised by grazing fees. On the basis of past use
records, Nicholson calculated that this fee should be about
5.25 cents per A.U.M. rather than the five cents previously
charged. But 50 per cent of the five-cent fee had gone to the
states and had usually been returned to the district advisory
boards for range improvement. Nicholson therefore suggested
that the fee be set at six cents per A.U.M. with $12\frac{1}{2}$ per cent
reverting to the states, instead of 50 per cent, plus a two-cent
range improvement fee for a total of eight cents per A.U.M.

While Nicholson's proposal was accepted by the advisory boards and by the Department of Interior it did not carry the same weight with Congress. In fact, by 1956, Congress had not yet appropriated enough funds to satisfy even the skeleton force recommended by Nicholson.

The acceptance of the Nicholson-BAE formula had generally undesirable effects for the administration of the federal range. It acted as a double-edged sword both to prevent the establishment of a realistic grazing fee and to restrict the activities of the administration. If grazing fees were to be determined by the cost of administration, and if the cost of administration were kept low, obviously there would be no point in raising the fees. On the other hand, the administrative costs could not be expanded because to do so would be to exceed the amount collected in fees.

It should also be noted that a fixed fee inevitably becomes out of date with changes in cost of living and the value of the dollar. Even if the Nicholson estimates had been adequate when first proposed, the rising costs of wages and other expenses would have quickly outmoded the original figures. But the fee remained static and the administration of the range suffered. Certain congressmen have long believed that grazing fees on the public domain are too low. These congressmen ordinarily oppose any increase in appropriations for the grazing activity unless grazing fees are also raised. Other (western) congressmen are interested in keeping grazing fees low. These two groups, properly manipulated, have tended to cancel out each other's efforts; fees have not been raised substantially and neither have appropriations. The Nicholson report had the effect of formalizing this dual concept into departmental policy. Thus no expansion of grazing activities has been possible without an increase in fees—and increased fees have, of course, been resisted. The stockmen who were represented by advisory boards generally accomplished their objectives: they obtained just enough federal supervision to keep outsiders off the range but not enough to hamper their own activities seriously, and at the same time they held down the cost of grazing fees. In the process they also established a *right* to free use of the range because supposedly they were not paying for using the range—only for administering the Grazing Service. Because of inadequate appropriations, the Grazing Service has not been able to carry out the duties with which it is charged under the Taylor Grazing Act. The shortage of staff has also forced administrators to be especially dependent upon advisory boards for information and also for securing compliance with administrative regulations and decisions, thus further enhancing the power of the advisory boards.

In 1948 a recalcitrant Congress did not supply even the meager appropriations recommended in the Nicholson report. A new director, Marion Clawson, stated that "appropriations for the coming year are still approximately $200,000 short of providing the organization recommended by Rex L. Nicholson."[42] Mr. Clawson also noted that during the 1947 fiscal year, the appropriation afforded only two graziers for each state plus contributions from the industry which made it possible to maintain one grazier in each district. The 1948 appropriations was sufficient to maintain one grazier and one clerk in each district.[43] Table 4, a summary of personnel as-

TABLE 4

### TOTAL PERSONNEL ASSIGNED TO THE GRAZING ACTIVITY, BLM, NORTHWEST REGION

|                          | 1950 | 1951 | 1952 |
|--------------------------|------|------|------|
| Regional Office          | 2    | 4    | 6    |
| Idaho Grazing Dist. #1   | 3    | 5    | 5    |
| #2                       | 3    | 4    | 4    |
| #3                       | 3    | 4    | 4    |
| #4                       | 3    | 3    | 3    |
| #5                       | 3    | 4    | 3    |
| Oregon Grazing Dist. #1  | 3    | 3    | 3    |
| #2                       | 3    | 3    | 4    |
| #3                       | 3    | 4    | 5    |
| #5                       | 2    | 3    | 4    |
| #6, 7                    | 2    | 2    | 3    |

Source: Minutes, Oregon state advisory board meetings, November 14, 1951 and December 15, 1952.

signed to the northwestern regional office and the grazing districts during 1950-52, will give some idea of the inadequacy of staffing under the Nicholson plan.

F. R. Carpenter was an accurate prophet when he stated at Vale, Oregon, in December, 1934: "It is proposed to administrate the Taylor Act with a tiny personnel of Federal officials and a tremendous backing by the personnel of the stockmen as a class and their local advisory committees."[44] Yet in the face of this depleted staff situation the demand for decentralization still continued with charges of "long-handled" administration from Washington. Clawson himself spoke of the need for decentralized administration and an "administrative structure of greatly strengthened local offices."[45] Presumably, Clawson was speaking of other functions of the BLM. Surely he was not suggesting that the bulk of administrative decision-making be delegated to the lone grazier and his single clerk in the grazing district office. In his annual report for 1949, Clawson again emphasized the benefits of decentralization and the progress being accomplished toward a decentralized administration. Carpenter's reports, in the days of the infant Grazing Division, had also stressed the decentralization theme.

In 1952 Clawson suggested the need for a long-term program of range rehabilitation (reminiscent of the Forsling plan) at an estimated cost of $450,000,000.[46] But 1953 brought a new administration, a new director, and a new reorganization plan which, strangely enough, emphasized the need for a more decentralized administration.

On October 16, 1953, the Secretary of Interior established a survey team to study the organization and operations of the Bureau of Land Management.[47] The survey was headed by Floyd Hart, president of Timber Structures Corporation. Other members were Robert K. Coote, a former BLM employee; Paul Hunt, former lieutenant governor of Nebraska; Philip McBride, a Seattle attorney; Theodore Taylor, and Robert Efteland, secretary. Probably none of these men, with the possible exception of Robert Coote, had any considerable experience as a responsible public administrator.

This team was concerned with all the operations of the BLM—of which grazing is only one part. On December 18, 1953, the survey team submitted its recommendations, which were approved by the Secretary of Interior. On January 26, 1954, the Secretary instructed the director of the BLM to proceed with the reorganization proposals embodied in the Hart report. [48]

The new organization plan eliminated the six staff sections which had previously existed in the Washington office and substituted two assistant directors and nine staff and auxiliary officers. One of the assistant directors is in charge of "technical activities." His division, or branch, is headed by five staff officers for land, minerals, forestry, range, and cadastral engineering. These are staff officers in the accepted sense of the term—that is, their functions are advisory only, and they do not issue orders or instructions except in the name of the director.

The other assistant director is in charge of "operations," which includes budget and accounting, personnel, administrative services, and the land office.

The seven old regional offices were abolished and three area offices substituted. It may be more accurate to say that eleven state offices were substituted for the seven regional offices and that the three area offices were superimposed on the state offices for policy development and coordination. At any rate the jurisdiction of the three area offices is as follows:

Area 1, Portland, Oregon: states of Washington, Oregon and California.

Area 2, Salt Lake City, Utah: states of Idaho, Nevada, Utah, and Arizona.

Area 3, Denver, Colorado: states of Montana, Wyoming, Colorado, and New Mexico. [49]

In the old organization the chain of command went from the director to the regional administrator to the district manager. Now it goes from the director to the area administrator to the state supervisor to the district range manager. [50]

The Hart report stated that "there still remains too great a concentration of operations in the Washington and regional offices. The number of supervisory and operating personnel should be reduced. . . . Operations should be decentralized to the field."[51] Consequently, most of the work formerly done by the regional offices is now performed by state offices and

district offices. Both the area administrators and the state
supervisors have staff sections comparable to that of the Washington office. As presently organized, the BLM is an almost
exact prototype of the usual military line and staff organizational system.

Each area administrator has a range and forestry staff officer (as well as other staff officers). This staff officer usually
has two assistants: one forestry technician and one range technician. The same pattern is repeated at the state level. Just
why there should be a range and forestry staff officer to supervise the work of the range officer and the forestry officer
is something of a mystery. As far as speed and operating efficiency are concerned this arrangement can only act to slow
down the communication and decision-making processes because it interposes two additional clearance points between
the director and the district range manager. On the other hand,
it does reduce the number of persons reporting directly to the
area administrator and the state supervisor. Probably the rationale behind this arrangement was that the combined post
of range and forestry would result in better coordination of the
two programs. This may be true. It is possible, however, that
the range and forestry officer at both area and state levels
concentrates primarily on whatever program is of greatest
importance 'n his area or state. If this suspicion is correct
the practical result will be two forestry staff officers and one
range staff officer in one situation and two range staff officers
and one forestry officer in another situation. There may be
nothing wrong with such a system; it may, in fact, provide a
desirable flexibility.

The organizational chart on page 93 may clarify the organizational structure which we have been considering.

### Decentralization

Throughout most of its history the federal grazing service
has emphasized a decentralized organizational structure. When
F. R. Carpenter organized the old Grazing Division he established what he thought was a decentralized organization
but some other directors have tried to decentralize still further.

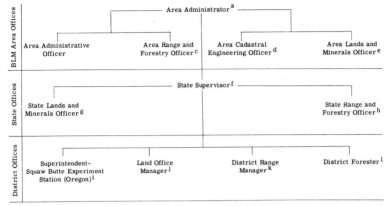

Fig. 1. Functional chart of Bureau of Land Management area, state, and district offices, Area I (Oregon and California), 1955. Source: Department of Interior, Bureau of Land Management.

a. Responsible for the effective administration, supervision, and coordination of all activities of the Bureau of Land Management in the area. Develops long-range programs and plans for the management and conservation of the land and its resources under his jurisdiction.

b. Responsible for general business management of the area (including state and district offices)—budgeting, finance, personnel, property utilization, record management, and general administrative services.

c. Responsible for staff advice and over-all technical supervision of range and forestry programs and policies. Analyzes and coordinates range and forestry programs of states into over-all area program.

d. Responsible for direction of cadastral surveys within the area, technical direction of mineral surveys, including technical examinations, appointment, and bonding of mineral surveyors. Maintains office of record for public survey, Area I. Supervises cartographic drafting section.

e. Responsible for staff advice and over-all technical supervision of land and mineral programs and policies, and of adjudication activities.

f. Responsible for directing all Bureau's operating programs within the state except cadastral engineering and general administration. Develops long-range programs for the state regarding use, management, and disposal of the public lands and resources. Coordinates the Bureau's programs with the state's. Represents the Bureau in dealing with the state government and other public and private agencies.

g. Responsible for staff advice and conduct of the lands and minerals program within the states. Classifies lands for agricultural homestead, grazing, forestry, recreational and wildlife uses. Appraises mineral lands for leasing and patenting, and supervises field examinations.

h. Responsible for staff advice and technical direction of range management (grazing administration, soil and moisture conservation, range fire protection, range improvement, revegetation, weed control, research, and conservation surveys) and forest management (forestry activities on public domain lands; timber sales; forest protection against fire, insects, and disease; special timber salvage programs; forest access roads; forest development and improvement; forest inventory; reforestation; watershed protection), and multiple-use management of public lands.

i. Responsible for range research and demonstration programs, carried out in cooperation with the Oregon State Agricultural Experiment Station.

j. Responsible for land office activities. Receives and takes action on applications and claims for lands and for the use of lands, and receives payment due the government in connection therewith. Adjudicates applications for land and mineral use or disposal. Custodian of local public lands records and other information relating to public lands.

k. Responsible for administration of land resources under his jurisdiction. Receives and acts upon applications filed by stockmen for grazing on public lands both inside and outside of grazing districts. Promotes economic use of the federal range through proper range management. Conducts soil and moisture conservation; range improvement; weed control; range protection, including fire control. Supervises all other activities involving conservation of surface resources within his jurisdiction.

l. Responsible for administration of forest and land resources under his jurisdiction, primarily sustained-yield management and protection of forest resources from fire, insects, and disease. Administers timber sales, forest development and rehabilitation, watershed protection, trespass control, forest land exchange, special land use permits; access roads, rights-of-way; and receives payment due the government in connection therewith.

In his remarks to the National Advisory Board Council on April 6, 1955, BLM director Edward Woozley said, "A major objective of the reorganization was the decentralization of functions in an effort to place administration closer to the level where the work was done."[52]

Six years earlier, Gordon Griswold, chairman of the National Advisory Board, had complimented Marion Clawson and the BLM on their progress in decentralizing the administration of the grazing activity.[53]

From the point of view of administrative efficiency and service to clientele, there are certain undeniable and rather obvious advantages in a decentralized organization. The local administrator is more familiar with local problems, personalities, and situations than a more distant administrator. When he is not familiar with a local problem he can make a study "on the ground" with little time loss. This knowledge of local matters may enable him to make more intelligent decisions. Discussion of problems "across the table" may give the public a better understanding of the program, make the administration seem less cold and impersonal, and result in a higher degree of acceptance of and compliance with the administration program. Less time may elapse from receipt of a case and final disposition because less travel time is involved and less time is lost while the case is being shunted around in a large, production-line office. This does not mean that fewer man hours are expended on the case by the administration; in fact the opposite is likely to be true. The genius of American production involves increasing specialization in all lines of activity. We need not belabor the advantages of specialization in increased speed and quality of work. Generally speaking, the lower the point of decision-making and "processing" the less specialized the worker must be. Since he is less specialized, his work will be slower and his decisions less intelligent; he cannot be an expert in all things. From the point of view of operational efficiency, these disadvantages may overbalance the advantages of proximity to the problem. This conclusion, however, may be legitimate only in proportion to the consistency of the cases processed, that is, the more deviations from a consistent pattern, the less successful a highly specialized, production-line office is likely to be. We have all encountered the bureaucratic indigestion which almost inevitably results in the large office when an unforeseen contingency arises or a unique problem is introduced. Instances like these cause the red tape to become snarled and make it appear that the bureaucracy is less efficient than it really may be. Specialization may also tend to create an intellectual isolation with attendant lack of adaptability.[54] These observations seem to indicate that centralization is likely to involve increased specialization and that increased specialization is likely to result in greater efficiency, but also greater rigidity.

The more decentralized the administration, the more flexible and adaptable it is likely to be. But if this adaptability is carried far enough it results in local autonomy and lack of consistency in policy implementation. Such inconsistencies and deviations not only may have disastrous effects on the operational effectiveness of the program but also may result in unfavorable political repercussions from other grass-roots clientele groups who will complain they have been treated unfairly or have been discriminated against.

The location of the optimum point for most effective administrative decision-making cannot be found by consulting management manuals. It will vary with space, time, situation, and personality. It seems likely that in its zeal to decentralize, the federal grazing service may have pushed the decision-making level below the point of reasonable expertise and below the point at which reasonable expertise might be acquired. The district range manager is not an expert on all the phases of the operation upon which he is called to make decisions, and he does not have time to become an expert. Yet he is forced to make decisions which are as binding as if made by the Secretary of Interior. Inevitably some of these will be unsound decisions simply because the district range manager has been "spread too thin." It this situation does exist, it could, of course, be rectified by the assignment of sufficient specialized staff to the district office. However, moving specialists from an area or state office to a district office does not solve the problem caused by lowering the point of decision-making because, where the expert formerly used his specialty throughout a whole region (now area) or state, he now can utilize his special skills only throughout a single district. The other districts no longer have the benefit of his specialized services. On the other hand there will probably not be enough work in his specialty within a single district to keep him busy. He will therefore be assigned other additional duties in which he has little or no training and experience. The net result may be that highly trained and highly competent specialists are not utilized at their highest level of capability and that the same people are used in areas where they have a low level of competence. This may mean that more faulty decisions will be made and work may be done poorly and slowly. The backlog thus created might require the employment of additional personnel—who will also have little experience.

After the present decentralized program has been in effect for some years these deficiencies will gradually tend to disappear as employees learn their new jobs.

We have noted that one advantage of decentralization is that it brings the decision point to the front line where the situation is known or knowable, where the facts are most easily accessible, and where people can be dealt with "across the desk." This very proximity, however, may be a disadvantage. The local administrator, bogged down in detail, may not be able to comprehend and attach enough significance to the overall problem. The local manager cannot help but develop sympathies, and antipathies, likes and dislikes, which will color his judgment. "Man-to-man" dealing may be more satisfying, but personalities will influence issues. Firsthand knowledge of local problems and issues is an invaluable asset to the decision-maker—but it tends to make his decisions less impartial.

We have so far considered only the purely administrative or "efficiency" aspects of decentralization. It is entirely possible, however, that decentralization may be desired for its greater susceptibility to interest-group action. Some western congressmen from stockraising districts have maintained an almost continuous harangue about "swivel-chair cowboys" and the communistic tendencies of land-grabbing bureaucrats. The National Advisory Board Council and the stockmen's associations have maintained continual pressure for greater decentralization of grazing administration, which gives greater power to local stockmen in the management of individual grazing districts. This power is exerted mainly through the district advisory board. Advisory board members are commonly members, and frequently officers, of the stockmen's associations. As such, they will ordinarily reflect association views. Since the advisory boards are the "local governing agency as to all matters of a range regulatory nature" it is not necessary for them to exert pressures on the administration in the usual sense because they are a legally constituted part of that administration. The clientele group and to some extent the formally organized associations have thus become institutionalized as a part of the administrative structure.

We should also note that field officers are likely to be more susceptible to pressures than are officers of the headquarters.[55] There are numerous reasons for this belief. The field officer is often a resident of the state or locality in which he serves. In the grazing activity such residence is a requirement.[56] Consequently he is likely to have political alliances with local groups and is likely to identify himself with them. He may, in fact, have secured his position through the influence of state politicians. His attitudes and sympathies are likely to be closely akin to the prevailing interests in his area, especially if his clientele group is also a dominant local group. A local situation is less likely to have competing pressures than is the headquarters. The local official is apt to be less politically sophisticated than is the headquarters official. The local official is in constant and personal contact with local pressure organizations so impersonal and objective judgment is made more difficult. Since the local official usually has a lower rate of pay and occupies a lower rung on the prestige scale he may be "less well placed to resist pressure or influence, particularly when it takes the more subtle forms of flattery, extreme deference, personal assistance, and social favors."[57]

The continued emphasis on decentralized organization in the administration of the public lands has probably resulted in a lower level of efficiency than would otherwise have been possible. More important, however, is the likelihood that decentralization has enabled the stockmen to maximize their influence in the determination of range regulatory policy. Thus a structural device has been used to accomplish policy objectives.

It is unlikely that the many reorganizations of the federal grazing activity have produced any significant improvements in efficiency of operation, if for no other reason than the frequency of the reorganizations. Organizational changes of any consequence are almost certain to result in initial confusion and uncertainty, dislocations and lowered morale, with a consequent drop in over-all effectiveness. While these consequences are somewhat temporary, a succession of reorganizations cannot help but result in a loss of momentum. It seems evident, however, that the primary objectives of the frequent reorganizations of the grazing activity were not increased efficiency but rather that changes in structure were accomplished to realign political forces in such a manner as to produce policy changes or to thwart attempted policy changes.

# 5. GRAZING DISTRICT ADMINISTRATION

The grazing district is the point of implementation for all the planning and coordinating that takes place at higher levels. It is here that plans take shape and are translated into action. It is here too that formally enunciated policies are tailored to fit local conditions. Here also is the point of greatest contact with the users of the range.

This chapter describes grazing administration at the district level and concludes with an account of a succession of advisory board meetings in a particular district. The problems considered by this advisory board and the environment in which it functioned are considered to be fairly representative of grazing district administration.

The district range manager is the final responsible line officer in the organization of range administration. Under the new decentralized plan he is also responsible for forestry activities in his district and has final authority in various other transactions which were formerly carried out in the districts but forwarded to higher echelons for "processing" and final approval. Generally speaking, the district range manager is responsible for the protection and development of all the surface resources in his district. Probably the major functions carried on in a grazing district are grazing management, range conservation, range improvements, forestry management, fire control, and wildlife management.

Once the boundaries of a district have been set, it is the district range manager's duty to ascertain the carrying ca-

Fig. 2. Grazing districts. Approximately 156,000,000 acres of federal range are included; there are an additional 13,000,000 acres of rangeland (not shown) outside the districts which have been leased under section 15 of the Taylor Grazing Act. The checkered area in western Oregon represents intermingled private lands and revested Oregon railroad grant lands, which form one of the nation's greatest reservoirs of Douglas-fir timber.

Source: United States Department of Interior, Bureau of Land Management, *Rebuilding the Federal Range* (Washington: Government Printing Office, 1951), p. 7.

pacity of the range. There are several methods by which this may be accomplished. Probably they fall into two general categories: visual estimates and estimates arrived at through the use of measuring devices. One common measuring device is a hoop about eight feet in diameter. This hoop is thrown out at random over various parts of the range and all the grass inside the hoop is clipped off. It is then dried and weighed. The multiplication of the dry weight of the grass within the hoop by the proper factor will indicate the number of pounds of grass per acre. By using a generally accepted formula which includes the number of pounds of grass necessary to maintain an animal in good condition, one determines the carrying capacity. Obviously, the more samples taken, the more accurate the estimate will be. Human discretion in deciding where to throw off the hoop may also affect the accuracy of the survey. Notwithstanding such defects, a measuring system will generally be more accurate than an estimate based on visual inspection. Some oldtime stockmen tend to scoff at such methods and contend that a stockman with years of experience on the range can estimate carrying capacity with more accuracy than can a "college boy with a microscope."

When the carrying capacity of the range has been determined, the next task is to apportion the use of the range to the various applicants for permits. Rather elaborate criteria determine the selection of permittees and the number of stock each is allowed to run on the federal range. These guidelines for awarding grazing permits were considered in some detail in a previous chapter. At this point we need only note that grazing privileges are allotted to lands, and not to individuals, and that permittees must be able to maintain their stock on other properties when they are not grazing on the district. We should also note that the determination of grazing "rights" is often a highly complicated and time-consuming process.

When the permits have been issued, the administration must keep up with continued range surveys to establish the trend of range condition. Range utilization checks are also necessary to determine the actual amount of use regardless of the number of permits issued. Since permits are granted on the basis of commensurate property the district range manager (hereafter referred to as the DRM) must maintain a record of private property transfers and production and use records of private commensurate properties. He must also make frequent inspections to see that livestock are being grazed in the areas assigned to them, that permittees are not exceeding the numbers allotted to them, and that other stockmen are not trespassing on the federal range. When stockmen exceed the numbers allotted to them, "turn out" early, or when stockmen without permits run stock in the district, they are cited for trespass and fined. The grazing district office also calculates grazing-fee charges, notifies the permittees, and makes collections. Seasons of use for various units of the range and for different classes of livestock must also be designated.

The district office is responsible for the leasing of section 15 lands (isolated tracts) and for cooperative agreements with both public agencies and private individuals for the inclusion of their lands within the district.

The DRM is also responsible for conserving and improving the range. A range improvement program may include wells, reservoirs, detention dams, ditches, water spreaders, storage tanks, pipe lines, spring developments, watering troughs, fences, corrals, loading chutes, dipping vats, cattle guards, weighing scales, riders' cabins, bridges, truck trails, stock trails, stock driveways, water-hauling roads, firebreaks, contour furrowing, check dams, diversion dams, subsoiling sagebrush eradication, plowing and range reseeding, noxious and poisonous weed control, rodent control, insect control, predatory animal control, reseeding of logging roads and skid trails, brush burning and reseeding, and eradication of brush stands by chemical spraying.

Range conservation and improvement projects may be financed from several different funds among which are soil and moisture conservation, range improvements, and funds for the control of halogeton, a poisonous weed. Improvements may also be undertaken by cooperative agreement with the users, by advisory board contributions and by agreement with other country, state, or federal agencies. Once established, such improvements need to be maintained in good repair.

In grazing districts which produce commercial timber the DRM must maintain an inventory of these resources and must institute management plans to utilize the timber on a sustained yield basis. He must also supervise cutting operations and provide access roads.

Fire control is also the responsibility of the DRM. In some districts cooperative arrangements for fire protection have been arranged with national forest and local fire-protective associations. In others, district personnel and temporary employees carry out fire protection activities.

The Federal Range Code requires that sufficient grazing capacity be set aside in each grazing district to provide for a reasonable number of game animals. Wildlife management is ordinarily the responsibility of the fish and game department of the various states. As a consequence the management of game on grazing districts becomes a cooperative undertaking of the state and the grazing district. Thus the district assists in game counts, game range surveys, range-use adjustments, transplanting of big game, and makes recommendations on hunting seasons, allowable kill, and other such matters. Each grazing district advisory board now has one member to represent wildlife interests.

None of these activities is ever completed: range surveys must be periodically redone; commensurate properties change hands; improvements must be maintained to protect the original investment. Grazing district administration is a continuing responsibility.

The niggardly appropriations for the grazing activity over the years have prevented any really significant conservation activities and only a token amount of the necessary range administration has been accomplished. According to an organization and management study team report in 1955:

. . . lack of information with respect to grazing activity, dependent property qualifications, range condition and trend, forage utilization, forest inventory and other basic resource data precludes effective management planning and range-use supervision. As a result, grazing and other privileges are more often than not granted on the basis of prior Bureau actions, Advisory Board recommendations, general observations and personal opinions of the District Manager and staff members. . . .

In recent years staffing has been increased as a result of additional funds for range conservation and improvements and Halogeton control. However, the districts have remained consistently shorthanded and each permitted increase in staffing has been largely offset by the assignment of additional work and responsibility.[1]

While we have listed the multitude of activities for which a district range manager is responsible, it is obviously ridiculous to expect him to carry out these responsibilities (over an area larger than some states) with his pitifully small staff and the meager funds at his disposal.

The stockmen naturally wish to encourage range improvement, but at the same time they apparently desire minimum regulation of grazing and a low grazing fee. These objectives place the stockmen in a somewhat ambivalent position: if increased appropriations are obtained for range improvement it is likely that closer supervision of grazing will also result. Increased appropriations are also likely to produce demands for increased grazing fees. The stockmen have generally attempted to advance these somewhat conflicting objectives by securing "earmarked" funds, by advisory board control of funds returned to the states, and by cooperative arrangements for range improvements between the BLM and individual permit-holders. In the latter instance the BLM ordinarily furnishes required materials, and the permit-holder supplies the labor. Most important, however, is the fact that the stockmen have apparently "settled" for a most limited range improvement program as the price for retaining relative freedom from regulation and supervision of their grazing activities.

We have previously noted that decentralization has been used as a device to help the stockmen maximize their control of grazing administration. Along with the movement toward greater decentralization of the grazing function, however, there has also been a similar decentralization of some other BLM functions. One result of these various decentralizations has been the consolidation of these several functions in the district grazing office.

These multiple duties should act to change the DRM from a range specialist to a generalist in natural resource administration. As such he may become a balancer of competing or complementary interests rather than a specialist whose interests revolve around a single land use. This change in responsibilities may result in important and unforeseen long-run consequences.

The following section contains observations of three district advisory board meetings during 1955 and 1956. This commentary may provide some insight into the ecological circumstances and day-to-day problems of a typical grazing district.

Oregon Grazing District 1 is located in south central Oregon with district headquarters at Lakeview, Oregon. This area is an old stockraising section which has been grazed continually by domestic animals since the latter part of the last century. Many of the present ranchers are descendants of the first pioneer cattlemen who entered the area in the '70's and '80's.

The district comprises a gross area of about 5, 800, 000 acres—more than Massachusetts and Rhode Island combined. Of this total about 3, 300, 000 acres are federally owned with the balance in state or private ownership. The district is about 120 miles long by about eighty miles wide. Most of the district lies within Lake County and the remainder in Harney County. Both these counties are sparsely settled. Lake County with an area of 8, 270 square miles has a population of about 6, 500. Harney County covers 10, 132 square miles and has a population of about 6, 000. Lakeview, the county seat of Lake County, has a population of about 2, 800—almost half the total population of the county.

The grazing district is bounded on the west by Fremont National Forest and on the north by the Deschutes Game Refuge and the Deschutes National Forest. The district also encompasses the Hart Mountain Antelope Refuge.

The area consists generally of a series of long, narrow ranges or high ridges alternating with broad basins. Most of the ridges run in a north-south direction. They are usually steep on one side and slope off gradually on the other. Because of the steep slopes, some of these ridges, or fault blocks, are called "rims." Abert Rim and Winter Rim are among the more spectacular examples.

Originally this area was mostly bunch-grass range, but overgrazing has caused much of the bunch grass to be supplanted by sage brush, rabbit brush, greasewood and other less palatable plants. Consequently, some of the range is now of little value for cattle and only of limited value for sheep.

Fortunately, very little dry farming has been attempted in this district, except in the northern part around Fort Rock, so the range has been spared this kind of destruction. In the Fort Rock area some dry farming was attempted about 1908 but was generally unsuccessful. Areas which were plowed at that time have now gone back to grass (or brush). Some small areas are being used to raise rye for hay.

In 1955 the grazing district licensed 119 operators for 232, 415 A.U.M.'s for an average of 1, 953 A.U.M.'s each.

Of this total the Chewaucan Land and Cattle Company (known as the ZX Outfit) was licensed for 44,002 A.U.M.'s and the Warner Valley Livestock Company for 41,000 A.U.M.'s. These two livestock companies accounted for about 35 per cent of the total A.U.M.'s licensed in the district.

Ordinarily the grazing season is considered to be of seven months duration. If all licensees had used the range seven months and if cattle had been the only livestock licensed, the district would have supported 33,200 cattle in 1955. More realistic figures are available by class of livestock for 1954. In that year the district licensed 46,552 cattle, 702 horses, and 32,225 sheep for a total of 203,825 A.U.M.'s.

The average number of livestock per permittee in this district is considerably larger than the average for the state of Oregon. During the year ending June 30, 1955, 112 cattlemen were licensed for an average of 413 cattle each as compared with the 1,190 cattlemen in BLM grazing districts in the state who were licensed for an average of 217 head. Eight sheepmen in the Lakeview district averaged 4,184 sheep against the total in grazing districts in the state of sixty sheepmen with 2,265 head each.

*Composition of the Board*

Of the eight stockmen on the board five were cattlemen, one was a sheepman, and two ran both cattle and sheep on the grazing district. Three of the board members were among the ten largest permittees on the district. The two largest permittees had A.U.M. allotments that comprised about 35 per cent of the total. Neither of these permittees was represented on the board. Although representatives of these two large cattle companies had been nominated several times, neither of them had been elected except once during the last eight years. The individual elected at that time served out his term but was not re-elected. The biggest permittee on the board ran 6,940 A.U.M.'s on the district; the smallest, 855 A.U.M.'s. Board members ran an average of 3,644 A.U.M.'s on the district as compared with a district-wide average of 1,953 A.U.M.'s.

The youngest board member was about thirty and the oldest about sixty-five. With one exception they had spent all their lives in the stock business. In several cases their fathers, and sometimes grandfathers, were also in the stock business in the same area. Certainly they were expert stockmen. This expertise, however, did not necessarily extend to the administration of a grazing district with all its problems of finance, budget, personnel, soil and moisture conservation, forestry, fire control, and legal matters. The wildlife member was a lawyer. Of the nine members, four were commonly thought to have assets of over $500,000.

*Board Meetings*

Ordinarily the board meets three times during each year. The first meeting is primarily an organizational meeting; the second considers applications for grazing permits; and the third is an appeal or protest meeting on decisions made during the second meeting. The board may also meet at other times as desired or required. Probably most of the board's time is spent in passing upon questionable applications for permits or disputes between permittees. The board also considers recommendations on wildlife matters, range improvements, and general administration problems.

The supervisory staff of a grazing district office is ordinarily composed of a district range manager, one or more range managers, a soil and moisture specialist, and where the situation warrants, one or more forestry officers. The district range manager is the over-all supervisor and is responsible for all the activities carried on by the grazing district office. The range managers are responsible, in particular, for grazing activities as distinguished from forestry or soil and moisture conservation. Both the district range manager and the range managers are termed range managers in civil service job titles. Through usage, however, the term "district range manager" has come to mean the responsible officer, as distinguished from the more specialized and subordinate range manager. The district range manager and/or the range manager make up the agenda for the meetings, but board members feel free to bring up any matter they desire.

In this particular district the range manager was the former district range manager and had been in residence for eight years and had been a member of the federal grazing activity almost since its inception. He was thoroughly familiar with the topography, condition of the range, local practices and personalities.

The range manager and former district range manager was about sixty-two years old. His adult life had been devoted to the livestock business. He entered the old Grazing Division as a range rider soon after the passage of the Taylor Grazing Act and had been a member of the organization since that time. He had been the district range manager of the Lakeview district for about eight years prior to the appointment of the present district range manager the summer before.

*Advisory Board Election*

The advisory board consists of nine members, three of whom are elected each year for three-year terms. The advisory board election for this district for 1955 was held on November 15. The election booth was located in the rear of a room in which the Lake County Cattleman's Association was holding its annual meeting.

To encourage participation the election was held on the same day and in the same place as the cattleman's association meeting. Most of the bigger operators were members of stockmen's associations and nonmembers were mostly small operators. Approximately 75 per cent of the permittees were members of the cattleman's association. Some permittees ran both cattle and sheep and could be members of both associations. Eligible voters were those persons who held valid permits to graze livestock on this particular grazing district. There were 119 such permittees entitled to vote. Of this number only twenty-nine cast a ballot. The total vote cast in 1954 was thirty-two, and in 1953 the vote totaled forty-nine. Twenty-six permittees voted in 1952 and forty in 1951. During these years the number of eligible voters varied from 115 to 120.

The grazing district is divided into four precincts. Each precinct has two members on the advisory board. The ninth member is the wildlife member who is appointed by the Secretary of the Interior on the recommendation of the State Game Commission.

Nominations were made orally from the floor by permittees from the precinct concerned. However, permittees from all precincts voted by class of livestock on the persons thus nom-

inated. After the nominations were made, cattlemen voted for
cattle representatives and sheepmen voted for sheep representatives.[2] The names of persons nominated at this election were
posted on a blackboard opposite the position to be filled. Voting was accomplished by write-in on blank slips of paper. The
vote could be written in secret by stepping away from the table.

In this election there were four positions to be filled: the
three positions caused by expiration of terms and one vacancy
caused by death. The three former incumbents were renom-
inated and were unopposed in the election. The fourth member, nominated to finish out the unexpired term, was also unopposed.

*Discussions at Three Advisory Board Meetings*
The advisory board meeting of November 16, 1955 was held
in the district manager's office. The previous chairman was
re-elected for the coming year and one board member was
elected to serve on the state advisory board. There were no
other nominations for either position. The board then considered a dispute between two permittees over the construction of a fence; the various ways in which funds for soil and
moisture conservation could best be utilized; an application for
a temporary winter range permit; and a study report on BLM
administrative and personnel procedures.

The district manager next described the district's physical
plant facilities, which he considered highly inadequate. He
then began a discussion of the kind of facilities that would be
most suitable for district headquarters. The board was drawn
into this discussion and offered several suggestions. The district manager then "wondered" if the board might be interested
in doing some construction out of funds under its jurisdiction.
The board instructed the manager to draw up plans for the
kind of plant he thought most suitable and to include estimated
cost figures. These plans were to be submitted to the board
at a later meeting for further discussion and possible decision.

The second meeting of the board, February 2, 1956, was
held primarily for the purpose of acting on applications for
grazing permits. The range manager opened the meeting by
saying it had been the policy of the board in the past to consider first whether any changes in the grazing capacity of the

district were necessary. Apparently no member of the board had any definite opinion on the necessity for any change. By unanimous agreement, or rather by lack of dissent, the total capacity of the district was left unchanged. There was practically no discussion.

The range manager then stated that it had been the policy in the past to use range improvement funds to maintain existing improvements first and then to use whatever funds remained for new improvements. He suggested this policy to be followed and that funds remaining for new improvements be used primarily for the construction of fences. There was little discussion and no dissent, so it was assumed that the range manager's suggestions would constitute the policy for expenditure of range improvement funds for the year.

Applications for grazing permits were considered next. The range manager stated that he had separated all the applications which contained changes from previously approved permits. He then described these applications and requested the board's advice. Some of these changes were of a minor nature, but he apparently felt that any kind of change on an application should receive the board's attention.

The range manager then read a list of eighty to ninety names of applicants for grazing permits which he said were in order and identical with permits previously approved. Since these applications had all been previously acted on by the board, he assumed that "everything was O.K." and that it would be unnecessary to consider each case separately, unless some member of the board wished to have any of the cases reviewed in more detail. Two members requested that two cases be pulled out to receive further consideration. There was no objection to any of the rest of the names on the "no change" list. So, in effect, this list of applications was approved by the board without review or discussion.

After all the cases involving grazing permits had been disposed of, the district range manager raised the question of adequate storage, shop, and office space for the district office. He proposed that the advisory board purchase a certain piece of property (with advisory board money) from the State Highway Commission and construct an office building on the property. The board reacted to this proposal hesitantly and

with some skepticism. Finally the board recommended that
the manager investigate the matter further and report back at
the next meeting.

The third and last official advisory board meeting of the
season was held February 29, 1956, to hear protests from
decisions of the previous meeting. However, only one permittee appeared in protest—mainly to object to the actions of
another stockman rather than to any particular decision of the
advisory board. This dispute was solved by the range manager's offer to develop three additional waterholes so the two
stockmen would not need to use the same watering facilities.

The board then discussed maintenance of fences and approved sixteen late applications for grazing permits. Next
considered was the district manager's proposal to purchase
land and construct an office building. The board authorized
purchase of the land but postponed decision on the proposed
building. Finally, it authorized the creation of a fifth voting
precinct within the district. There were no dissenting votes.

No formal agenda had been prepared for the meetings. The
district range manager had some notes on his desk which he
consulted occasionally. The range manager had no visible
notes except a stack of case files. Consequently, the board
members had no warning or previous knowledge of cases on
which they would be asked to make a recommendation. The
range manager stated the problem orally and supplied such
information as he thought pertinent from memory and with oc-
casional reference to a case file. Some of these files were
voluminous, and rapid reference to a file during the course
of a meeting was practically impossible. On several occasions
the range manager was forced to respond to a question by saying that he could not answer without a detailed study of the
file which might take several hours. The range manager showed
a definite tendency to rely on memory or to refrain from referral to the record. He frequently used phrases such as, "I figure about, " "as I recollect, " "around about that, " "just about
practically all, " and the like. Some board members also tended
to rely on memory, general observations, and approximations. Two board members tended to ask for "the facts in the
case, " or a "detailed review of the record. " The district range

manager, on the other hand, depended almost entirely on the record or attempted to quote and identify statements made by local authorities. However, he had been in the district such a short time that these were about the only sources of information available to him.

A map of the district was available but the physical arrangement of the meeting made reference to it somewhat difficult. Few of the members made any effort to consult the map, and relied on their memory of "that territory back of _____ butte" or "up to the draw" from a certain spring. The members' recollections of certain areas was frequently hazy.

In considering possible changes in the over-all carrying capacity of the range there was no reference to, or consideration of, range surveys, dependent property surveys, range utilization checks, or range condition and trend studies. It is entirely possible, of course, although unlikely, that everyone present was so familiar with such data that discussion was unnecessary.

If the range manager desired to keep the advisory board from becoming too well informed on district matters, the withholding and monopolization of the "facts and figures" might be one method of accomplishing that objective. By dealing in generalities, approximations, verbal remarks, and memory, he made available to the board very little exact information. Such an approach might not only have practical consequences but might also have the psychological effect of bolstering the range manager's ego by making him the "only man who knows."

If the primary function of the board is considered to be public relations, then the procedures outlined above may be adequate. However, if the information and advice of the board are genuinely desired, such methods are not likely to produce it. Extemporaneous verbal presentation must necessarily result in superficial, off-the-cuff recommendations and a lack of information and advice on matters to which board members might otherwise be able to make real contributions.

It is likely, however, that the above observations may not be applicable in this particular case. One or both of two other possibilities may offer an explanation. Part of our folklore involves a distrust, resentment, and sometimes contempt, for "paper work," "two-bit clerks," excessive details, "red tape," and officialdom. Probably this attitude is most prevalent and most pronounced among rural people. Ranchers, especially big ranchers with cultural roots back to the days of the cattle barons, tend to be contemptuous of "minor" details. In the old west particularly, there was a tendency to rely on verbal statements. After a lifetime on the range, the range manager has undoubtedly absorbed much of this old western folklore and may at least subconsciously identify himself with the oldtime stockmen. Certainly some members of the board held these attitudes.

Still another explanation may be that the range manager found through long years of experience with stockmen that frequent referral to the record created nothing but annoyance. He may also have found that stockmen did not read written materials that were submitted to them. Persons who do not make frequent decisions on the basis of written data are likely to demand face-to-face verbal presentation of a problem before they make a decision.

The range manager did not depend upon the board to supply him with information. He did look to the board for opinions, suggestions, and ideas. He used the board primarily to make decisions that he may have been disinclined to make or take personal responsibility for, as a sounding board for contemplated policy, and as a public-relations body. The range manager may not have been consciously aware that he was using the board for these purposes. Usually the district range manager or the range manager has a monopoly of the official information and the manner in which he presents this information makes some board decisions predictable in advance. Some of the questions submitted to the advisory board could have been decided by the district range manager alone and decisions of the board can be overruled by him.

In Oregon District 1, the board believed it was making the decision when it passed upon a proposal. The board, when asked its advice, did not feel that it was giving advice, but that it was making a decision. It was essentially correct in this belief, because the range manager had overruled the board's "decision" only once during eight years as district range manager. In one other case he broke a tie vote.

This hand-in-hand working relationship between the range

manager and the board may indicate that (1) the range manager manipulates board members so successfully that they render "decision" only on items he chooses and in accordance with his wishes, (2) the identifications, interests, and objectives of the range manager and the board may be identical, or, (3) the range manager may accept "decisions" of the board even though they may be contrary to his findings and possibly contrary to BLM policy. In the sample district, it appeared that the range manager tended to identify himself closely with the stockmen, that he was skillful in manipulating the board, but that once the board rendered a "decision," he carried out that decision if at all possible.

To summarize, the range manager decided what issues the board would act upon; he attempted to influence their decisions through the selection and presentation of information; and he appeared to follow decisions of the board even though they may have been contrary to his own previous decisions.

According to the range manager, board members very seldom attempted to use their position for their personal advantage. When such an "accident" happened, the offending member was "straightened out" by the other members and was not reelected at the next election. Board members in this district did not attempt to give advice or exert pressure in such matters as personnel or purchasing. Neither did they attempt to bypass the manager by obtaining information from his subordinates or by giving instructions to them.

The fact that there was only one protest from decisions of the board on about 120 applications for grazing permits would seem to indicate that the BLM grazing permit system had been generally accepted throughout the area and that livestock operations had become stabilized. It might also mean that the permittees knew they had been granted all the range would carry and consequently realized there was no point in applying for more numbers which would overstock the range. It could also mean that ranchers generally paid their token tribute (fifteen cents per A.U.M.) to the BLM, operated generally as they pleased, and settled disputes among themselves.

While there are very likely some smaller operators who consistently trespass on the grazing district, there are probably other small operators who apply for permits, pay their fees, and take what they get without complaint—whether they have grounds for complaint or not. Ordinarily these smaller stockmen have no clear understanding of the Federal Range Code and the opportunities that may be available to them. Although stockraising is a business, probably many small stockmen are not businessmen in any sense of the word.

In an old rural society, class lines may be more clearly drawn than in an urban society. As a consequence these people are likely to "stay in their place." After a lifetime of "staying in their place" complaints tend to be expressed as vague and general gripes rather than as specific charges. Furthermore, there tends to develop in these small stockmen an attitude of "what's the use? The big outfits have got everything sewed up and there's nothing we can do about it." Last, many of these stockmen would rather take a substantial cutback than suffer the embarrassment of appearing before a board in protest.

While the lack of protest may indicate a stabilization of the range industry in this district, it could also indicate a subservience to the users, or to certain dominating users, or the dominance of the advisory board over both the stockmen and the administration. We have noted that no reference was made to range surveys, dependent property surveys, range utilization checks, or range condition and trend studies. It seems likely that no such current studies existed. If this conclusion is correct, the board accepted past decisions as the sole criterion for present conditions. Some of these decisions may have been many years old and, even when originally approved, may have been based on questionable data. If, through ignorance, inertia, or fear of losing something, the permittee reapplies for the same range privileges year after year and if the board automatically accepts any application which has been previously approved, there will be few reasons for protest. Such a situation may present a smooth, unruffled front, but it may also serve to hide an inefficient range management program, gross inequities among users, and a deteriorating public range.

It seems likely that neither the administration, the advisory board, nor the users had any accurate, up-to-date information on dependent property, range use or range condition. The niggardly appropriations available for the grazing activity for several years had probably made impossible the collection of data necessary for intelligent decisions. This being the case, the administrators were forced to rely on the opinions of the advisory board because they had no better source of information.

Relations among the board members appeared to be cordial and friendly. There was no evidence of personal rivalry or antagonism. Neither was there any evidence of factionalism. Relations between administrators and the board also appeared friendly. There was no evidence of personal antagonism nor was there any evidence that any board member was "carrying the ball" for the administrator.

Generally speaking, the district range manager and the range manager did not initially present problems in sufficient detail to make an immediate decision possible. They either began what first appeared to be a somewhat aimless discussion which later led to the "discovery" of the need for making a decision or they stated the question with no substantiating information at all. After the question had been presented, the administrators and the board embarked on a kind of cooperative investigation. In the process of this investigation the solution gradually seemed to emerge.

This approach tended to create a receptive attitude among the board members. They asked questions, made suggestions, and generally reacted in a positive manner. They were drawn into the discussion and became, in effect, participants rather than judges. If a more direct approach had been used, wherein the management presented all the facts and then called for a decision, the response probably would not have been as favorable. The board may have been more inclined to assume a negative or critical role.

Partly because of the methods used by the administrators, and partly because of the sensitivity of the chairman, all the decisions of the board were unanimous. The chairman in each case allowed the discussion to continue until he felt a consensus had been reached. He then called for a motion and got a unanimous decision.

# 6. HOME RULE ON THE RANGE

In chapter 4 we noted the origins of an advisory board system which Congressman Taylor called "home rule on the range." The use of advisory bodies of some sort is, of course, rather commonplace in administrative history. Administrators have frequently used such groups to provide information, technical advice, advice as to the acceptance of current and projected programs and to act as a public relations medium to inform and explain administrative actions. The advisory board device has also been used to gain the cooperation of a clientele by co-opting influential members to serve in an advisory capacity.

In varying degrees, advisory boards in the federal grazing activity have served all these purposes but the co-optation process has been carried much farther than usual. Probably Congressman Taylor's use of the term "home *rule*" was more accurate than he realized.

During the first four years of the Grazing Division, F. R. Carpenter used a system of advisory boards who served at the pleasure of the Secretary of Interior. These advisory boards were not provided for in the statute but were established by Carpenter through administrative directives. Carpenter was able to find several phrases in the act which, by implication, might be construed as granting the Secretary authority to establish an advisory board system. Section 9 provides for "cooperation with local associations of stockmen" and for "local

117

hearings on appeals from the decisions of the administrative officer." Section 2 gives the Secretary authority to "enter into such cooperative agreements, and do any and all things necessary to accomplish the purposes of this Act." Carpenter explains his reasons for establishing the system and some of the methods he used in the following statement:

> . . . it was impossible to approach such a complicated project in the usual bureaucratic method of sending out field men to find out what was going on and report back to Washington. The intense interest of the range people required immediate action, and just to bring the matter to a crisis, the other federal bureaus, seeing the drawstrings were about to be pulled on what had always been a free grab-bag for them all got busy and put in claims for the range land to round out and increase their kingdoms. The Forest Service asked for 29 million acres; the National Parks, 17 million; the Indian Service, 12 million; and the Biological Survey, 10 million. The total of these claims was 68 million acres. This meant that if these claims were satisfied almost no acreage would remain for grazing districts, and, what was of real importance, no land left for western livestock whose owners would all be put out of business.
>
> Something had to be done at once or there would be nothing left to do. The example of the Selective Service Act of 1917, where local draft boards performed practically all the work of raising an army and the Federal officials acted only in a coordinating and directing capacity, seemed appropriate. No one knew much about the range except the local users and inhabitants, and they knew more about their own parts of it than any official could learn in years.
>
> Accordingly, 33 districts were set up in the ten states, their average size about that of the State of Connecticut. They were precincted into their natural range units and elections were held to select representatives of the industry to act as an advisory board to the Department for the distribution of range privileges in that district. The number of cattlemen and sheepmen were kept even on each board and goats and horses were allowed representation where their numbers justified it. The election rules were copied directly from the Colorado School Law for third class school districts, and proved effective. A federal official presided at all meetings and voted in case of a tie.
>
> By this method, almost overnight 483 district advisors were selected, the number of members averaging 14. Many of the members had university or college degrees; some were judges, bishops and holders of offices of trust in their communities; nearly all were men with an established reputation for fairness. They brought to their meetings an intimate, first-hand knowledge of the range and the operators, and a desire to do the job right and with thoroughness and dispatch.

Anyone with experience in adjudicating the waters of a small stream who has seen the infinite number of adjustments and differences that arise when a use in common has to be made of a natural resource, will appreciate that the distribution of grazing rights over 142 million acres of land in ten states might well become the work of a decade. When I give you the figures of the accomplishment you will appreciate the value of the decentralized method used.

The act was passed on June 28, 1934. It was explained to the stockmen in a series of meetings in the ten states, culminating in a general meeting in Denver, Colorado, on February 9, 1935. The grazing districts were created by proclamation and set up by June 1, 1935. All applications were acted upon and the entire range adjudicated by September, 1935, just over one year and two months after the Act was passed. Licenses had been issued to 14,221 operators for over half a million cattle and 6 million sheep; and while some districts have since been added and minor changes made, the original and first adjudication remains substantially as it was then made. Only thirty-eight cases were appealed to the Director, and three from him to the Secretary of the Interior.

While the local district advisors had no final authority, but only a recommendatory one, in practice their advice was followed in 98.3 percent of the cases. They were sworn in as part-time members of the Department and drew five dollars per day while on duty plus travel expense. Applicants were notified by mail of the board's action, and if dissatisfied, could appear in person before them and argue their case. This appearance in person before a board of the applicants' neighbors was a great discouragement to imaginary or outlandish claims and had a tendency to keep facts on a rock bottom.

Some of the boards' actions reflected the genius of the American people for organization if given an opportunity. Friendships sprang up between cattlemen and sheepmen heretofore enemies, and all matters were handled in as impartial a manner as possible. [1]

In the above remarks Carpenter said the boards had only recommendatory powers, but in his report for the year 1935 he characterized the boards as "the local governing agency as to all matters of a range regulatory nature." [2]

In a more recent statement, Carpenter stated, "At all times I warned the boards they were 'on trial'—that they had no final authority and that they were like jurymen performing a public service and a civic duty." He further stated, "Ickes approved [the advisory board system] with tongue in cheek, believing they would keep the heat off him and that he could abolish them as soon as the reorganization was complete and running."[3] Apparently the stockmen also feared that Ickes would abolish the boards. To preclude such a possibility, Senator McCarran introduced an amendment to give the boards full statutory recognition. The amendment, as finally passed in 1939, provides for an advisory board of five to twelve local stockmen in each grazing district. These advisers are appointed by the Secretary of Interior on recommendation of the users of the range through local elections. The Secretary may remove any adviser from office if, in his opinion, such removal would be for the good of the service. The boards are to

. . . offer advice and make a recommendation on each application for such a grazing permit within its district: PROVIDED, That in no case shall any grazing district adviser participate in any advice or recommendation concerning a permit, or an application therefor, in which he is directly or indirectly interested. Each board shall further offer advice or make recommendations concerning rules and regulations for the administration of this Act, the establishment of grazing districts and the modifications of the boundaries thereof, the seasons of use and carrying capacity of the range, and any other matters affecting the administration of this Act within the district. Except in a case where in the judgment of the Secretary an emergency shall exist, the Secretary shall request the advice of the advisory board in advance of the promulgation of any rules and regulations affecting the district.[4]

The amendment also provided for the appointment of one adviser for each board to represent wildlife interests.

While the bill was being considered, Secretary Ickes said he had no objection to legal recognition of the boards if it was clearly understood that they would remain advisory.[5]

The amendment provided for district advisory boards only—no mention was made of a higher echelon of boards. However, in July, 1940, representatives from the various districts met in Denver to consider proposed revisions to the Federal Range Code. At this meeting the delegates organized a national association of advisory board members headed by a board of directors. The charter for the organization stated in part: "The purpose of this organization is to further the interest of users of the public domain under the jurisdiction of the Grazing Service in the public land states, and for such other purposes as from time to time may be determined upon by the Board of Directors."[6]

Although the charter specifically stated that the organization was not a part of the Grazing Service it offered its services to the Secretary should he need them on matters of public interest in the range country.

Gordon Griswold of Nevada was elected president, A. D. Brownfield of New Mexico first vice president, and Dan Hughes of Colorado, second vice president. Members of the first board of directors included Frank O'Connell of Montana, Pat Cecil of Oregon, Kelso Musser of Colorado, and Floyd Lee of New Mexico.[7] These men remained on the council for several years and played a prominent role in the development, or lack of development, of the federal grazing activity.

Within a month after the organization of the National Advisory Board Council (hereafter referred to as the NABC) the director of the Grazing Service began to worry about the powers which this new organization might acquire. In a letter of August 20, 1940 to all the regional graziers, Director R. H. Rutledge said:

The National Advisory Board Council was organized primarily to aid in connection with national defense matters if and when the President, the Secretary, and this Service might request action by them. I have noted, however, that there is a growing disposition to figure that the Council may be used to handle a lot of problems with which the Grazing Service is confronted. . . . We must exercise a great deal of caution in regard to the requests we make of the Advisory Council, and it seems the best strategy and the proper procedure . . . to clear all such requests through this office.[8]

Shortly after the formation of the NABC, state boards were formed in each of the federal range states.[9] By 1949 both the NABC and the state boards were officially recognized in the Federal Range Code.[10] Since the NABC and the state boards had been functioning unofficially in the interim period, however, the Federal Range Code of 1949 simply recognized an existing situation. In fact, the most crucial decisions of the NABC may have occurred during the years prior to its official recognition.

The three board levels are chosen as follows: holders of permits in each district elect a board of advisers for their district. These advisers select two from their own membership to represent them on the state advisory board. One adviser is to represent sheepmen and goatkeepers and the other

to represent cattlemen and horsemen. The process is repeated
in the state board. Each state board selects two of its members to represent the state in the NABC. Thus each member of
the NABC is also a member of a state board and a district
board. The only board member who is not elected by permittees is the wildlife member who is appointed by the state supervisor, BLM. The various district wildlife members in a state
elect one of their own members to serve on the state advisory
board. The various state wildlife members, in each of the
three areas, select one of their own members to the NABC. As
presently constituted, the NABC has twenty advisers and three
wildlife members.

We might pause here to recapitulate some of the distinctive
features of this advisory board system. First, the boards are
accorded legal recognition in the statute. The statute and the
regulations spell out the duties and authority of the boards in
some detail. Board members are elected by the users (clientele) of the federal range. They are sworn in as federal employees and serve regular three-year terms. Members of the
state boards are chosen from the district boards and members of the NABC, in turn, are chosen by and from the state
boards. Members may be removed on due notice by the Secretary of Interior. Vacancies which occur through death or
resignation are filled by the state supervisor, BLM, on recommendation of the remaining board members. [11]

As we have noted, district advisers are elected by persons
in their grazing district who hold valid grazing permits. Each
permittee is allowed one vote regardless of the number of animal units he owns or runs on the federal range. Elections
are conducted in accordance with the General Procedures for
Grazing District Advisory Board Elections as approved by the
director, BLM, and published in the Federal Register. [12] The
actual voting practice, as conducted in one district, was described in the preceding chapter. The rate of voting participation has generally been low. The data on page 113 show voting
participation in Oregon and Idaho grazing districts in 1951. [13]
While these participation percentages seem low, they actually
indicate a higher average rate of participation than occurred,
because the higher voting rates are from the more sparsely
populated districts. The average voter participation for the two

| Grazing District | Per Cent of Permittees Voting |
|---|---|
| Idaho #1 | 7.9 |
| #2 | 10.8 |
| #3 | 7.2 |
| #4 | 4.9 |
| #5 | 4.7 |
| Oregon #1 | 22.6 |
| #2 | 20.7 |
| #3 | 16.3 |
| #5 | 12.3 |
| #6 | 12.9 |
| #7 | 24.5 |

states was only 9.9 per cent.[14]

When the above voting data were presented to the Oregon state advisory board in 1952, the members found nothing alarming about the low voting rate and one member suggested it indicated the users were satisfied.[15] Bureau of Land Management officials, however, appeared to desire more active voting participation and cast about for some method to encourage voting. Naturally the board members were not likely to be critical of the system that put them in office. It is not known whether the administration was interested in getting rid of some advisers who had been elected for several terms and hoped that a heavier vote might accomplish such results. At any rate the administration experimented with a system of balloting by mail, on a trial basis, in three grazing districts in 1953. One of the "test" districts was Oregon grazing district 5 at Prineville, Oregon. The balloting by mail system included two phases: nomination and final election. Each permittee was first mailed a nomination sheet and invited to nominate an advisory board member for his class of livestock. Persons making nominations were required to sign the nominating sheet. The nomination sheets were opened and the nominees listed by a board of three permittees. Ballots were then prepared listing the nominees in alphabetical order and with space for a write-in and mailed out to each permittee with a letter of instructions. The permittee marked his ballot, placed it in a plain, sealed en-

velope, which in turn was placed in an outside envelope on
which the permittee wrote his name and return address. When
the letters were received at the district office the permittee's
name was checked off the eligible list and his plain envelope,
containing the ballot, was placed in the ballot box to be opened
and counted on election day by a panel of election judges. This
system was first used in the Prineville district in 1953 and
was continued in 1954 and 1955. The results in voting participation, over a fourteen-year period were as follows:

| Year | Number of Votes Cast |
|------|----------------------|
| 1942 | 5 |
| 1943 | 13 |
| 1944 | 25 |
| 1945 | 13 |
| 1946 | 17 |
| 1947 | 17 |
| 1948 | 23 |
| 1949 | 22 |
| 1950 | 25 |
| 1951 | 28 |
| 1952 | 28 |
| 1953 | 214 |
| 1954 | 162 |
| 1955 | 135 |

   In 1953 there were 234 permittees eligible to vote in the election and about the same number in 1954 and 1955. The high
voting record in 1953, when the plan was first issued, seemed
to indicate that the new system was a rousing success. But
the sharp drop in 1954 and the continued decline in 1955 may
indicate that interest subsided after the novelty of the first
election. Even so, the vote in 1955 was about five times as high
as the highest vote obtained under the old system. One might
have expected the tremendous increase in 1953 to result in
the election of a new set of advisory board members. This
did not happen. Voting patterns and preferences remained
about the same as before.
   The administration has decided that balloting by mail is a

successful method, however, and has made polling by mail an optional method.[16]

The rate of turnover on advisory boards is generally extremely low. In the 1952 elections in Oregon and Idaho thirty advisers were elected. Of this number, twenty-six were reinstatements and only four were replaced by new members.[17] The rate of turnover on state advisory boards also appears to be slight, if Oregon is a fair example. The first Oregon board, elected in 1940, included David T. Jones, James Wakefield, W. S. Leehman, Andrew Greeley, Sam Ross, and John Achabal. Wakefield, Leehman, and Ross were still members in 1954. Of the 1959 membership, three individuals had been on the board for ten years or longer.[18]

The same kind of continuity has prevailed on the NABC. The first NABC of 1940 included Gordon Griswold, A. D. Brownfield, Dan Hughes, Frank O'Connell, Pat Cecil, Kelso Musser, and Floyd Lee. In 1959 A. D. Brownfield, Dan Hughes, Frank O'Connell, and Floyd Lee were still members of the board. Here again, membership for ten years or more has been the rule.[19]

As one would expect from the foregoing, the chairmanship of the boards also remains relatively static. Gordon Griswold remained chairman of the NABC from 1940 to 1949. A. D. Brownfield, elected as first vice president in 1940, has been chairman since 1950.[20] The minutes of the Oregon state advisory board meetings from 1940 to 1955 do not reveal a single instance of a contested vote—either for the chairmanship of the state board or for delegates to the NABC. In every case there was only one nomination for each office. If someone other than the incumbent was nominated for an office, the incumbent ordinarily seconded the nomination or moved that nominations be closed.

We may recapitulate voting participation, tenure of members, and tenure of officials in the advisory board system by noting that the percentage of voting participation is generally very low, the tenure of advisory board members is long—ten years is common, and officials of the boards also tend to have long terms in office.

Do these conclusions indicate that the advisory board system is "home rule on the range?" Or do they suggest the presence of a rural caste system which decentralized administration has strengthened and crystallized? Decentralization does not necessarily imply democratization. Bringing government "closer to the people" does not necessarily mean a more democratic government. When we decentralize and "bring government down to the people" de we simply bring it to the local power-holders and thus aid in buttressing a caste system by discouraging vertical mobility in the society?[21] These questions are not answered by the repetition of euphonic slogans.

The powers and duties of advisory boards, as outlined in the Taylor Grazing Act, require some elaboration and explanation. The Federal Range Code spells out these responsibilities in some detail:

District advisers shall advise or make recommendations on the following matters:

1. The qualifications, classification, and requirements of base property.

2. The transfer and relinquishment of base property qualifications.

3. The grazing capacity of the Federal range in the district.

4. Applications for all types of grazing licenses or permits, including nonuse, or extension of use, except applications of district advisers.

5. Cancellation of grazing licenses or permits when related to: failure to use base property, loss of all or part of lands used in year-round operation, range depletion, failure to offer base property or to validate a license or permit, or failure to use grazing privileges.

6. Agreements as to the extent of individual grazing privileges, when such agreements have been reduced to writing and found to be equitable and in substantial compliance with the provisions of the Federal Range Code for Grazing Districts.

7. Variance in range improvement fees in accordance with the character and requirements of the district or portions thereof.

8. Requirements for unit or allotment boundary fences and apportionment of costs between the benefiting licensees or permittees.

9. Proper rules of fair range practice.

10. Allotments of range by classes of livestock or for community or individual use.

11. Seasonal use of the Federal range or any part thereof.

12. Cooperative agreements or application for the construction or maintenance of improvements on the Federal range under section 4 of the act and assignments thereof.

13. Work plans under the range improvement, weed control or soil and moisture conservation programs.

14. Any recommendations made by local associations of stockmen in the district.

15. Reservations of grazing capacity of Federal range for wild game animals, including any agreements in connection therewith proposed for execution with State or Federal wildlife agencies.

16. Special rules for the district, within the meaning of section 161.16.

17. Any other matter which they may desire to bring to the attention of the Director, or on which their advice may be requested. [22]

The code further specifies that the state advisory boards shall make "recommendations on grazing administration policies or problems affecting the state as a whole," and repeats essentially the same terminology with respect to national policies and the NABC.

Some of these provisions merit particular emphasis. First and most important is the provision in the act which requires that the boards be consulted "in advance of the promulgation of any rules and regulations affecting the district," and also that "each board shall further offer advice or make recommendations concerning rules and regulations for the administration of this Act."[23]

In practice, the boards have acted in much the same fashion as a legislative body. "Bills" are drawn up by members or submitted by the administration. The boards then act on them in much the same way as does a legislature. Recommendations or "bills" passed by the boards are then submitted to the Secretary of Interior who in effect signs or vetoes the recommendation. In brief, the advisory boards are the legislative body for the grazing activity of the BLM. According to Gordon Griswold, president of the NABC from 1940 to 1949 "the revised [Federal Range] Code was written in its entirety by livestock men at the first meeting in Denver. The Grazing Service even asked if we would rather they weren't there."[24] This procedure is considerably different from the usual administrative rule-making practice wherein the top administrators establish the regulations within the framework of the statute. It hardly seems necessary to remark the power inherent in this kind of arrangement.

As we have noted, the Federal Range Code gives the boards specific authority to make recommendations on most matters which are likely to occur in the administration of grazing districts. But the code also provides that the boards may bring to the attention of the director "any other matter which they desire . . . or on which their advice may be requested." This means that no area of the administration is closed to the boards. Matters which receive most attention at the district level are range carrying capacity, awards and cancellation of grazing permits, range improvements, and control of trespass. District boards may also be consulted, however, on managerial questions and on such matters as bureau-wide personnel policy. An example was the study report mentioned above, which was primarily concerned with staffing and organization and methods. This report was referred to all the district advisory boards for their comments.

State boards consider primarily major policy matters and make recommendations to the Bureau and the NABC. A partial list of the items discussed by the Oregon state advisory board over a fifteen-year period follows: use of state-owned lands, revision of the Federal Range Code, reorganization of the grazing service, staffing, grazing fees, congressional bills affecting public lands and grazing, wildlife in grazing districts, congressional appropriations, public relations, range improvement, trespass control, abandoned horses, weed control, advisory board elections and bureau personnel.

The NABC was concerned with essentially the same problems except that it tended to concentrate more on congressional bills, grazing fees, appropriations, organization of the grazing service, and revisions of the Federal Range Code. However, NABC members have not hesitated to introduce matters of a purely local interest to the council. NABC member Sam Ross of Oregon once objected strenuously to the actions of A. K. Hansen, DRM in Ross's home district.[25]

The Taylor Grazing Act and the Federal Range Code give the advisory boards recommendatory powers only. How powerful are these recommendations? No definite answer can be given because the boards have had varying degrees of effectiveness depending upon the issue involved, the personalities of the director and the Secretary of Interior, and the effectiveness of their congressional supporters. The case studies which follow in chapters 7 and 8 portray some of the strengths

of the boards in specific situations. Some generalizations seem
appropriate here. Carpenter clearly intended to create something more than a consultative group when he established the
advisory boards. In his remarks at Vale, Oregon, in 1934,
he said:

> Now we come down to the proposed method of administration of the
> grazing districts. District advisory boards of stockmen will be elect-
> ed by the permittees. These boards will devise rules, subject to ap-
> proval by the Secretary of the Interior. The total personnel proposed
> for the Grazing Division at present is only twenty-one. You realize
> the government men are only going to be coordinating and supervi-
> sory agents in governing these grazing areas. We will have to, and
> are going to, depend on the local committees to apply these prin-
> ciples in classifying these applications, and to apportion out the per-
> mits in a fair manner. [26]

The users of the range apparently came to believe that they
were to administer the program through the advisory boards,
and it does not appear that the language of the amendment of
1939, giving the boards only advisory authority, made any
particular impression on the stockmen. Every director of the
grazing activity has been careful to praise the boards on every
appropriate occasion. C. L. Forsling spoke of the boards as
"an important part of the Grazing Service Organization" and
as having "aided materially in the administration of grazing
districts."[27] Marion Clawson spoke of the advisory board system as a "democratic approach" and one that "has proved successful both from the standpoint of the administration and that
of the industry."[28] The Nicholson report, which formed the
basis for organization and operation of the federal grazing activity for several years, was mainly a restatement of advisory
board recommendations.

The monies accruing to the states from a percentage of
grazing fees are ordinarily returned to the advisory boards
to be used for range improvements. These funds are spoken
of as "advisory board money." They are actually state funds
and the board serves as an agent of the state in supervising
their expenditure. The board, not the DRM, determines how
and for what purposes the money will be spent. In the activities carried on with these funds, the DRM is actually serv-
ing as the board's foreman.

The **DRM** may legally overrule the board's recommendations on grazing permits. How often does this occur? No statistics are available, but the following statements give some clue as to the board's powers in making decisions on grazing permits. At a congressional hearing, Dan Hughes, one of the original members of the NABC, was asked:

> What has been your experience as to whether or not the decisions of the Board have been set aside by the Grazier, or Chief Grazier, or any agency of the Grazing Service?
>
> Mr. Hughes. As a rule, I would say it has not been possible; 5% of the decisions have been set aside, make it 10%, but as a rule they follow our decisions. [29]

Hughes's use of the word "decisions," rather than "recommendations" may be significant.

In the same series of hearings, Gordon Griswold, Chairman of the NABC, was asked:

> The Chairman. . . . do you recall actions of your advisory board that have been overruled or set aside by your grazing authorities?
>
> Mr. Griswold. Not to my knowledge, there has been—the advisory board has never been overruled. [30]

In the same hearing the following interchange took place:

> Senator O'Mahoney. I take it . . . that the recommendations of the Advisory Boards with respect to the issuance of permits would be practically controlling.
>
> Mr. Rutledge, Director of the Grazing Service. Right, right, it is controlling. [31]

Advisory board members have, at various times, also given advice on the appointment of personnel. Thus one regional administrator wrote the director in the spring of 1948,

> I believe it well to recommend that the announcement of the person selected to head the Division of Range Management be withheld until after the members of the Advisory Council have had an opportunity to express their approval. Otherwise there will be opportunity for criticism because of failure to carry out what [some NABC members] seem to regard as a firm commitment on the part of Secretary Krug. [32]

In testifying before a House subcommittee on appropriations in the spring of 1947, J. M. Jones, executive secretary of the National Woolgrowers Association, said:

> The two national associations together with the National Advisory

Board Council and the Joint Land Committee named Dan H. Hughes of
Montrose, Colorado . . . for the director of the Bureau of Land Management and Ed Kavanaugh . . . for Chief of Range Development. It
was understood that when the matter of appointments would be taken
up by Secretary Krug, we would be advised. [33]

Jones then went on to say that apparently Dan Hughes was disqualified because he was a successful stockman and a permittee and that it looked as if the administration preferred men
who had gone broke. Jones then complained because the two
appointments made "were not acceptable to the livestock interests."

The boards not only use the administration to further the
interests of the stockmen but are themselves occasionally used
by the administration to help get support for administration
measures or help defeat measures the administration considers undesirable. In a letter of May 26, 1948, for example,
Marion Clawson asked for the assistance of the NABC with
reference to two bills then pending in Congress.

The late Bernard DeVoto in his March, 1951, "Easy Chair"
column in *Harper's Magazine* accused director Clawson of col-
laborating with the livestock associations in the preparation
of a bill which DeVoto considered most undesirable. Clawson
replied in the "Letters to the Editor" column of the June issue, expressing proper indignation—but he did not deny the
charge. There is, of course, nothing unusual in joint preparation of bills by a government bureau and its clientele. This
may, in fact, be the usual procedure as carried on through an
informal consultative process. But in the Bureau of Land Management the process is more advanced and regularized than
in most agencies.

In his remarks to the NABC in their 1954 meeting, Director
Woozley reviewed congressional bills and gave the board the
department's point of view. [34] In so doing, he was not only explaining the department's stand on the various bills, but also
soliciting support for the administration's position.

In any discussion of the advisory boards the relationship
between the boards and the stockmen's associations inevitably
arises. How much influence do the associations exert on advisory board members? In the first place it is not necessary
for the associations to "work on" the boards from the outside

because most board members are either members of the National Woolgrowers Association or the American National Livestock Association. As one ascends the board hierarchy, it is more likely that board members will also be association members. Some individuals have been members of an advisory board and officers in a stockmen's association simultaneously. Others have held office in a stockmen's association either before or after service on an advisory board. The following list suggests the closeness of the relationship between the advisory boards and the stockmen's associations.

| *Name* | *Position Held in Advisory Board System* | *Position Held in Stockmen's Association* |
|---|---|---|
| A. D. Brownfield | First Vice-President, NABC<br>President, NABC | President, New Mexico Cattlegrowers Association<br>President, American National Cattlemen's Association |
| Gerald Stanfield | Chairman, Oregon State Advisory Board<br>Member, NABC | President, Oregon Woolgrowers Association |
| J. C. "Pat" Cecil | Member, NABC<br>Secretary, NABC | President, Oregon Cattlemen's Association<br>Member, Executive Committee, American Cattlemen's Association |
| Stanley Ellison | Member, Battle Mountain (Nevada) Grazing District Advisory Board | President, Nevada Woolgrowers Association<br>Member, Executive Committee, National Woolgrowers Association |
| Sam C. Hyatt | Member, NABC | President, American National Cattlemen's Association |

| | | |
|---|---|---|
| Milford C. Vaught | Member, NABC | Member, General Council, American National Cattlemen's Association<br>Member, Executive Committee, American National Cattlemen's Association |
| Brunel Christensen | Member, NABC | Member, General Council, American National Cattlemen's Association |
| W. F. Garrison | Member, NABC | Member, Executive Committee, American National Cattlemen's Association |
| Fred Strosnider | Member, NABC | Member, Executive Committee, American National Cattlemen's Association |
| Floyd Lee | Member, NABC | Member, Executive Committee, American National Cattlemen's Association<br>Chairman, Public Lands Committee, American National Cattlemen's Association |
| Frank Meaker | Member, Monticello Grazing District District No. 9 Advisory Board | President, Colorado Woolgrowers Association<br>Member, Executive Committee, National Woolgrowers Association |
| Leonard Horn | Member, NABC | Member, Executive Committee, American National Cattlemen's Association |

| | | |
|---|---|---|
| Gene Etchart | Member, NABC | Member, General Council, American National Cattlemen's Association |
| Julian Arrien | Member, NABC | President, Oregon Woolgrowers Association<br>Chairman, General Resolutions Committee, National Woolgrowers Association |

The above list could be expanded considerably. We should not assume, however, that complete unanimity exists simply because advisory board members may also be members and officers of the associations. State associations, for instance, occasionally disagree with the national association. Generally speaking, however, it seems safe to say that the association views expressed in the NABC are the views of the association's national headquarters.

F. R. Carpenter used the stockmen's associations to help form the first organization committees. The following exerpt from his remarks illustrates the procedure used:

> I am going to ask Mr. Wayne E. Phillips of Keating, Oregon, representing the State Wool Growers, if he will suggest the names of four sheepmen from the state at large for membership on his committees.
>
> Mr. Phillips. Garnett Barrett, Morrow county; Ben Taylor, Willow county; Gene Hammond of Klamath county; F. C. Vaughn, Baker county.
>
> The Director. If it is satisfactory with you, I would like to add the name of Mr. Wayne E. Phillips. [35]

Carpenter maintains, however, that "they were never consulted afterwards and while we allowed their representatives to attend all meetings, participation was confined to permittees." [36]

Representatives of the associations do commonly attend meetings. J. M. Jones, former executive secretary of the National Woolgrowers Association, regularly attended NABC meetings. F. E. Mollin, former executive secretary of the American Livestock Association, also attended. These association executives, and occasionally other officials of the associations, have sometimes been called upon to address the NABC. In fairness, we should mention that Ira Gabrielson, representing competing wildlife interests, has also addressed the NABC.[37] The Oregon state supervisor, BLM, customarily invites the presidents of the stockmen's associations and also the state wildlife officials to state advisory board meetings.

Further evidence of the close relationship between the boards and the associations appears in the scheduling of meetings. The 1951 NABC meeting was held December 2 in Portland to coincide with the National Woolgrowers Convention which was held December 4-7 in the same city. The 1953 NABC meeting was originally scheduled for January 8-9 at Kansas City to follow immediately after the American National Livestock Association convention. This meeting was postponed at the last minute to enable the director to meet with Secretary-designate McKay.[38]

When Director Forsling attempted to raise grazing fees in 1944, the NABC joined with the two associations to form the "Joint Livestock Committee on Public Lands" for the purpose of combating the proposed increase. Since that time the two associations and the NABC have united in a "stockmen's grazing committee" to promote the passage of an act known as the "Uniform Federal Grazing Land Tenancy Act." A. D. Brownfield was the chairman of this committee and also the chairman of the NABC.[39] We need not belabor further the various interlocking relationships which exist between the stockmen's associations and the advisory boards.

It may be worth while to pause here to summarize our observations of the advisory board system. The boards are accorded legal recognition in the statute and the statute and the regulations spell out the duties and authority of the boards in some detail. Board members are elected from, and by, the clientele group for regular terms as federal officers. The percentage of voting participation for advisory board members is very low. The rate of turnover of board members and board officials is extremely low. The boards appear to be the dominant rule-making (policy-formulating) body in the federal grazing service. The boards also are involved in managerial details and, in fact, no part of the administration appears to be barred from their surveillance. The boards determine how range improvement funds are to be expended and their decisions on individual grazing permits are rarely overruled. The boards are influential in the selection of administrative personnel. The relationships between the boards and the two livestock producers organizations are so close that leadership in the associations and the boards is frequently embodied in the same persons.

From these observations it would appear that, primarily through the administrative process, a small interest group has been able to establish a kind of private government with reference to federal grazing districts. It would appear that they formulate the broad policy, make the rules, and superintend the execution of these rules and policies.

The advisory boards naturally consider the public lands to be primarily range lands of little interest to anyone but the permittees. But at least theoretically the federal range is directly and indirectly the concern of every resident of the United States. These lands will become increasingly important as population pressure increases. To date, only wildlife and conservation groups (aside from the stockmen) have taken an active interest in the administration of the grazing districts. On several occasions they have been able to muster enough congressional support to defeat measures which they believed gave the stockmen too much control and jeopardized wildlife, recreation, and conservation values.

In this section we have considered a particular kind of political activity which might be called administrative politics, as distinguished from legislative or judicial politics. We have observed some of the devices which were used by an interest group (the western stockmen) to gain a considerable degree of political power primarily through administrative processes. As we will see later, the interest group also exerted its influence in the state legislatures and in Congress but basically the case involves bureau politics.

Bureau politics partially dispenses with the competition of the ballot box and the competition of the market place as means of social and economic adjustment and democratic control and substitutes for it a system of competition between interest groups or clientele blocs.[40] The same statement could be applied to pressure group influence on the legislative bodies but with lessened validity because the competition of the ballot box still has some considerable influence there. The legislator still has to confront a public which has votes and which is more diversified in interests than that which typically faces the administrator. The legislator may not face a competitive political market, in the sense of the economist's use of the term "competition," but he will usually be faced with an oligopoly, or competition between a few conflicting pressure groups. The administrator, on the other hand, is likely to be confronted with a duopoly or monopoly situation with regards to interest group competition. For want of a better term we may designate such a situation as "monopolitical."

In a monopolitical situation the administrator is in substantially the same position as the consumer who is confronted with a monopoly producer. He has no real alternatives. His public is narrow and restricted. In the case of the Federal Grazing Service that public is confined to the western stockmen and a few sportsmen and wildlife groups. Very likely few people outside that public know anything about the affairs of the grazing service and care less. The administrator and his staff are alone—except for the stockmen who are with them always. As time goes by, they are likely to identify themselves closely with the stockmen. When they make decisions of a regulatory nature they are forced to consider essentially the same factors as do their clientele so, over time, such decisions will tend to come closer together.

Monopolitics is a kind of political activity which has received little attention. People no longer believe that ours is a democracy in which all citizens participate equally in public decisions. The general impression among the populace is that we do not have a pure democracy because we delegate most of our public decision-making powers. Others, more politically sophisticated, may describe the democratic process in the United States as a resolution of the objectives of competing and conflicting pressure groups. This last may be a reasonably accurate description of that phase of the political process which primarily concerns legislatures. It does not accurately describe bureau politics because there are often no effective competing or conflicting pressure groups. So there is no conflict to resolve—at least within the bureau. In the affairs of the grazing service there is only one really effective public—the stockmen. The wildlife public has carried on an intermittent campaign of harassment but has generally been unsuccessful.

It appears that we have two general kinds of politics: competitive politics and monopoly politics. These two kinds of political activity tend to produce two kinds of government: general government and special government. The special governments, however, have all the sanctions and symbols of the general government and the public assumes that they are, in fact, a part of the general government. The leaders of the special governments, if they are rational individuals, will attempt to use the powers of the general government to maximize the satisfactions of the citizens of the special governments. This means that the special governments will tend to act like private organizations, but they will retain the powers of the general government. We may characterize these two categories as special private governments and general public governments.

Probably no interest group can be completely monopolitical. In the case of the Federal Grazing Service the wildlife organizations have occasionally snapped at the heels of the stockmen and have also been able to throw up a few congressional roadblocks. Their over-all effectiveness, however, can be judged from the strength of the stockmen's advisory boards.

Wildlife now has representation on the advisory boards but it is very definitely in the minority. This concession to the wildlife interests was not forced upon the stockmen. The NABC voted for wildlife representation on the national board in 1954. The stockmen seemed to believe that if they could get the wildlife people to sit in on board meetings and thus gain a better understanding of the stockmen's problems a more sympathetic attitude would result.

As long as a government agency is restricted to administering a single clientele for a single purpose, the observations set forth in this section seem applicable. However, if the agency is consolidated with others, or assumes additional functions, the monopolitical characteristics of the original clientele group may become weakened and the vitality and effectiveness of the special private government diminished. When the old Grazing Service was combined with the General Land Office to form the present Bureau of Land Management, the advisory board system may have begun to lose some of its strength. In recent years a concept of multiple land use has been growing. By the administration, at least, the grazing districts are no longer considered as grazing reserves only. It seems probable that this trend may continue. If this happens there will be increasing pressure to broaden or diversify representation on the advisory boards. Diversified advisory board representation could mean a return to competitive politics and a diminution of the strength of the stockmen.

# 7. THE BATTLE OF SOLDIER CREEK

The case study which follows describes a controversy over grazing permits which illustrates some of the generalizations of earlier chapters. It also further illustrates the activities of advisory boards and gives some indication of the attitudes of permittees and administrators and the roles and identifications of each.

While the case is not a typical example of grazing district administration because of the frequency of conflict situations, it is by no means unusual or abnormal.

## *The Soldier Creek Grazing Unit*

Soldier Creek is one unit of federal grazing district 3 in southeast Oregon. On most maps this area is blanked out by the legend. The closest town is Jordan Valley, which has a population of about three hundred. Jordan Valley was named for a pioneer stockman who was killed by Indians in 1864. At that time the town was already well established.

Most of the present residents of this section are descendants of pioneer stockmen who settled the area a century ago. There has been little migration into the area since that time. Families are often interrelated and are, of course, intimately acquainted with each other's affairs. Jordan Valley is still somewhat provincial partly because the nearest railroad is some fifty miles distant. People still speak of "going to the railroad" rather than of going to the city.

The Soldier Creek grazing unit is a triangular shaped section bounded on the east by the Oregon-Idaho state line, on
the southwest by the Owyhee River Canyon, and on the north
by Jordan Creek. The Jordan Creek valley is taken up by irrigated farms and ranches, some of which have grazing privileges on the range land to the south. The Owyhee River to

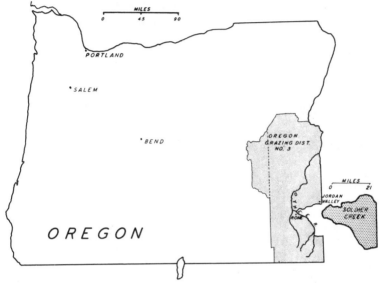

Fig. 3. The Soldier Creek Grazing Unit

the southwest runs through a box canyon. There are no bridges,
fords, or other crossings on this canyon for the whole length
of the Soldier Creek unit. The Owyhee canyon, then, forms a
natural barrier on the southwest. Four creeks, one of them
Soldier Creek, converge and flow into the Owyhee at about the
halfway point. There are a few private holdings scattered
along these creeks and along the northern border, but most
of the unit is federally owned range land. The unit comprises
an area of 205,066 acres. To the west of the Soldier Creek
unit lies the Jackie's Butte grazing unit. Some stockmen in
the Jordan Creek area use this unit by trailing through the gap
at Rome, Oregon.

This is an extremely dry region with average annual rainfall
between eight and ten inches. It is hilly, rolling country cov-

ered by an old lava flow so that the surface is somewhat rough
and broken. The high points, Whitehorse Butte, Juniper Point,
and Parsnip Peak, are along the southern and eastern boundaries. Originally this was bunchgrass country and was used
mainly as winter range because of the lack of summer watering places. As a consequence the grass was not "beat out, " because plants were able to grow to maturity before they were
grazed. In the early part of the century stockmen considered
the Owyhee region to be among the best portions of the remaining federal range.

### Preliminary Skirmishes

On March 3, 1945, the following letter was dispatched to the
White House:

Dear President Roosevelt
Sir
    Just a few lines to see if it ever acured to you how to get a lot of
our boys started on a sef-suporting ranch . . . Now what is runing
the cattle and sheep industry is the Taylor Grazing Business. What
they do out here they have a Board and no one sits on it but the Big
Cattle man all they have done has put the Little Cattle man out of business they have killed the raising of all of 30 thousand head of Beef
that would be mighty hand right now before long. There will not be
enough Beef to supply this country not saying any thing about *abroud.*
. . . now take me for instant I have 10 head of cattle and that is all
I can have as I haves to keep them up in pasture all the times as I
can't get no point to run cattle as I did not apply when the Law first
started so all I can do is just keep 10 head. They brag and tell all they
do and dont do nothing except draw that check evry month and hold
meeting evry month or so and all the Big Cattle men meet and have a
big blow out in the Boise Idaho or Salt Lake no little man has a chance
now I though we all had a equil chance but as it is just a few . . . so
as it is what chance has a man no anie. The Tailor Grazing will have
evry thing run by just a few stock men and they cant supply all the
needs. . . . you may not be ablt to read this but I hope so I know you
do not know all that is going on and I dont expect that of your But rem-
ber what I am saying there will be no steaks or mutton in 10 years.
                            Yours sincerely
                            /s/ (name withheld)
P.S. I would like to hear from you. Now for example take Sam Ross
at Jordan Valley in Oregon a big cattle man He has 2 ranchs one put
up about 300 tons Hay as the other is only a Grazing Ranch No here is

what the Taylor Grazing did for him. The alloted him 2000 acres and furnish all the post and wire and the CCC fenced all his alotment and developed all the springs for water in side of this 2000 acres. Now he turns out on other alotments and run his cattle till the feed and springs dry up Then he gathrs his cattle and put in his new fenced alotment. They evry bodies cattle that is out on the off range and dry springs has to get by as strong can But Sam Ross has a good pasture for his cattle that has been developed by the Taylor Grazing for his cattle. Now do you see any justice in that and giving a man a equival right? Resevores [reservoirs] for him and another public grant at his other ranch and is going to fence about 1500 acres more for him so he will have all the pick land around him fenced and all the water fenced in also. Then all out side cattle will have to go about 4 miles to get watter now do you call that just or not I do not. I am safe to say that the Gov., has spent 10,000.00 developing property for Sam Ross alone, The CCC builds new rodes in to their door for them So what do you think about the way the Taylor Grazing is doing You may say I am jelous But I am not. Treat evry body alike. . . . And let evry farmer rais cattle sheep and you would have plenty meat without ration same and could ship meat to the Forin Country and help the whole Nation what I want is to help the whole nation excep our enemies, as I have 2 Boys over there fitting for the freedom of the country sam as you. So please think this over and see if ther cant be something don

                                                    As evr yors
                                                    /s/ (name withheld)

The range referred to in the letter is Oregon grazing district 3, in southeast Oregon.

Originally the present district 3 was divided into two districts—Oregon 3 with headquarters at Vale, Oregon and Oregon 4 with headquarters at Jordan Valley. The boundaries of the Soldier Creek unit were decided at a meeting of February 17, 1936, at which Sam Ross presided.[1] This is the Sam Ross referred to in the letter. Ross is a Jordan Valley stockman who served as a member of the district advisory board from 1936 to 1956. During much of that time he acted as chairman of the district board and was for several years a member of the Oregon state advisory board and the National Advisory Board Council. Ross did not own any property in the Soldier Creek unit but was said to hold two ranches on unsatisfied sales contracts and two more on mortgage loans during part of this time. He also acted as a kind of "field man" for some lending agencies during a period when practically every ranch was heavily mortgaged and additional loans were being most urgently sought. Consequently, as one rancher expressed it, "he sort of had us over a barrel."

One month after the Soldier Creek unit was formed, twenty-two cattlemen filed the first of a long series of protests from that unit. This particular protest objected to the presence of sheep in the unit and demanded an earlier opening date.[2]

Trouble between cattlemen and sheepmen in Soldier Creek continued. Marvin Klemme, the regional grazier, thought it necessary to call a special meeting of the Soldier Creek stockmen in an attempt to reach some agreement but was unsuccessful.[3] According to Klemme, "The Soldier Creek unit was overstocked and overgrazed at the time the district was set up. Legitimate priority and commensurability existed for more than twice the number of animals the unit could properly carry."[4] Klemme had previously worked for the Forest Service. He had become acquainted with F. R. Carpenter during an assignment in Colorado and transferred over to the newly formed Grazing Division after Carpenter's appointment as director.

At this time all the grazing districts in Oregon were administered from a regional office in Burns, Oregon. In the fall of 1938, however, five district offices were established, one at Jordan Valley for district 4. Regional grazier Marvin Klemme chose S. R. Bennett to be the first DRM for the Jordan Valley district. Bennett had spent several years with the Forest Service and had resigned in 1924 to operate his own cattle ranch. Klemme chose Bennett for this particular district because "he was an experienced cattleman and spoke their language" and "would be better able to get along with such a group than would any of the younger, college trained men."[5]

Shortly thereafter Klemme took a leave of absence and was replaced by Nick Monte. Monte was also an "experienced cattleman" and had been one of the originators of the Mizpah-Pumpkin Creek grazing district in Montana in the early thirties. The grazing district plan in the Taylor Grazing Act was patterned somewhat after the successful Mizpah-Pumpkin Creek experiment so Monte was indirectly one of the architects of the present federal grazing system.

Sam Ross continued as chairman of the district advisory board. In 1937 the board was successful in getting a Civilian Conservation Corps camp located in the district after Ross offered to lease suitable camp sites "for as long a term as the government wants."[6]

The C.C.C. was employed in building fences, developing watering places and generally improving the federal range in the Jordan Valley area. Chairman Ross apparently was not altogether satisfied with the work of the C.C.C. or with the district range manager; in an advisory board meeting of November 16, 1940, he stated that the main work of the C.C.C. camp had been the building of a road to Burns so that Bennett could make more frequent trips to that city. According to Ross, DRM Bennett spent most of his time in Burns and had worn out one car already driving back and forth and had many miles on another one. At the same meeting Ross stated that he had prepared a petition asking for the removal of Nick Monte (regional grazier) and S. R. Bennett from the Grazing Service.[7]

Sometime in December, 1940, Bennett notified the advisory board members that the next meeting would be held at Rome, Oregon. This precipitated the following letter to the Director, Division of Grazing, Washington, D.C.:

Dear Sir:

We the undersigned board members, of Jordan District, State of Oregon have received notice from S. R. Bennett, District Grazier, that our next board meeting will be held at Rome, Oregon, December 20. Jordan Valley is the most central and convenient place and has always been our meeting place. Mr. Bennett has taken it upon himself to make this change without consulting either the board or any of the users. . . .

We therefore refuse to change our meeting place and suggest you send a delegation from Washington to meet with this advisory board and investigate this situation as it stands here now. As both the users and the board are very unsatisfied by the way things have been going.

/s/ Sam Ross, T. T. Garlick,
Andrew Greeley, John
Achibal, Jr.

The director upheld Bennett's decision in a letter to each of the objecting advisers. This apparently was not an isolated case of disagreement between the board and the DRM because

Bennett later stated that, "A few letters like this [the director's letter] will do a lot to stop the disloyalty to the users and the service that we have had to contend with."[8] At the Rome meeting Ross again protested against the meeting place and objected to a general lack of publicity as to time and place of meeting.

At the same meeting Nick Monte, regional grazier, requested Ross to

. . . account to the advisory board for 42 spools of . . . wire taken from the Jordan Valley camp warehouse without proper authority, the wire having been requested and the receipt having been signed by Mr. Ross' hired man and issued by the CCC boy in charge without Mr. Bennett's knowledge or approval. Mr. Ross advised that the wire was obtained in order to replace that which he had furnished at his own expense on the Ross drift fence, which was constructed in 1937 by Mr. Ross on public domain lands.[9]

Ross then proceeded to inform the board that he had a district-owned windmill and some six-inch well casing which he was using on his Jordan Valley ranch. He agreed to return this equipment or replace it.[10]

When the minutes of the meeting just discussed were read at the ensuing meeting Ross objected to so many items that the board decided that henceforth minutes of meetings would be first written as rough drafts and submitted to each of the board members for corrections and additions before the final draft was prepared.[11]

Ross continued to serve as chairman of the district advisory board even though he requested in 1942 that some other member replace him. There had been some changes in the composition of the board during the first six years of its existence but Ross continued in office, not only in the district but as a member of the state advisory board.[12] While the board appeared to function quite smoothly at this time, its methods apparently were questioned by some administrators. One member of the grazing service recorded the following observations in a memorandum to the regional grazier:

During my recent assignment in the Jordan district I sat in on a meeting of the advisory board. . . . There were certain characteristics of this meeting which indicated possible underlying unhealthy conditions.

First, there was a marked tendency for board members to act as individuals rather than as a board, each member being tacitly given unquestioned autonomy in his precinct. One member repeatedly disavowed any interest and refused to join in making a decision when cases outside his own neighborhood were brought up. This resulted in most cases being settled on the opinion of the one or two board members personally familiar with them, without benefit of a review and opinion of all members.

Second, there was a further tendency to decide cases on the basis of whether this or that applicant was "a good fellow," and without a review of any kind of the base property involved. Use of this approach by the board chairman [Ross] was particularly noticeable. . . .

The personality and attitude of the board chairman have contributed largely to the tendency of the board to use a personal rather than a base property merit approach in many cases. [13]

At the organization meeting in January, 1943, Ross was promptly re-elected chairman for the ensuing year.

During the years of Bennett's tenure as DRM, considerable tension developed between him and the board chairman. Whether Bennett was transferred for this reason is unknown, but at the board meeting of March 25, 1943, Sam Ross proposed that the board submit a vote of thanks to Bennett for his services in Oregon grazing district 4. [14] Bennett was succeeded by Art J. Seale as DRM.

## The 1943 Agreement

During the intervening years the users of the Soldier Creek unit had been in more or less continual dispute. Between 1935 and 1943 the number of sheepmen operating on Soldier Creek was diminished by refusing permits to some operators because of lack of sufficient commensurate base property. Because of these reductions, additional range became available to some class 2 operators (those who had commensurate base properties but no history of use during the priority period). Some of these class 2 operators were old stockmen who had been forced to sell out or decrease their herds during the priority period. Naturally these stockmen pressed for increased range privileges. The method used to resolve this problem is best told in the words of Sam Ross:

It is a well known fact that the years beginning '29 and '34 were the toughest years on the livestock business that this country has ever seen, so a large per cent of the livestock people were practically out of business, and very few of the users could classify as Class 1 [those who had both commensurate property and history of prior use]. The Advisory board and the livestock people worked for three or four years trying to find an answer to this problem. Finally the district-grazier and the advisory board of the Soldier Creek district decided that the only fair thing to do would be to call a meeting of all users and set the range up by agreement. This group of users and the district grazier decided to throw Class 1 and 2 together and divide it up that way. The stock men and the range administrator then made a survey of the carrying capacity of the range in the Soldier Creek district which they finally agreed to be 45,000 A.U.M.'s. They then made a survey of base property demand which showed a demand of something over 77,000 A.U.M.'s. But we couldn't license over the carrying capacity of the range, which would be 45,000 A.U.M.'s.[15]

On the basis of this arrangement both class 1 and class 2 applicants were "set-up" in the district office records on an equal basis for the full amount their base properties would support. In other words, priority rights were ignored and the estimated carrying capacity of the unit was also ignored. Commensurate base property was the only factor considered. The total of these commensurate base property rights for Soldier Creek amounted to 77,419 A.U.M.'s. However, it was recognized that the unit would not support this total. The advisory board estimated the carrying capacity of the unit at 43,260 A.U.M.'s.[16] Ross has insisted, over the years, that the estimated carrying capacity was 45,000 A.U.M.'s but both the board and the administration generally accepted the 43,260 figure. The applicants agreed that the 77,419 figure would be used only as a starting point for making the downward adjustments necessary to keep licensed use within the carrying capacity of the unit. However, each permittee's "rights" were not *proportionately* reduced. Each permittee still had "rights," on paper at least, for the full amount his commensurate properties would support. There were two reasons, in 1943, for not proportionately reducing each permittee's "rights" to bring the total down to the estimated carrying capacity of the unit. First, the stockmen planned eventually to build bridges across the Owyhee Canyon and consolidate the Jackie's Butte area with Soldier Creek.[17] If this had been accomplished, the total capacity of Soldier Creek would have been increased considerably. Secondly, this system, or lack of system, permitted more flexibility in allocating annual licensed use. Thus, in a particular year, operator A might not desire to use the range at all so operator B could conceivably be licensed for the total amount his base properties would support.

The operators, in cooperation with the board, were thus able to work out informal agreements on an individual basis for the use of the range without overstocking it (at least on paper). Such an arrangement could work only as long as there was a high degree of cooperation among the permittees, or the decisions were made by someone in whom they had confidence and who could satisfy, or silence, the more contentious claimants. Sam Ross was able to keep this informal arrangement operating for several years without any formal appeals or serious complaints from the users. He was also able to hold down the licensed use below the estimated carrying capacity of the unit. The licensed use in A. U. M.'s on the Soldier Creek unit from 1943 to 1951 follows: 1943, 34, 132; 1944, 38, 970; 1945, 36, 095; 1946, 33, 561; 1947, 34, 542; 1948, 35, 964; 1949, 37, 122; 1950, 37, 867; 1951, 39, 768.[18] All these figures are considerably under 43, 260 A. U. M.'s, the estimated carrying capacity of the district.

In brief, it appears that grazing privileges in the Soldier Creek unit were not allocated according to the Federal Range Code but according to the discretion of the advisory board, and, more particularly, the discretion of the chairman, Sam Ross. Ross is reported to have made such statements as, "If I tell him to cut a hundred head—he'll cut, " or, "I told him to buy more stock to fill out his permit." One might compare this system with the old private government which existed on the range before the advent of the homesteader and the nomadic sheepman.

### Personnel Changes

District range manager Art J. Seale apparently had no particular difficulties with the district advisory board but he was replaced after about one year of service by DRM Tom Campbell. According to Campbell,

A few days after coming to the district . . . in October of 1944 I went
to Mr. Ross' residence for the purpose of getting acquainted. We . . .
spent several hours shooting ducks. . . . Mr. Ross told me he had
got along very well with Mr. Seale as District Grazier, but was very
critical of Mr. Bennett. He . . . stated that he had been instrumental
in getting a former employee by the name of Beers discharged from
the Service. He further stated that he did not get along very well with
the camp superintendent who was formerly in charge of the CCC camp
at Jordan Valley, and remarked that it had taken quite a while before
he got him fired. He also stated that he did not get along with Mr.
Bennett and that Mr. Bennett was no longer in the district. He said he
had not got along with Regional Grazier Nick W. Monte and that Nick
Monte had been transferred out of the district. I asked him, "what are
you trying to tell me Sam?" Ross replied, "Oh nothing. I was just
talking." I said, "I think I understand."[19]

For several years the problem of wild or abandoned horses
received much attention because of their alleged damage to the
range. At one time Sam Ross presented his certified check
for $5,000 to the advisory board as his bond and guaranteed
that he would rid the district of wild horses. He said that he
would "get 90 per cent of them, and if the board insisted, he
would go out and shoot the rest." Ross proposed that he be giv-
en exclusive rights to rid the district of wild horses and that
he be allowed to keep all the horses he caught. DRM Campbell insisted, however, that neither he nor the advisory board
had authority to give Ross rights of ownership to the horses
he caught because many of them were branded and, even though
they were trespassing on federal range, they were still private
property. The advisory board nevertheless recommended that
Sam Ross be authorized to rid the district of wild horses in
accordance with his proposal.[20]

At another meeting the board (with Ross absent) decided to
employ one Shirley Scoggins as range rider and pay him in
part with advisory board money.[21] That morning Scoggins
had visited Ross to "ask him what his stand was." Ross supposedly assured Scoggins of his support and suggested that if
anyone "blocked the deal" it would be the DRM. However, when
Ross heard of the board's decision he objected to the range
rider working under the supervision of the DRM or any other
member of the Grazing Service. DRM Campbell tried to explain that any personnel employed by the district would have to

be responsible to him. But Ross insisted that the board would spend the money on county roads or "let it pile up" rather than pay a man who would work under the supervision of "Tom Campbell or any other Grazing Service man." As a consequence, the matter was dropped.[22]

Campbell apparently attempted to get some of the advisory board members to "stand up to Ross" during this meeting, but none of them was willing to do so. Supposedly they were afraid that if Ross was sufficiently antagonized he might be able to cause the removal of Campbell and the appointment of a DRM more amenable to his wishes. If this were to happen some board members were said to fear their personal interests might suffer.

Campbell writes, "On June 30, 1945 when I was at his [Ross's] home he said, 'In the first board meeting we held after you came to the district . . . I made up my mind then you would not last long.'"[23]

According to advisory board member Gerald Stanfield,[24] "All this friction between the users and the Service or District Graziers generally ended in a change of Graziers. I believe it was in 1947 that the Director, Marion Clawson, consulted me relative to consolidation of District 3 and District 4 with one advisory board and Grazier [DRM]. That was done."[25] DRM Campbell was let out in this consolidation and M. H. Galt, the DRM of district 3, now became responsible for both districts.

Galt almost immediately took exception to the method used in allocating permits in the Soldier Creek unit. At an advisory board meeting of February 18, 1947, Galt explained that "commitments were made in 1943 considerably in excess of the carrying capacity of the federal range in the Soldier Creek unit. A readjudication will be necessary as . . . the demand can be satisfied only to the extent of the carrying capacity of the range."[26]

No readjudication was attempted, however, and the advisory board's recommendation that the existing procedure "be allowed on a temporary basis this year" was accepted.

Galt was not reconciled to this state of affairs and complained to regional grazier Kelso Newman that a "situation had developed [in the Soldier Creek unit] which must be clari-

fied. "[27] Newman replied, "you have no recourse except to let
the matter rest until you have more help available . . . until
such time arrives I suggest the matter be left in status quo. "[28]

From 1943 to about 1950, "everybody was satisfied and it
went along fine, " according to Sam Ross. In the meantime,
however, many of the users of the Soldier Creek unit forgot
about the estimated carrying capacity of the range and, as one
Jordan Valley rancher expressed it, "every rancher thought
he had about twice the right he actually had. "[29]

When the two districts were combined, W. W. Scott, former chairman of the district 3 board, was nominated for chairman of the combined districts. Sam Ross promptly seconded
the nomination. Ross was nominated but withdrew his name.
He was then elected vice chairman by a unanimous vote. Sam
Ross and Gerald Stanfield were elected to the state advisory
board.[30] The same pattern prevailed the following year except that Ross nominated Scott for chairman and Stanfield for
vice chariman. Both were elected.[31] The following year Scott
was elected chairman and Ross vice chairman by unanimous
vote.[32] During all three years Stanfield and Ross were elected
to the Oregon state advisory board.

In 1946 the General Land Office and the Grazing Service
were combined to form a new Bureau of Land Management.
The organizational structure in the grazing activity remained
about the same as before except that the director now headed
the combined agencies. One change that is pertinent to this
case was the consolidation of Idaho and Oregon into one regional office.

In 1948, Marion Clawson, director of the Bureau of Land
Management, became aware that some disharmonies existed
in Oregon grazing district 3. According to Clawson:

There were too many livestock on the range when the Taylor Grazing Act was passed, their numbers were not reduced, the regulations
under the Act were not followed properly, the Board had too much
influence in the administration of the District, and two men dominated
the Board more than should be the case on a well-functioning board.
The old Grazing Service may properly be criticized for having allowed such a situation to develop and continue, although there were
extenuating circumstances—shortage of personnel, and especially of
well-qualified personnel, being a major one. We discovered this situation in 1948, in a quick inspection made of grazing districts in this

region, and in 1949 a detailed inspection revealed the details and the magnitude of the problem. It was evident that some personnel moves in the district and at the regional office were necessary if the situation was to be corrected, and we made those personnel changes. [33]

These personnel changes are best described by Gerald Stanfield.

After the consolidation of Idaho and Oregon into one region, Mr. Seely [regional grazier] was moved in from Utah . . . and we had more trouble over Soldier Creek. This ended in the removal of Mr. Galt, District Grazier, to a district in Utah, and bringing Mr. Hansen to District 3-4. Then real trouble began. [34]

## The Opening Campaign

The new district range manager, A. K. Hansen, had been sent in to do a job and he lost no time in getting started. According to Sam Ross, "at our first board meeting he made the statement, 'This range is depleted and I am going to cut the use fifty-six per cent.'"[35] The protest meeting which followed lasted four days.

A. K. Hansen described the Soldier Creek system in these words:

In so far as the individual licensee was concerned, his recognized potential use could have been the greatest number that had been recognized from the production of his base properties. This leaves the potential amount of 77,419 A. U. M.'s which could be applied for but could not be considered for licenses beyond 43,260 A. U. M.'s. The A. U. M.'s applied for above this figure would be reduced proportionately to each licensee each year. This presents a very unstable method of licensing and creates an impossible administrative problem. It is also illegal in that licensees with unquestionable qualified grazing privileges would be rejected for a portion of their number to admit licensed use of those who would not be justly qualified under the provisions of the Federal Range Code.

Since the advisory board insisted that this method of licensing continue, complete studies of base properties and ranges were required to obtain facts on which the advisory board could be overruled. These studies have been completed and are being used in an attempt to establish legal qualification. [36]

In the summer of 1951, DRM Hansen brought in a crew of range conservationists who made a survey of the grazing capacity of the Soldier Creek unit. This survey team computed the grazing capacity of the unit at 31, 284 A. U. M. 's. This was considerably less than the 1943 estimate of 43, 260 A. U. M. 's or Ross's estimate of 45, 000. It was, of course, less than half the 77, 419 A. U. M. 's to which many stockmen believed they were entitled.

The accuracy of the range survey was questioned primarily on the basis that it was taken too late in the season. According to advisory board member David T. Jones, [37] "We usually have a heavy growth of weeds in the range country in eastern Oregon—even on the desert. These weeds are annuals. About the end of June they dry out, shrivel up, and blow away. But sheep practically live on these weeds during the early part of the season."[38]

Armed with this range survey, Hansen attempted in the fall of 1951 to obtain a recommendation from the advisory board for a decrease in total grazing privileges on Soldier Creek. David T. Jones described the proceedings as follows:

An advisory board meeting was called and convened on the Monday before Thanksgiving. Mr. Hansen had a series of maps on the walls. He wanted to know how much this district or locality should be cut and how much another unit should be cut in numbers of livestock. On Monday, Tuesday, and Wednesday there was a complete deadlock between Mr. Hansen and the advisory board. In other words—no recommendation from the Board. Mr. Hansen appeared to be very peeved. On Wednesday evening Hansen came in and asked if the Board had any recommendations and if they would come back Friday, the day after Thanksgiving. The Board was unanimous on the matter of not coming back until Monday. When we arrived on Monday someone whispered around that the Director of Grazing, Mr. Clawson, had arrived at Vale. Pretty soon Mr. Hansen and Mr. Clawson arrived. . . . Mr. Clawson stated he was glad to meet us all. He made a nice talk. . . . But he wound up his talk with the statement that, "You members of the Advisory Board had better cooperate with your range manager," and that, "he has a right to veto any recommendation that the Board makes." Well, after Clawson left there was hardly any doubt but that Hansen had sent for him. But still there was no cooperation.[39]

Hansen did not immediately proceed to cut grazing privileges to the 31, 284 A. U. M. 's shown in the survey. In an effort to gain the cooperation of the board and the users, he accepted the 43, 260 figure and reduced permits *proportionately* to total that level. In actuality then, this was the same ceiling that had been used since 1943, except that the possibility of making "adjustments" in individual licenses was eliminated. In the meantime, the actual demand for the range had increased to about 49, 000 A.U.M.'s. Although this was only about 6, 000 A.U.M.'s more than the 1943 carrying capacity estimate, it was 28, 000 A.U.M.'s less than the 77, 419 "paper rights" to which many ranchers believed they were entitled. Again, a protest meeting in February, 1952, lasted for four days with feelings running high. Fred Eiguren, for instance, threatened the board with, "I'll tear up the whole set-up in the Soldier Creek unit and I'll start right here around this table."[40]

Hansen's compromise move to placate the board and the users was of questionable legality. As long as the 1943 estimate remained as the official carrying capacity of the range there could be little rational objection to the enforcement of that ceiling. But when a new survey showed the capacity of the range to be about 12, 000 A.U.M.'s less it would appear that, technically, Hansen would have to limit grazing to the new survey or nullify that survey with another one. As we have seen, he did neither but attempted to secure compliance by authorizing permits in excess of the capacity shown by the new survey.

At the protest meeting in February, 1952, a Soldier Creek delegation appeared and offered to reduce their time on the range from seven to five months. Ross objected and stated in part, "Who is the Grazing Service? You have seen them come and go. Are you going to accept the new survey or are you going to keep the old one of 43, 260 A.U.M.'s?"[41] We should note that both Stanfield and Ross of Oregon grazing district 3 were at this time members of the National Advisory Board Council and the state advisory board as well as the district advisory board and that Ross had objected strenuously to DRM Hansen's actions in a NABC meeting held the previous December.[42]

Following this meeting, the first of a long series of complaints to Washington began. One stockman wrote:

Since Mr. Hansen has been in charge of the Taylor Grazing Office at Vale, they say I have no right what-so-ever.

What I can't understand is why all of a sudden I have *no right*, when men right beside of me—having same water right and almost same amount of tillable acres have 200 head right for 12 months—winter and

summer—How can some obtain such big rights and leave cattle out 12
months on the range. . . .

Could you please explain this to me. How can the board just pick out
certain ones and give them what they want and stop others entirely. [43]

That spring, one Stewart Elsner was cited for trespass on
the grazing district and informed that no license or permit
would be issued until he had made payment to the United States
for trespass. Elsner did not take this citation lying down. Later
in the summer he complained to United States Senator Herman
Welker, referring to Idaho grazing district 5.

There were several hearings held over these cuts in time on the
range. These hearings were just mockery with the best liar winning.
At this the Grazing Service seemed to be professional. Under such
dictatorship we couldn't operate there any longer so sold our ranch
and moved to Vale, Oregon. Neighbor stockmen here said they had
been getting along OK but that conditions were getting worse under
Taylor Grazing. We thought nothing could be as corrupt as District
No. 5 in Idaho. [44]

Tension between the administration and the board continued
to increase. In the fall of 1952 the Bureau of Land Management sent most of its "heavy artillery" to attend the organizational meeting of grazing district 3. Among the representatives of the Bureau were Gerald M. Kerr, head of the Division of Range Management; Chesley Seely, regional director;
W. J. Anderson, range conservationist; and DRM A. K. Hansen. The board re-elected its former slate of officers and
again elected Gerald Stanfield and Sam Ross to the state advisory board. Feelings ran high in this meeting as is evidenced
by the following interchange:

Kerr. The administration has always recognized the findings of
range technicians who have been educated and trained in range surveying. We don't intend to tell the stockmen how to run their cattle or
sheep but it is our responsibility to determine how many stock can
graze the federal range and how long.

Ross. The Soldier Creek range has improved steadily since 1935.
Men have paid high prices for ranches for the grazing rights and are
now being put out of business. There will be ranches and range long
after you are gone.

Kerr. If we have our way there will be better range.

Ross. We don't want better range. We are doing alright [sic] now. [45]

By this time it appears the board had decided to "get" DRM Hansen. Gerald Stanfield maintained in the meeting that Hansen's appointment was a violation of section 17 of the Taylor Grazing Act in that Hansen was not a resident of Oregon at the time of his appointment.

After two days of fruitless discussion, adviser Archabal remarked, "Lets make some kind of a recommendation on this Soldier Creek unit." Ross vetoed this suggestion by saying, "I don't want any Board recommendation." Gerald Kerr then asked in the board had any objection to transferring full responsibility to the DRM for the adjudication of the Soldier Creek unit.[46] Ross replied, "That's what I'm trying to force him to do." Stanfield objected to leaving the decision with the DRM but Ross insisted,

It's your problem. Now go ahead and work it out. For seventeen years these men have used the range under the Grazing Service and everything has been all right and everyone has been satisfied. These men were set up in the 1943 adjudication and . . . according to the code their rights cannot be molested. I am not going to have a decision passed against anyone in Soldier Creek. You are the ones who want the change . . . you go ahead and make up a table showing what each man's rights are but you won't force it down anybody's throat.[47]

At another point in the meeting Ross addressed Hansen directly: "Mr. Hansen, you were sent here to this district to straighten this out. Now shoot your own gun. Jerry Kerr said yesterday you were sent here to straighten this mess out. Let him tell you how to do it."[48]

In commenting on this meeting one BLM official wrote:

. . . I recall few, if any, more frustrating experiences. . . . This board consumed two and one-half days, in argument, bickering and criticism of the range manager. Furthermore, the board refused to make a recommendation on the Jackie's Butte case until one of the members who operates in the unit had an opportunity to contact all the users in the unit to learn what their wishes were.

Such delaying tactics and refusal to take responsibility for recommendations prior to consultation with the range users affected seems to be fairly typical of many of the members of this board. Those who are differently disposed are reluctant to take strong issue with the evident leadership of Gerald Stanfield and Sam Ross. A further disturbing attitude relates to the preponderant weights given by the board, or certain members of it, to the immediate welfare of the users as opposed to the proper and constructive uses of the Federal Range. . . .

Stanfield was very critical of Hansen's proposal to reverse the board. . . . From his remarks it is quite evident that he feels the range manager should accept and approve the recommendations of the advisory boards, irrespective of the propriety or legality of them.

Both Mr. Ross and Mr. Stanfield resent having Mr. Hansen in this district, principally, I feel sure, because they are unable to over-persuade or push him around.[49]

Two months later (December, 1952) Sam Ross did make a recommendation on Soldier Creek. He moved "that for the purpose of determining priority among the applicants for grazing privileges in the Soldier Creek unit, the 1943 adjudication of 77, 419 A. U. M.'s be used and reduced proportionately to 45, 000 A. U. M.'s." The motion was accepted by the board and it so recommended. DRM Hansen promptly overruled the recommendation on the grounds that it violated that provision of the Federal Range Code which provides that, "No license or permit will confer grazing privileges in excess of the grazing capacity of the Federal range to be used."[50] As matters stood when the meeting closed, the board had made a recommendation and it had been overruled by the DRM.[51]

The meeting continued informally in a hotel room afterward with only part of the members present. Sam Ross was asked to withdraw his motion for a ceiling of 45, 000 A. U. M.'s and is said to have replied, "Not over my dead body." He then charged he was being threatened in an attempt to force him into withdrawing his motion. The administration apparently believed that the 43, 260-A. U. M. ceiling had some legal validity because it had been the estimated carrying capacity since 1943. If they could get the board to consent to this figure they seemed to believe they could overlook the ceiling of 31, 284 A. U. M.'s, established by the 1951 survey. The 45, 000-A. U. M. ceiling recommended by the board was clearly and obviously illegal. A majority of the advisers were brought around to this way of thinking in the hotel room meeting and grazing permits for 1953 were allocated by the DRM using 43, 260 A. U. M.'s as the carrying capacity of the range.

When the board next met formally in January, 1953, it was

faced with this *fait accompli* and could do little except to ratify
the informal agreement. Gerald Stanfield moved that the board
recommend "that the carrying capacity of the federal range of
the Soldier Creek unit be set at 43, 260 A. U. M. 's and licenses
be issued accordingly. " Ross promptly seconded the motion
(which he had previously said would be passed only "over his
dead body"). He then moved that the 1943 adjudication of 77, 419
A. U. M. 's be reduced proportionately to 43, 260 A. U. M. 's. This
motion also passed.[52] This last motion requires some explanation. It will be recalled that the 1943 figure of 77, 419 A. U. M. 's
was established on the basis of commensurate properties only;
priority of use was disregarded. This meant that class 1 permittees (who had both priority of use and commensurate properties) and class 2 permittees (who had commensurate properties but no priority of use) had equal grazing privileges. As
long as those ranchers who were entitled to prior use preference (class 1) were granted privileges up to the full amount
of their commensurability they had no complaint. But when
their privileges were reduced by this action of the board, they
recalled that they did have a legal preference based on customary use of the range during the priority period. The reac-
tion of one user, Tex Payne, is typical:

> I'm not going to stand for a cut of any kind unless you go back to
> the priority from 1929 to 1934 giving the old original ranches their
> rights set up for them according to the Taylor bill during the priority
> years. Then if there is a shortage in feed I am willing to take my
> proportionate cut until the range can be built up to its original carrying
> capacity. . . .
> I am certainly not going to give up any part of my rights just to let
> someone else in who probably never ran a cow until prices started
> coming up and then went into the cow business. As I see it the only
> way this can be done is to go back to the priority years from 1929 to
> 1934, and stay with it as should have been done from the start. Until
> this is done, I'm sure going to hold my Class 1 rights for 275 head
> of stock and I don't figure on giving it away or having anyone steal it
> from me.[53]

Thus the administration, in attempting to conciliate the advisory board, antagonized some of the old users in the process.
We shall return to Tex Payne and his complaint as the case
progresses.

## *Extension of the Battle Line*

In January, 1953, a new administration was in office with
a new Secretary of Interior—from Oregon. Whether this fact
influenced the attitude of the district 3 advisory board is, of
course, conjectural. However, in its first meeting in January,
1953, the board seemed to be especially independent. At this
meeting the board expressed its opinion of the hearing examiner by reiterating a recommendation it had submitted six
years before. At that time the board approved an extension
of time on the range for David T. Jones. The DRM had overruled the board and Jones had appealed only to have the hearing officer sustain the DRM's decision. Gerald Stanfield now
moved that the action taken by the board in the David T. Jones
case on January 7, 1947, "still be considered as the recommendation of the Board at this time." Sam Ross seconded
the motion and it carried. While this motion had no effect on
Jones's time on the range, it did express the board's defiance
of the hearing examiner's decision.

At the same meeting a delegation of thirteen stockmen from
Soldier Creek appeared to protest the recent reductions on the
range. They also went on record as "rejecting" the results
of the range survey.

At this point in the meeting Gerald Stanfield lectured the
board and the administration on the position and authority of
the advisory boards. According to Stanfield:

> I appreciate very much that the advice of the advisory board is
> vital and should be given every consideration possible in every case.
> I wish to submit that advisory boards are provided for in the law. The
> advisory boards were not made a part of the management for the pur-
> pose of not being considered at the time the law was written. They
> are as much a part of the management as any other official that is
> serving or is having anything to do with the grazing service or the
> users of the Federal range. . . . I wish to comment that at the time
> I participated in the amendment of the act in 1948, this part was dis-
> cussed with members of Congress drawing the Act, the position of the
> Advisory Board relative to the advice that was to be given. I asked
> specifically of the members of Congress present, as to how binding
> the advice of the Board might be and I was assured that the advice of
> the Board was binding upon the District Range Manager or those ad-
> ministering in all cases, and the reason for the exception in the last

clause was wherein the Secretary might come in and asking the advice
of the Board and it was determined that the range was being depleted,
then the Secretary should take action. [54]

On January 23, 1953, David T. Jones appeared before the
DRM and the board and said he was that day sending the following two wires:

Honorable Douglas McKay
Secretary of the Interior
Washington, D. C.

Honorable Secretary:
Please contact Senator Cordon relative to action taken by Mr. A.
K. Hansen BLM, Vale, Oregon. Appeal program too slow. Need im-
mediate investigation. Some stockmen feel that Hansen must be suf-
fering mental derangement because of recent illness. Please contact
G. E. Stanfield, President Woolgrowers Association, Vale, Oregon,
Sam Ross or other stockmen.

/s/ David T. Jones

Senator Guy Cordon
U. S. Senate
Washington, D. C.

Program presented advisory board here by A. K. Hansen, Range
Manager, calls for from 30% to 50% reduction in Federal range in
Malheur County. Hansen was formerly state operator now range manager, BLM, Vale, Oregon. Must be stopped. If not, following results
possible Ontario and Portland sales yards will be glutted with livestock both sheep and cattle for the next three months. Financial institutions here very much concerned over new program. If Hansen's
program prevails there is a possibility of a runaway panic in the livestock industry. Please contact Douglas McKay.

/s/ David T. Jones[55]

The next day Jones sent the following telegram to Representative Sam Coon:

In utter disregard of advisory board recommendation A. K. Hansen,
Range Manager, BLM, Oregon Grazing District #3, insists from 25
to 52% cuts in livestock in Federal range here. District 3 embraces
all Federal range in Malheur and part of Harney counties. If Hansen's
program prevails, sale yards in Ontario, Vale, Nyssa, and Portland
will be glutted with livestock for the next 3 months and tend to create
a runaway panic in livestock operators in eastern Oregon. This with
already depressed markets is serious, contact McKay, investigate.
Hansen's program is serious. Financial institutions here very much
concerned. [56]

Two days later Senator Cordon wrote Director Clawson asking for a report on the situation. On the same day Representative Sam Coon contacted Clawson directly, presumably by telephone, and also wrote a letter transferring Jones's telegram to Secretary Douglas McKay. Excerpts from Representative Coon's letter follow:

Dear Doug:

. . . Mr. David T. Jones, who sent this wire, is a former president of the Oregon Woolgrowers Association and I have also received a letter from Gerald Stanfield, who is president of this organization. Also many other permittees in the area have talked to me in the past year concerning the matter and apparently the district grazier is disregarding all recommendations of the Advisory Board.

This is one of the few grazing districts where the management is not getting along with the permittees, but in this district they seem to have been at loggerheads since Mr. Hansen has been there. I shall appreciate your looking into this matter and assisting in any way possible. With all best wishes to you I am,

Sincerely yours,
/s/ Sam Coon[57]

On January 28, 1953, Director Clawson gave his support to Hansen in a memorandum to his chief, Secretary McKay. This memorandum stated in part,

The seriousness of the degree of range depletion and over-grazing in this district had been recognized long prior to the investigation in 1951. When it was found that corrective action could not be obtained from the man then in charge of the district he was transferred to another area, and Mr. A. K. Hansen was transferred to the Vale office on September 15, 1950 with the understanding that it was imperative that the public ranges be brought into proper use and management. In his endeavor to carry out this admonition Mr. Hansen has incurred the enmity of Messrs Gerald Stanfield and Sam Ross, members of the Advisory Board. This is understandable when it is recognized that, during the term of the former District Manager the Advisory Board, and these gentlemen in particular, controlled in large measure the activities of the Range Manager. It appears that almost invariably the recommendations of the Advisory Board were adopted, irrespective of their conformance to the provisions of the Taylor Act and the regulations thereunder, or with principles of good range management. On the other hand Mr. Hansen has consistently refused to accept recommendations of the Advisory Board which were clearly contrary to the regulation or productive of misuse of the Federal range.[58]

Similar letters were forwarded in response to the queries of Senator Cordon and Representative Coon.

In the meantime other complaints from Soldier Creek were being directed to the Secretary. On February 14, 1953, M. F. Hanley wrote:

> I am taking this opportunity to bring to your attention the unjust persecution we are receiving from the Bureau of Land Management through the local Grazier. . . .
> The result is that all the users of the Soldier Creek unit will be out of business. [59]

On February 15, 1953, Mr. and Mrs. Richard Staples of Jordan Valley complained that their range rights had been reduced from 302 to 143 cattle; that they could not pay for their ranch with this amount of cattle; and demanded a reinstatement or the "removal of the present grazier who has shown no consideration for the livestock man."[60]

On February 15, 1953, Jaca Brothers[61] complained to the Secretary:

> If Hansen has his way, 75 per cent of the stockmen in the country will be completely out of business. We feel this is unconstitutional and even Communistic. . . . So far as all of the people out here are concerned, he is just a holdover from that old gang that Eisenhower and men like yourself kicked out of office, and if this man isn't replaced with someone with common sense, our whole future is in danger.
> Why not let the Advisory Board, who actually know the conditions personally, run the business and have the District Range Manager merely carry out their order?[62]

In a letter of February 24, 1953, Fred Morton, president of the Dry Creek Basin Cattle Association, asked the Secretary:

> Now Mr. McKay, why do we have to put with this man Hansen? He will not in any way cooperate with us. He is nothing more than a dictator in this office, to the point of being abusive with that power, that the office affords him. . . . He is not qualified for this job, and spends the taxpayers money as though it was water. Since he has been here (2 years) the office force has grown to about 10 men and 2 stenographers, where 5 years ago it was run by 2 men and 1 stenographer. . . .
> I was born here in this area, my folks were among the earliest of the pioneers, and to me there is no place like Oregon. But I'm losing faith rapidly when I can look in the future and see my very existence being choked out by a bureau with the wrong man in office. You might

know my brother Estis L. Morton, who was with the First Nat'l bank
. . . in Salem. . . .

Please have him removed and give us someone here we can work
with. [63]

The administration seemed to believe that these complaints
were not spontaneous but part of an organized drive to oust
Hansen.

During the month of April, a BLM official in a personal letter said:

The main point is that Sam Ross kept them [the users] bedded down
in promises that if they'd be good neighbors and leave the licensing
only in total figures year after year, they could locally and internally,
fill up. If one operator is down one year, someone else could put out
a few more head, and the Bureau wouldn't need to adjudicate the base
property qualifications. . . .

Sam still feels that the Soldier Creek Unit is his own personal af-
fair, and that the Bureau shouldn't be meddling in his affairs.

During 1953 there were forty-one operators in the Soldier
Creek unit. Nine appealed the decisions of the DRM to the
hearing examiner.

Stewart Elsner[64] wrote to the Secretary of Agriculture (in
error) saying:

To cut the Grazing Service personnel about 90% would be a great
saving to the government and should reduce the grazing fees for the
stockmen.

The people of the U.S. elect a president thru a congress. Then congress can over rule the president if they see fit. Here in the livestock
business the government hires some exstockmen or some green college
boy as district grazier and the stockmen elect a board of advisers. But
this grazier has the power to over rule them but does not have the
ability to run a stock business of his own. . . . Lets have some action
here. [65]

The complaints continued. Dr. A. D. Woodmansee, a Salem,
Oregon, dentist wrote:

One of your crew—a Mr. Hansen—in the grazing office at Vale, Oregon should either be canned or moved. He repeatedly demonstrates
his complete failure to understand the cattlemans problems. Over
rules the boards recommendations and levies quotas that make it
tough on the folks trying to make a go of things, and they are sure
having a tough time. This fellows qualifications seem to be that he
went broke running sheep somewhere in Utah. [66]

The Soldier Creek Livestock Association in a resolution of December 17, 1953, contested the validity of the 1951 survey.

### Truce, Resumption of Hostilities, and Treaty of Peace

According to Gerald Stanfield, "when a change of Administration came in and we got a new Secretary of Interior, a request for a change of Director of Bureau of Land Management was made. The Secretary appointed Mr. Edward Woozley as Director."[67] As we have seen, Marion Clawson was familiar with the Soldier Creek situation and had supported Hansen's efforts to operate the district according to the Federal Range Code. With Clawson gone and Woozley an unknown quantity, Hansen's position grew more insecure. He still had the support of Chesley Seely, regional chief of the division of management. As late as December 23, 1953, Seeley wrote: "I would certainly like to add again the thought of my confidence in the program you have initiated."[68]

On January 14, 1954, the *Malheur Enterprise* editorialized:

As guardian of the public's interest in the range lands, the Bureau of Land Management has a vital function to perform, but that function must be performed with more understanding than has been exercised in the past. . . . Once a grazing allotment has been established for a base property, there must be the greatest assurance that it will continue without capricious interruption on the part of public officials.

On February 9, 1954, the Malheur County Court addressed a letter to Secretary McKay, Senator Cordon, and Representatives Walter Norblad, Homer Angell, Harris Ellsworth, and Sam Coon. This letter said in part:

The thing which bothers us the most is that the DRM made the cut against the advice of and contrary to the wishes of the Advisory Board. These men are all experienced stock men—all are operators—they know the range capabilities—they are interested, even more than the Manager, in a long time operation. Certainly it was never the intention of Congress that this one bureaucrat should over-ride the considered judgment of the cumulated experience of the members of the Advisory Board. The manager and his paid personnel should furnish the information and the Board should fix the policy.

If this is not the theory, it should be. [69]

In response to a query from Senator Cordon on the Malheur County Court complaint Director Woozley wrote:

On February 4, W. G. Guernsey, Regional Administrator, Region
I, and I, met with Congressman Coon concerning the Vale situation.
He suggested that Mr. Guernsey meet with representatives of the Cow
Creek and Soldier Creek Units to hear their side of the story. Such
a meeting was held February 17 at Vale by Messrs. Guernsey, Doyle,
Seely and Hansen of the Bureau of Land Management with the Oregon
District No. 3 Advisory Board and some 50 permittees of the Cow
Creek and Soldier Creek Units. . . . No further action to reduce graz-
ing privileges will be taken during the next five years, since that pe-
riod is considered necessary to evaluate the benefits to be derived
from the range improvement program.[70]

In May, 1954, DRM A. K. Hansen resigned from the Bureau
of Land Management.

Later that year the General Accounting Office objected to
the five-year moratorium on range reductions in the Soldier
Creek unit as instituted by Director Woozley and regional administrator W. G. Guernsey. The General Accounting Office
Report concluded by saying:

We believe that the basic principle here involved [Cow Creek and
Soldier Creek Grazing Units] is identical to that involved in Departmental Decision A-26532 of Director's Decision of May 29, 1952, applicable to the case of A. K. Anderson, et al. In that case the Director
said:

"The Range Manager attempted to soften the impact of the 45% reduction in grazing use by allowing the range users temporary annual
license for an additional 20% for an interim adjustment period. But
section 161.6 (c) (3) of the Code provides, 'No license or permit will
confer grazing privileges in excess of the carrying capacity of the
range to be used.' The carrying capacity having been established at
45% under the authorized use, the issuance of temporary licenses for
any amounts in excess of the range was erroneous and improper. To
that extent the Range Manager's decision of October 27, 1950 should
be reversed."

Since the decision to set aside the range survey data applicable to
the Cow Creek and Soldier Creek units and make only partial reductions in the grazing privilege is contrary to departmental policy as
well as to the Federal Range Code, we recommend that the Bureau
reconsider its action.[71]

By the time the General Accounting Office report reached
the director's office, W. G. Guernsey had been moved up to
the Washington office as assistant director, BLM. In issuing
instructions to the Oregon office relative to the General Accounting Office report, Guernsey (then acting director) said:

In view of these and other comments contained in the report, you should carefully review the procedures followed in District No. 3 and advise me of the action taken during the past year and those which are contemplated in the future in the Soldier Creek and Cow Creek Units, as well as in other units in the district. [72]

It will be recalled that Tex Payne and some other operators, who had used Soldier Creek during the priority period, had appealed the decisions of the advisory board and the DRM. These were the decisions which disregarded the priority period, established the total "rights" at 77, 419 A. U. M.'s, and later reduced all operators proportionately to 43, 260 A. U. M.'s. These were the compromise decisions made by A. K. Hansen in an effort to conciliate certain members of the advisory board rather than reduce the ceiling to the 31, 284 A. U. M.'s as established by the range survey of 1951. As we have seen, these compromises failed to conciliate the advisory board partly because Hansen had warned that further reductions would be necessary unless the range showed improvement. These were the decisions which were frozen by Director Woozley in his five-year moratorium on reductions in the Cow Creek and Soldier Creek units. While these decisions were advantageous (in the short run at least) to those stockmen who had no history of use during the priority period, they were a disadvantage to the class 1 permittees. This disadvantage had not been seriously felt when permits were issued under the "paper" ceiling of 77, 419 A. U. M.'s. When this "paper" ceiling was proportionately reduced to 43, 260 A. U. M.'s and the limit of each permit specifically reduced accordingly, the old "priority period" stockmen lost the advantage which use during the priority period legally conferred upon them.

One of the appellants, Loveland Brothers, in his appeal charged:

That the District Range Manager, Oregon Grazing District No. 3 and the Advisory Board thereof, since the advent of the Taylor Grazing Act and up to and including the present date, have passed upon and determined grazing applications in total disregard of the standards established by said Act and by the Federal Range Code; that said Range Manager and Advisory Board have made little effort to obtain the facts regarding the operations and base properties of the various applicants upon which lawful and equitable determination could be made . . . that the failure of the DRM and the Advisory Board of Oregon Grazing

District No. 3 to adhere to the law and to regulations of the Bureau
of Land Management promulgated thereunder has operated to the pre-
judice of your appellant; that the decision here appealed from is affected by and is the product of many years of arbitrary, unlawful and
capricious acts.

In a decision of February 4, 1955, the hearing officer upheld the appellants. Pertinent parts of the decision follow:

3. Each of the appellants is entitled to Class I grazing privileges
determined under the provisions of section 161.2 (g), 161.4 and 161.6
of the Code and limited by the provisions of sections 161.6 (c) (3),
(9), (10) and (11) of the Code.

4. Each of the appellants is entitled to participate in the award of
Class 2 grazing privileges in an amount determined on an equitable
basis of any forage in the Soldier Creek unit of Oregon Grazing District No. 3 which is in excess of the qualified demand of Class I licensees or permittees. . . .

This matter is remanded to the District Range Manager for a determination of appellants' grazing privileges in conformity with this
decision. [73]

This decision had the effect of nullifying the compromise
agreements carried out since 1943 and reversing Director
Woozley's five-year freeze of grazing reductions in Soldier
Creek. The decision said, in effect, range privileges will
henceforth be allocated in accordance with the Federal Range
Code and not by negotiations between the administration and
the advisory board.

When A. K. Hansen resigned in 1954, he was replaced by
DRM Derrel Fulwider. Fulwider was transferred in from a
grazing district in Nevada where he had served as DRM for
several years. When he assumed his new duties he was aware
of the urgency of the Soldier Creek problem and the necessity
for an early solution. At the same time he was unwilling to
take any action until he became thoroughly familiar with the
situation and had all the available facts at his disposal. He
therefore assigned a member of his staff to make a detailed
study of the problem. This study consumed almost one year.
By January, 1956, however, Fulwider was ready to act.

A meeting of the district advisory board and the users of the
Soldier Creek unit was called for January 10, 1956. Fulwider
came to this meeting flanked by members of his staff who had
worked on the study and armed with a base property survey

which showed the qualifications of each piece of property in the Soldier Creek area. The first day of the meeting was taken up with a statement and an explanation of the grazing entitlement accruing to each applicant in conformance with the hearing examiner's decision and the Federal Range Code. While there were objections to some of the DRM's allocations he was, in each case, able to marshal an imposing array of data to substantiate his decision. There was no estimating or "remembering."

The survey showed a total class 1 eligibility of slightly over 20,000 A.U.M.'s which meant that only about 11,000 A.U.M.'s were available for class 2 operators. The Soldier Creek stockmen were informed that the hearing examiner's decision left only two alternatives open: grazing privileges could be granted to class 1 operators for 20,000 A.U.M.'s with the balance of 11,000 A.U.M.'s being divided between class 1 and class 2 operators according to the productivity of their commensurate base properties; or the users of the Soldier Creek unit could disregard the priority period and enter into a written agreement, approved and signed by every user, which specified the grazing privileges of each one and which did not exceed a total of 31,284 A.U.M.'s.

As we have previously noted, strict adherence to the priority period for allocation of class 1 privileges would work a serious hardship on some ranchers but, unless the users could unanimously agree to accept some other distribution, the administration would now be forced to apply the priority period rule. Those persons who had a history of use during the priority period would obviously suffer a reduction in grazing privileges by signing such an agreement.

The class 1 operators declined to sign any agreement decreasing their entitlement, while the class 2 operators refused to accept the schedule set forth by DRM Fulwider. The meeting continued on into the evening, with no decision forthcoming, and recessed to the following day. The second day was a repetition of the first and again continued on into an evening session. During this time frequent caucuses and individual conferences were held and several unacceptable counterproposals were advanced. Finally, when the meeting seemed to have reached a hopeless impasse, S. K. Skinner, a class 1 operator, gained the floor and volunteered to take a reduction of 250 A. U. M.'s in his entitlement.[74]

When the heretofore highly contentious stockmen recovered from their surprise at this dramatic offer, others followed suit. Jaca Brothers offered to "cut" 140 A. U. M.'s. Dick Staples took a voluntary reduction of twenty-seven A. U. M.'s. The successful appellants, Raymond Gluch, M. F. Hanley, Loveland Brothers, Tex Payne, and others volunteered to reduce their entitlement.[75]

The upshot of this controversy is recorded in the following news article from the *Malheur Enterprise:*

Grazing officials and stockmen of the Soldier Creek Grazing unit conferred for three days and nights last week in a successful effort to straighten out a fifteen year old dispute on grazing rights within the unit.

All range users in the district entered into a use agreement. . . . In order to arrive at the final allotment of range rights a group of stockmen took voluntary range cuts amounting to a total of 1701 A. U. M.'s. In addition, range users accepted an over-all 4 percent reduction in range rights as well as a shortening of some 15 days in the grazing season.

"The voluntary cuts taken by a large group of stockmen were made solely in their desire to see the problem solved," DRM Fulwider said, "They did not have to take the cuts, but did so in the spirit of community cooperation. It was a fine thing."[76]

# 8. THE GRAZING FEE CONTROVERSY

In our discussion of private special government in chapters 6 and 7 we focused our attention mainly on activities within the bureau. In this chapter we will review a series of incidents which are concerned with the relationships between congressional committees, interest groups, and the bureaucracy in attempting to resolve the problem of grazing fees on the federal range.

Students of politics have for some time seriously questioned the concept of "the public." Instead they prefer to think of a pluralistic society in which there are many publics. No one contends that these various publics are separate and isolated entities. It is recognized that there is considerable overlap and that the same individual may be a member of several different publics. It is not usually so clearly recognized that the members of the various publics move within a complex of behavioral patterns which have a high order of consistency. These consistencies may be explained by law, tradition, custom, or habit. Whatever the explanation, there does exist this commonalty within which the various publics function. While this chapter is concerned with a particular public which may have somewhat unique objectives, it should be recognized that these objectives are pursued according to generally accepted "rules of the game" and that this particular public is not, in fact, isolated but is a part of the national community.

Along with our acceptance of the notion of a plurality of publics we have come to accept the idea of a plural legislature.

While we continue to speak of "the Congress, " we are aware that most of the work of Congress is done in committees. The membership of these congressional committees tends to become specialized according to industry, location, or some other grouping of interests. The congressional committee, then, tends to become a private special congress which represents one or a few particular interest groups. This representation does not, of course, confine itself to those things which are ordinarily considered to be purely legislative functions. The committees also attempt to oversee the administration of legislation which affects the interest groups they represent.

To be realistic we may need to particularize still further and recognize that sometimes the committees themselves are also general subsystems which may be further divided into still more specialized subsystems. We may find, in fact, that one senator or representative may constitute a subunit of the subsystem and may for most purposes be considered as "the Congress" for a particular bureau or interest group. [1]

The case study which follows involves the interactions of congressional subunits, bureau executives, and the leaders of an interest group bureaucracy in their attempts to resolve the problem of grazing fees on the federal range. While this problem may appear to be of interest to a restricted group only, it seems likely that many problems which confront the Congress and the administration may be of a similarly restrictive nature.

The case history also suggests that the level of administrative decision-making is determined by the amount or intensity of actual or expected controversy, that every administrative problem is at least a potential political issue, [2] that technical conflicts are often resolved through a political process, and that congressional oversight of administration is likely to be specialized according to the interests of individual congressmen and their constituents.

When the Taylor Grazing Act was under consideration by the House Committee on Public Lands in 1933, Secretary Ickes was asked: "Is it contemplated that the government will derive revenue from this measure?" Ickes replied: "Yes; just the expense of operation. We are not trying to make money out of it. "[3] The following year Ickes reiterated his position that "We have no intention of making this a revenue producer at all. We would like for the range to pay for its own administration but nothing more. "[4]

These early remarks of Secretary Ickes initiated the concept that grazing fees should be tied to the cost of administering the range. Ickes further stated that

The cost of administration will depend largely upon the character and intensity of administrative operations. It is believed that these should be kept at a minimum and by reason of operations already carried on by the Department of the Interior throughout the public land area the cost can be held to a very nominal figure and perhaps can be defrayed entirely from normal appropriations made for the Land Department. [5]

Possibly these statements were designed to encourage passage of the bill but, whatever the motive, western stockmen came to understand that grazing fees were to be fixed according to the cost of administering the program, and that the cost of administration would be negligible.

As finally passed, the Taylor Grazing Act provided:

The Secretary of the Interior is authorized to issue or cause to be issued permits . . . upon the payment annually of reasonable fees in each case to be fixed or determined from time to time. . . . Such fees shall consist of a grazing fee for the use of the range, and a range-improvement fee which, when appropriated by the Congress, shall be available until expended solely for the construction, purchase, or maintenance of range improvements. [6]

In commenting on the fee question in December, 1934, F. R. Carpenter said:

If we charge no fee it would amount to a government subsidy, and a government subsidy is always subject to scrutiny, criticism and investigation. You stockmen should set some fair fee, so that you can go before any committee from Boston, or Newport, or anywhere else, and show it is fair. Otherwise you are never going to be away from constant criticism from the people in the east and middle west, who feel that the way to solve the question is to throw all the cattle and sheep off the public domain. They pass resolutions to that effect, and they mean just what they say. So, we will want fees for our own protection.

The only kind of a fee which ever met with any degree of satisfaction on the part of the stockmen is that such as they have in the forests, based on a sliding scale; whereby it is apportioned according to the price of beef and mutton. It is my belief that that is the fairest way to have the fee. In other words, the expenses should be in accord with the income. [7]

We should notice that Carpenter said, "you *stockmen* should set some fair fee, " and also, "*we* will want fees for *our* own protection. "

No grazing fees were levied in 1935, nor did the Secretary of the Interior attempt to establish "reasonable fees" for grazing privileges at that time. Instead, the advisory board members were called together in a mass meeting in Salt Lake City on January 13-14, 1936, to decide upon a set of regulations to govern the new agency. Among other matters, the advisers agreed upon a uniform grazing fee of five cents per animal unit month (A. U. M. : five cents per month for a cow or horse and one cent per month for a sheep or goat). The Secretary accepted this recommendation and the five-cent A. U. M. fee became effective during the 1936 grazing season. At this rate the cost of grazing a cow for seven months (an average grazing season) would be thirty-five cents. This may seem to be an excessively low rate today, but it was considered fairly reasonable in 1936 because of the low prices then prevailing for livestock products and because of the generally depleted condition of the federal range. While this fee may not have been unreasonable in 1936, it was not raised until 1947.

Nevada stockmen objected even to this low fee and obtained an injunction from a Nevada District Court "restraining the Regional Grazier from interfering with their free use of the range. "[8] The action of the contending Nevada stockmen requires some explanation. Nevada stockmen, as well as some ranchers in other states, had built their livestock operations on the assumption that they would continue to enjoy free use of the federal range. Persons who had purchased ranch properties had done so assuming that the public lands would remain free. Ranchers also maintained that, since property values (and hence assessed values) were based on capitalized income they had in actuality, been paying property taxes on federally owned lands. Objecting stockmen also contended that a uniform fee for all parts of the range was unfair because of the great variations in value of the forage.

The action of the district court was appealed to the Nevada Supreme Court, which sustained the action of the lower court and held that grazing fees for temporary licenses were unauthorized in the Taylor Grazing Act and that a uniform fee for all districts and all users did not conform to section 3 of the act, which provides for "the payment annually of reasonable fees in *each case.*"[9]

The case was appealed to the United States Supreme Court which reversed the decision of the Nevada Court on May 26, 1941. Mr. Justice Roberts, in delivering the opinion of the Court, held that "repeated appropriations of the proceeds of the fees . . . not only confirms the departmental construction of the statute but constitutes a ratification of the action of the Secretary as the agent of Congress in the administration of the act."[10]

The decision of the Supreme Court was of particular importance to Nevada stockmen. Nevada has within its borders not only the largest amount but also the highest percentage of federal land of any of the states. In 1944, Nevada also licensed more A.U.M.'s than did any other state but was sixth in total number of permittees.[11] In 1955, Nevada was still almost one million A.U.M.'s ahead of the next largest user of the federal range but had slipped to seventh place in total number of permittees.[12] In 1944 the five largest permits issued by the Grazing Service were issued to Nevada operators and fifteen of the fifty largest permits in ten states were alloted in the state of Nevada.[13] Nevada stockmen used the federal range more than did stockmen in other states and they were bigger operators than in any other state. Along with mining and the tourist trade, stockraising is an industry of major importance in Nevada. Stockmen's families are among the oldest, wealthiest, and most influential in the state.

One of the most effective advocates of the interests of the Nevada stockmen was Senator Pat McCarran. Senator McCarran had ridden in with the Democratic party in 1932. Until 1940 he appeared to have had no particular complaint against the Grazing Service. He had been interested in the organiza-

tion, however, and had successfully introduced an amendment
to the original act which prohibited cancellation of permits
when used as collateral for loans and the amendment which
gave statutory recognition to the advisory board system.

While the *Dewar* v. *Brooks* case was awaiting consideration by the United States Supreme Court, Senator McCarran
rallied to the support of his constituents by introducing Senate
Resolution 241. This resolution demanded an investigation of
the Grazing Service to determine the extent to which:

(3) the Federal bureaus and agencies administering the public lands
have been enlarged and extended and bureaus within bureaus have been
created for such purpose;

. . .

(6) administrative rules and regulations have been established under
the provisions of section 2 of the Taylor Grazing Act which have resulted in extending the authority of the administrator of such act and
which have evaded the limitations and restrictions placed upon such
administrator by other specific provisions of such act;

(7) administrative authority has been abused for the purpose of
circumventing the jurisdiction of the courts in which the legality of
such authority is being determined, by attempting to coerce the Federal courts or to use such courts for coercive purposes in connection with such determinations, or by attempting to coerce individual
litigants with respect to matters pending in the courts;

(8) representatives of the Department of the Interior have attempted
through coercive tactics to bring about the reversal of views expressed
collectively in regularly called representative meetings relating to the
creation of grazing districts; and

(9) there has been interference with the established principles relating to supervision of the livestock industry which have long been
applied by governmental bureaus and agencies charged with administering public lands, and there has been a disregard of the principles
which are essentially necessary for the purpose of providing stability
of the range-livestock industry which is in competition with non-range-
livestock operations not under Government supervision. [14]

The resolution was adopted in May, 1941, and Senator Mc-
Carran embarked on an investigation which lasted until the
fall of 1947. [15]

While the Grazing Service was awaiting the Supreme Court's
decision on the legality of the uniform grazing fee, it instituted
a study of grazing fees on the basis of range appraisals. One
of the objectives of the study was to determine the practicality

of fixing "reasonable fees in each case." J. H. Leech of the Grazing Service and Mont Saunderson of the Forest Service conducted the survey. Essentially, they attempted to make an estimate of the average value of the forage on the federal range in each of the range states. In making the study 214 ranches in the ten range states were surveyed. The results of this study are summarized below:[16]

|  | *Base Value for* |
| *State* | *Grazing Fees per A. U. M. (cents)* |
| Utah | 12.0 |
| California | 13.8 |
| Nevada | 12.4 |
| Oregon | 14.0 |
| Idaho | 16.7 |
| Montana | 16.7 |
| New Mexico | 7.3 |
| Colorado | 18.5 |
| Arizona | 8.4 |
| Wyoming | 15.8 |

It was also recommended that the fee be varied from year to year in accordance with changes in beef and mutton prices.

By the time the Saunderson-Leech study was completed in June, 1941, the Supreme Court had upheld the legality of the old uniform five-cent fee so that there was at least no legal compulsion to change the rate from state to state or "in each case" as claimed by the Nevada Supreme Court.

The Saunderson-Leech range appraisal was considered by McCarran's investigating subcommittee on public lands in its meetings at Casper, Wyoming; Salt Lake City; Reno; and Las Vegas in the fall of 1941. According to Senator McCarran,

The findings of the Range Appraisal study were subjected to critical analysis by the livestock men in several hearings before my subcommittee in 1941. These analyses disclosed that the results of the study furnished little or no support to the recommendation for increasing the fees. . . .

In the report of that study it was announced that the most important finding was what the report called the "startling data as to the commercial lease costs of an animal unit month" of feed. The finding was startling only because it was not a fair or honest comparison in any sense of the term. It was an attempt to compare dissimilar things. [17]

By 1941 the advisory board system had been expanded to include state advisory boards and a National Advisory Board Council (NABC).

No immediate action was taken by the administration to implement the findings of the Saunderson-Leech range appraisal. Instead, the study was submitted to the various state advisory boards for their comments.

The state boards generally approved the intent of the study but, without exception, voted against any increase in fees. Most of them did contend, in explaining their position, that they considered the sample inadequate and that a broader coverage of ranches should have been surveyed. [18]

Following its consideration by the state advisory boards, the range appraisal was next presented to the NABC on January 5, 1942. By this time the nation had entered World War II. Following the lead of the state advisory boards, the NABC passed a resolution approving the study and the efforts of the Grazing Service to establish a reasonable fee but suggested that further study was desirable. They went on to say:

> (2) We advise and recommend against the applications of the findings in Range Appraisal as to a "reasonable fee" until the present emergency is past. We feel that the livestock industry should not be disturbed while the stockmen are making every effort to assist in the defense of our country by producing the maximum of livestock products and by financing to the limit our Government by taxes and other methods to the best of their ability.
>
> (3) . . . we pledge ourselves to sit down with the Grazing Service when the present emergency is past and give our full assistance in determining and applying a reasonable fee. [19]

Possibly influenced by the findings of Senator McCarran's investigating subcommittee on public lands, Grazing Service Director R. H. Rutledge accepted the NABC's recommendation, as did Secretary Ickes. In a letter to Senator Hatch of New Mexico (member of the Senate Committee on Public Lands and Surveys) dated April 2, 1942, Ickes wrote, "In view of the war situation, I believe that the fees for grazing upon the Federal range should not be disturbed for the present . . . however, I think that meanwhile the entire fee question should receive serious and comprehensive consideration."[20]

During the next two years meat prices continued to rise and demands for increased grazing fees also continued. Anticipating a revival of the fee question Senator McCarran tried without success to amend the Taylor Grazing Act to read: "The Secretary shall not make any changes in the fees payable for grazing livestock within any district unless the advisory board for such district has consented to such change."[21]

When Depue Falck of the Grazing Service appeared before the House subcommittee on interior appropriations in 1942 to defend his organization's appropriation request, he encountered an entirely different point of view from that which prevailed in the Senate subcommittee on public lands and surveys. The attitude of the House subcommittee may have been due in part to the knowledge that in fiscal year 1941 appropriations to or for the Grazing Service had totaled $5,197,128 as against $922,455 collected in grazing fees. Although over half the appropriation was allocated to the Civilian Conservation Corps for work on the public range lands there was still a wide disparity between collections and expenditures.[22] Possibly for this reason the House appropriation subcommittee was hostile and even insulting. Congressman Jed Johnson, Democrat from Oklahoma and chairman of the subcommittee, was particularly unsympathetic. Johnson had served in the House of Representatives since 1927 and had generally upheld the interests of the independent petroleum producers of the mid-continent area. During the war years he carried on a running fight with Secretary Ickes over the latter's petroleum program. Whether this antagonism carried over to include the Grazing Service is, of course, conjectural. At any rate, Johnson quibbled over the most insignificant items in the Grazing Service appropriation request. He objected, for instance, to the rental being paid for the Salt Lake City office. According to Johnson, "it happens to be a lot higher rent down in the main part of the city than it would be farther out and a little exercise of a few blocks, even if you had to walk, might be helpful."[23]

On February 29, 1944, Depue Falck again confronted a hostile House appropriations subcommittee. After hearing Falck's

justification for the appropriation requested, Chairman Jed
Johnson said:

> So despite the fact that we're at war and this committee has warned
> you to cut expenses wherever humanly possible, and refused to grant
> your request last year, you are back on our doorstep asking for more.
> Mr. Falck. . . . That is one reason why I would like to take a mo-
> ment off the record, perhaps, to look at this map.
> Mr. Johnson. All right; we will look at the map since that may be
> all you will get. [24]

Other members of the committee were almost equally cap-
tious. Representative Carter of California declared:

> . . . cattle have gone up. . . . Sheep have gone up, and it seems
> to me your grazing land has gotten much better. . . . Why should you
> not receive a better fee. . . . I want you to tell me why we give these
> operators $5,850,000 worth of service and why we have collected only
> $850,000. [25]

Arkansas Representative Norrell added, "I do not think you
are getting enough money from these cattle owners. There is
no reason why this program should not be self-sustaining."[26]

Representative Jensen of Iowa seemed to express the attitude of the committee when he said:

> I just do not see how we can justify giving you fellows an additional
> appropriation here, while at the same time the folks deriving the ben-
> efit of your service are not paying any more, at a time when they could
> afford to pay more. [27]

In May, 1944, Clarence L. Forsling was appointed director
of grazing. Forsling was recruited from the Forest Service
and had considerable experience with the grazing fee system
in that agency, which was considerably higher than the five
cents per animal month charged by the Grazing Service.

Forsling's appointment came as a surprise to the NABC.
Previous to the appointment, Assistant Secretary of Interior
Oscar Chapman had met with the NABC in Denver. At this
meeting the NABC had recommended Assistant Director Ed
Kavanaugh to be the new director of the Grazing Service. When
Forsling was appointed the members of the NABC suspected
that Chapman had known of the impending appointment of Forsling when he had conferred with them earlier that year. Consequently, they felt that their advice had not only been disregarded but that there had never been any intention even to

consider that advice. This disregard of their recommendation caused considerable resentment among the members of the NABC who had by this time come to expect that the Secretary of Interior would ordinarily follow their advice.

In November, 1944, Director Forsling revived the fee question at a meeting of the NABC. He proposed a trebled fee schedule which was to be based on the value of the forage in any subsequent adjustment. Forsling's proposal met with unanimous opposition from the assembled members of the twenty-man National Advisory Board Council. They maintained that the proposed increase in fees would violate an assurance made to the livestockmen by Secretary Ickes that he "had no intention of making the Act a revenue producer at all" and that the proposal repudiated promises from the Department of the Interior that the fees would not be raised for the duration of the war. The board members formally resolved that:

> This organization opposes such increase for the following reason:
> 1. Any fee finally fixed must be based on a direct relation to the reasonable cost of administering public lands for grazing purposes only and nothing more. Until the fact as to the cost of administration, together with the necessity therefor and their relation to grazing, are determined, no one can fix a reasonable fee as provided by the Act.
> We propose—
> (a) That the study of cost of administration of grazing lands for grazing purposes only be completed and presented to this council.
> (b) We agree when such a report is available to and approved by the council to assist in fixing a reasonable fee as provided in the Taylor Grazing Act, based upon the fair and reasonable cost of administering the public lands domain for grazing purposes only, but nothing more. [28]

When Senator McCarran heard of Forsling's proposal he replied with highly vocal indignation. The new proposal, said McCarran, "struck consternation into the industry and into the financial institutions which stand behind the industry" and resulted in an avalanche of telegrams to congressmen urging them to "do everything possible to prevent an increase of the fees during the present war." He also introduced a resolution, adopted unanimously by the Committee on Public Lands and Surveys, "that no increase in grazing fees should be imposed until the Committee . . . has had an opportunity to make a full and complete study of the subject."[29]

The Nevada legislature came to the support of its Senator
with a joint resolution passed in February, 1945. The resolution protested against the attitude of the Grazing Service which
justified the proposal "not on the cost of grazing administration but instead upon the value of the range" and urged Congress to repeal the Taylor Grazing Act "unless the officials
of the Department of the Interior and the Grazing Service speed-
ily and forthwith show a proper disposition to conform with
and carry out . . . assurances and promises in connection
with their administration of the Taylor Grazing Act." The
resolution also suggested that no further increases in Grazing Service appropriations be granted until "the question of
how much the stock-raising settlers . . . can afford to pay
[is resolved]."[30]

Senator McCarran elicited a promise from Secretary Ickes
that fees would not be raised until his committee had made an
investigation. This assurance from Ickes was the culmination
of a gradual retreat from his original position. In a letter of
December 15, 1944, he stated that he had "approved Director
Forsling's request that a representative group of the NABC
come to Washington to go over the entire matter with me and my
assistants. . . . In my opinion this will be much more satisfactory than to hold a series of public hearings in the West."[31]

Senator McCarran objected to this procedure on the grounds
that the NABC could not speak for all the stockmen on "so important a matter as the drastic increase in grazing fees proposed by the Director of Grazing and especially when closeted
with you in Washington, and . . . surrounded by an array of
department attorneys and officials." He therefore insisted
"that the whole matter be discussed in public hearings before
my subcommittee . . . at central . . . points in the West."[32]

By January 10, 1945, Secretary Ickes had apparently abandoned his plan to consult with the NABC and wrote Senator
Carl Hatch that "I have approved the Director's recommendation to postpone action on his proposal to increase the grazing
fees until May 1, 1945." On January 23, 1945, he wrote Senator Joseph C. O'Mahoney of Wyoming, "You may disregard the
statement in my letter of January 10 to Senator Hatch. . . .
I will not take any action on the question of raising fees without giving the committee advance notice." On the same date

Ickes disapproved a request of the McCarran subcommittee that the Department of Interior provide automobiles for use of the subcommittee in its hearings in the West.

In explaining his retreat from the May 1 deadline Secretary Ickes wrote that until recently he had been unaware of statements by former Director of Grazing Rutledge that fees would not be raised for the "duration." To this explanation Senator McCarran commented that

. . . there is no criticism coming to you growing out of this lack of knowledge of what is going on in the Grazing Service. I frankly wonder how one can carry on as much as you do carry on, and indeed I will go further and say that I wonder how one carries on as well as you carry on, on the much that you have to carry on.[33]

Again Senator McCarran's committee conducted a series of hearings throughout the western states on the question of increased fees. Friends of the Grazing Service maintained that Senator McCarran used these hearings primarily as a stage from which to blast the Grazing Service in general and the proposed fee increase in particular.

When Director Forsling met the appropriations subcommittee, in March, 1945, he testified that he believed increased grazing fees were necessary and desirable; that he recommended such an increase; and that increased fees had not yet been made effective because the Secretary of Interior had promised to withhold action until the matter had been studied by the Senate Committee on Public Lands and Surveys. He stated further that he expected a report from that committee by July, 1945. The committee was naturally favorably impressed by Forsling's views but Representative Norrell reiterated the committee's stand on fees when he said, "I do not see any reason why the people in some other states should be called on year after year to provide an increased contribution to the livestock growers of the West."[34]

While the appropriations subcommittee may have been pleased with Forsling's testimony, Senator McCarran considered it a treacherous attack on the stockmen. According to him:

Within a few weeks following the renewal of this pledge, [to maintain the five-cent fee] officials of the Grazing Service, when they appeared before the House Subcommittee on Appropriations, launched a determined campaign to force an increase in the grazing fees. The

larger fees were and are sought by the Grazing Service for one purpose; and that is that the increased collections may serve as a justification for still larger appropriations and further expansion of the
organization. The Grazing Service officials . . . presented to the
Subcommittee on Appropriations, wholly gratuitously and without any
proper explanation, grossly misleading figures intended to show that
the grazing district users were receiving forage values many times
in excess of the sums paid therefor in the form of grazing fees. [35]

The report of the McCarran committee, which Director
Forsling had expected would be completed by July, 1945, was
not submitted until the spring of 1946. The report found that
no increase in fees was justified; that fees should be based
on the cost of administration rather than on the value of the
forage; and that the cost of administration was too high. In
addition, McCarran charged the Grazing Service with unnecessary bureaucratic expansion and urged the dismissal of a "very
small handful of self-seeking opportunist administrators."

By this time Secretary Ickes had apparently given up. In a
letter to Senator Hatch, he wrote: "I have decided to take no
action to increase the grazing fees on the Federal range until
6 months after the discontinuance of payments for beef-cattle
production and for sheep and lamb production."[36]

When Director Forsling next appeared before the House
subcommittee on interior appropriations in March, 1946, the
committee's attitude toward him had drastically changed since
his appearance the year before. Chairman Jed Johnson thought
it was "just shocking that the Grazing Service will continue
to charge practically nothing. One cent per month for sheep.
. . . Can you imagine that."[37] It seemed to Johnson that "the
Grazing Service is to all intents and purposes, thumbing its
nose at this committee."[38] Johnson seemed to hold Director
Forsling personally responsible for the continuance of the
five-cent fee, and like Senator McCarran but for opposite
reasons, he apparently felt that Forsling had betrayed a trust.
He wound up by saying: "The best thing to do would be to abolish the Grazing Service and withhold any appropriation whatever for the next fiscal year." To which Forsling replied: "It
is the land that suffers and not me personally if that is done."[39]

Representative Rooney had "never thought or dreamed be-

fore that things went on in this government such as this Grazing Service. "[40]

Representative Jensen thought it "criminal for us to sit
here and appropriate money for this Service which is not paying its own way even. "[41]

Representative Norrell scolded:

> I would appreciate your testimony much more if you would just come
> before us and tell us that the reason why these fees have not been in-
> creased is because the western Senators and Congressmen objected,
> because that is exactly the situation, and you know it, and I know it.
> . . . I think we are going to have to cut the appropriation of this De-
> partment down to the amount it has paid into the Federal Treasury
> . . . before we ever get an increase in fees. [42]

This language could have been interpreted as an attack on
Senator McCarran and some of his supporters, as well as on
the Grazing Service. But McCarran agreed:

> . . . the only way, in my judgment, to get the Taylor Grazing Act
> back again to a solid foundation is not to increase this appropriation
> now, but to hold . . . [it] down where the House put it, until the In-
> terior Department sees fit to set up a Taylor Grazing Administration
> that will be worthy of the name and the object of the law. [43]

In the meantime the stockmen's associations and the advisory
boards had not been idle. A task force, called the Joint Livestock Committee on Public Lands, was organized to defeat
the proposed increase in grazing fees. This organization represented the National Woolgrowers Association, the American National Livestock Association and the NABC. The Joint
Livestock Committee on Public Lands not only resisted increased grazing fees but also approved the proposed drastic cuts in appropriations for the Grazing Service.

On May 8, 1946, Representative Jed Johnson attacked the
Grazing Service on the floor of the House:

> It [the Taylor Grazing Act] passed . . . after a certain former Sec-
> retary of Interior appeared before . . . Congress and assured us that
> it could operate on $150,000 a year and that it would be self-support-
> ing. Over and over we were told that the Grazing Service would be
> self-supporting. . . .
> But what did the Grazing Service do? They went out and practically
> turned it over to the big cowmen and the big sheepmen of the West.

Why they even put them on the payroll. . . . It is common knowledge
that they [the big stockmen] have been practically running the Grazing
Service.

 . . . we gave them $425,000, the amount they collected . . . and
we said to the Grazing Service: "Live up to your contract; live within
your revenue" and by the eternals they are going to do it whether they
like it or not.[44]

The following day, May 9, 1946, Senator McCarran blasted
the Grazing Service in a long speech in the Senate. He accused
the Grazing Service of misinforming the appropriations subcommittee and of driving for unwarranted increased grazing
fees for the sole purpose of using the increased revenues as
a basis for additional appropriations by which a very few grasp-
ing individuals (J. H. Leech and Director Forsling) could satisfy their lust for power by building a bigger empire.[45]

Director Forsling and the Grazing Service were caught in a
triple play between a Senate committee which refused to allow
increased fees, a House committee which cut appropriations
because fees were not raised, and a powerful interest group
which supported both committees. The result was inevitable.

The Grazing Service budget was cut approximately in half,
which meant that a roster of some 250 range examiners and
graziers was reduced to forty-odd men to police and regulate
142,000,000 acres of public land. Director Forsling was re-
lieved of his duties with the Grazing Service and was reas-
signed to the southwest field committee of the Department of
Interior.

On July 16, 1946, the Grazing Service was reorganized into
the Bureau of Land Management and ceased to exist as a separate organization. Grazing fees remained at five cents per
A.U.M.

The Bureau of Land Management was formed by the amal-
gamation of the Grazing Service and the old General Land Office. By this time Harold Ickes had been replaced by Julius
A. Krug as Secretary of Interior. Fred W. Johnson, the first
director of the Bureau of Land Management, characterized it
as a "modern administrative structure for more efficient handling of problems involving the Nation's public land."[46]

The new "modern administrative structure," as we have
noted, practically wiped out the Grazing Service. If the graz-

ing districts had been forced to rely on congressional appropriations entirely, the Taylor Grazing Act would have been
almost completely ineffective. But the advisory boards came
to the rescue of the administration and allotted about $200,000
of range improvement funds to help pay salaries of employees
in fiscal year 1947.[47] At that time, 50 per cent of the total
grazing fees collected were transferred from the Treasury to
the governments of states in which the grazing districts were
located in lieu of taxes. Most of the states then transferred
these monies to the advisory boards to be used for range improvements. These were the funds which the advisory boards
used to pay salaries of employees. Even with this contribution the grazing service operated as a skeleton force.

Reduction in appropriations and reorganization of the grazing activity into the Bureau of Land Management did not solve
the problem of grazing fees. In an attempt to find his way out
of the grazing fee dilemma, Secretary Krug appointed Rex
Nicholson, a California cattleman, to make a study of grazing fees, organization and personnel of the federal grazing
activity.[48]

This study produced the Nicholson report which we considered in chapter 4. Nicholson recommended that grazing fees
be based on the cost of administering the grazing function only;
that grazing fees be raised to six cents per A.U.M. plus a
range improvement fee of two cents for a total of eight cents
per A.U.M.; and that the percentage of fees to be returned to
the states be reduced from 50 per cent to $12\frac{1}{2}$ per cent of the
grazing fee. These recommendations were accepted by the
Interior Department and the Taylor Grazing Act was amended
to allow separate grazing and range improvement fees and to
reduce the percentage of grazing fees accruing to the states
from 50 per cent to $12\frac{1}{2}$ per cent.[49] Nicholson's recommendation of an eight-cent fee was adopted by the Secretary of the
Interior and put into effect in July, 1947.

Secretary Krug also obtained from the Bureau of Agricultural
Economics a statement which estimated that only 70 per cent
of the expenditures on grazing districts directly benefited the
stockmen while the other 30 per cent accrued to the benefit of
the general public. On the basis of this 70-30 formula the
BLM calculated that Congress should appropriate 142.85 per

cent of the amount the BLM deposited in the Treasury from grazing fee collections. In effect, the stockmen would pay for their 70 per cent of the benefits through grazing fees and Congress, according to this reasoning, should appropriate the other 30 per cent from general funds. Table 5 indicates that the BLM was unable to sell this plan to Congress during the next three years.[50]

TABLE 5

GRAZING INCOME AND APPROPRIATIONS, 1948-50
(in dollars)

|  | 1948 | 1949 | 1950 |
|---|---|---|---|
| Net Balance to Treasury from Grazing Fees and Sect. 15 Leases | 825,211 | 738,818 | 837,500 |
| Appropriations Warranted by 70-30 Formula | 1,178,873 | 1,055,454 | 1,196,429 |
| Actual Expenditure, Appropriation or Estimate for Grazing Administration | 640,241 | 941,850 | 1,030,550 |

F. E. Mollin, executive secretary of the American National Livestock Association, explained the low appropriation for the fiscal year 1948 in this way:

After the new 8-cent fee had been put into effect, on May 1, 1947, the Bureau of Land Management sat tight and failed to give any encouragement to moves to amend the law so as to bring the administrative cost and the fees retained by the federal government into balance, until it became apparent that the appropriation committees would not grant the funds desired for administration until this was done. In the meantime, permittees were urged by representatives of the Taylor Grazing Service to wire their congressmen demanding that the appropriations be increased. Many stockmen did not understand that the only way to prevent further increases in the grazing fee was to stand pat on the appropriation until the Bureau of Land Management saw fit to cooperate to get the law amended as contemplated in the Nicholson report.[51]

William B. Wright of Deeth, Nevada, president of the American National Livestock Association, testified before the House subcommittee on appropriations,

Our appearance here is for the purpose of urging upon your committee the limited appropriation for the branch of range management under the Bureau of Land Management not to exceed that appropriation made for the fiscal year 1947, which appropriations are substantially less than previous appropriations.

The reasons for our request are three-fold.

First. There exists a plan . . . known as the "Nicholson Report" . . .

This plan provides details surrounding the reorganization of the former Grazing Service and a basic principle upon which a grazing fee can be established. Such principle is not only equitable to the range user but to the public interest as well, by providing for ample range supervision to protect the range resource. In addition, it is sound to the point of restricting constant growth and ever-expanding bureau ambitions.

Second. Any increase for the fiscal year 1948 over the 1947 appropriation will jeopardize the prospects of working out a long-term grazing fee structure in accordance with the Nicholson report.

Third. During the past season the range users have been able to get by on a basis of the 1947 appropriation augmented by contributions from the industry to assist and sustain the minimum essential activities of the Grazing Service. While we neither subscribe to such practice as being good government nor wish to continue the practice for long, we feel so strongly the necessity of clarifying this entire fee policy, and setting up a grazing administration management to fit it, that we are willing to rock along on a temporary basis with inadequate service. [52]

After the Taylor Grazing Act was amended on July 30, 1947, in accordance with the Nicholson plan, Congress granted a supplementary appropriation of $300,000. [53]

As we have seen, the advisory boards and the stockmen's organizations were heavily committed to the Nicholson plan. They felt obligated, therefore, to try to make the plan work. By 1950 it became obvious that the plan had serious deficiencies aside from its "cost of administration" basis. Nicholson had recommended a static fee, but costs of performing the same functions did not remain static; they increased. The Nicholson cost structure was already obsolete the day it went into effect.

Nicholson had worked out a table of organization allocating definite grades to each position. This meant that personnel could not be promoted unless someone died or for other reasons vacated his position. Nicholson's estimated cost for his minimum organization of 242 persons was $1,147,896 in 1946. With rising costs, this amount could not have maintained even the minimum organization proposed. But Congress refused to appropriate even that amount. The BLM was never able to employ the 242 persons recommended by Nicholson. The nearest approach to filling this quota was in 1949 when 182 persons were employed. By 1950 the number was reduced to 176.[54]

The plan was a failure, not only because it was based on an unsound and unworkable concept, but also because of its rigidities in both revenue sources and expenditures.

By 1950 BLM officials felt they could sell the stockmen on another increase in fees, if for no other reason than that the prevailing fees failed to provide enough revenue to satisfy the minimum requirements of the Nicholson plan. In effect, they could say to the stockmen, "you agreed to provide us with funds enough to maintain a certain standard of operation—now we are asking you to live up to the terms of your agreement."

BLM officials also reminded the stockmen that the current eight-cent fee was considerably below the average fees charged by the Forest Service. Table 6 sets forth this comparison for the years 1936-50.[55]

TABLE 6

A COMPARISON OF GRAZING FEES ON NATIONAL FORESTS
AND GRAZING DISTRICTS
(in cents)

| Date | National Forest Grazing Fees | | Grazing District Fees | |
|------|--------|-------|--------|-------|
|      | Cattle | Sheep | Cattle | Sheep |
| 1936 | 13.05  | 3.36  | 5      | 1     |
| 1937 | 12.55  | 3.66  | 5      | 1     |
| 1938 | 14.98  | 4.24  | 5      | 1     |
| 1939 | 13.4   | 3.3   | 5      | 1     |
| 1940 | 14.89  | 3.69  | 5      | 1     |
| 1941 | 15.97  | 3.85  | 5      | 1     |
| 1942 | 18.9   | 4.6   | 5      | 1     |
| 1943 | 23.0   | 5.5   | 5      | 1     |
| 1944 | 26.0   | 6.25  | 5      | 1     |
| 1945 | 24.8   | 6.03  | 5      | 1     |
| 1946 | 27.0   | 6.25  | 5      | 1     |
| 1947 | 31.0   | 7.5   | 8      | 1.6   |
| 1948 | 40.0   | 10.0  | 8      | 1.6   |
| 1949 | 49.0   | 11.0  | 8      | 1.6   |
| 1950 | 42.0   | 10.75 | 8      | 1.6   |

The figures quoted for the Forest Service are nationwide averages. Consequently Forest Service fees, in some areas, may have been as low or lower than BLM fees. The figures are also somewhat misleading in that grazing lands in the national forests are generally superior to those of the BLM so grazing privileges are more valuable.

Director Marion Clawson, Gerald M. Kerr, and other BLM officials presented these complaints to the NABC on September 6, 1950. The NABC responded with the following resolution:

WHEREAS, according to the Nicholson plan and report, the number of personnel to adequately supervise and administer grazing under the Taylor Grazing Act was: department 8; regions 43; and districts, 191; for a total personnel of 242, and
WHEREAS, since such report, the cost has gone up, and
WHEREAS, we deem it necessary to adhere to the Nicholson plan as to personnel,
NOW THEREFORE, we recommend to the Director of the Bureau of Land Management that if an increase in fees is necessary to take care of said personnel, then such fee be put into effect, and in no case is said fee to exceed 12 ¢, of which 2 ¢ shall be for improvements. [56]

Sam Ross supported this resolution and, in an Oregon state advisory board meeting, voiced the opinion that stockmen should advocate the abandonment of cost of administration as a basis for determining grazing fees. Ross felt that this system of fee determination was making enemies for the stockmen and would ultimately work to their disadvantage. Sam Coon (then a member of the state board) concurred.

The increase in fees to twelve cents per A.U.M. obviously did not correct the inequities and the impracticality of the Nicholson plan. Director Clawson, therefore, instituted another grazing fee study in 1952. Clawson's study followed somewhat the same pattern as Mont Saunderson's study eleven years earlier except that it was much more extensive and was conducted by selected BLM employees, who devoted their full time to the study. The survey included 487 samples of private lands totaling 3,634,000 acres and samples of federal range totaling 7,500,000 acres. The purpose of the survey was to determine the value of the forage in the different areas according to average livestock prices received by the growers during the five-year period 1947 to 1951. The rates determined by this study ranged from twenty cents per A.U.M. to forty cents per A.U.M. for an average of twenty-eight cents.

By the time the report was completed Clawson was on his way out as director and the NABC was none too cooperative. At the meeting of February 16-19, 1953, the NABC passed resolutions recommending that the users decide the season of use and the carrying capacity of the range and vetoed any increase in grazing fees. [57]

In his first meeting with the NABC in February, 1954, the new director, Edward Woozley, resurrected the 1952 study and again broached the subject of a revised grazing fee. The NABC seemed receptive to a suggestion that the cost of administration basis for fees be abandoned and that a fee based on livestock prices be substituted. The matter was given further study during the summer and was presented again at a special meeting of the NABC on August 2-3, 1954. At this meeting the NABC agreed to a fee system based on the combined prices of cattle and sheep in the markets of the eleven western states. Thus if cattle prices average seventeen cents per pound and sheep fifteen cents per pound during a given year, the average of the two, or sixteen cents in this case, would be the grazing fee per A.U.M. during the following year.

According to this formula, the fee for 1955, based on market prices in 1954, would have been about eighteen cents per A.U.M.—six cents higher than the prevailing twelve-cent rate. Director Woozley considered this 50 per cent increase "too much of an increase at one time under present conditions" and suggested that he would seek Department approval of an increase to fifteen cents per A.U.M. for 1955 and 1956 with the understanding that the fee in 1957 would be adjusted to the combined average per-pound price of cattle and sheep in 1956. [58]

The NABC accepted Director Woozley's proposal, which was then referred to the various state advisory boards. The plan was endorsed by the boards of all the range states except Nevada.

The National Woolgrowers Association tried a last-minute delaying tactic by passing a resolution at its convention on December 6-9, 1954, urging the BLM to hold the new fees in abeyance until a study could be carried out on the legality of the proposed changeover. The Woolgrowers tried to get the support of the cattlemen in this move but were unsuccessful.

Nevada stockmen promptly formed a committee composed of representatives of the two associations and the state Farm Bureau to contest the legality of the new fee formula through court action. Roy Young, an Elko, Nevada, stockman, and five other permittees refused to pay grazing fees levied under the new formula. These stockmen then secured a temporary order from the District Court of Elko restraining the BLM from prohibiting the use of the range to the parties in suit. The case was removed to the United States District Court in Carson City and was argued before Judge John R. Ross on July 7, 1955. Judge Ross held that the Secretary of Interior was an indispensable party to the action but that he had not been made a party thereto and, on these grounds, dissolved the restraining order and dismissed the case.[59] The stockmen apparently decided that further action was likely to be unproductive and dropped the case.[60]

We have noted that the new fee system was to have become effective on January 1, 1955, but that a compromise fee of fifteen cents per A. U. M. was adopted instead, with the understanding that the new formula would become effective in 1957. However, application of the new fee formula was again postponed, this time to 1958, because of severe drought conditions during 1956. Grazing fees therefore remained at fifteen cents per A. U. M. during 1955, 1956, and 1957.

On November 21, 1957, the Secretary of Interior issued Circular No. 1988 amending the Federal Range Code in accordance with the new grazing formula. The grazing fee for 1958, based on average livestock prices during 1957, was set at nineteen cents per A. U. M.[61]

After two decades of uncertainty and bitter dispute it appears that a method for determining grazing fees has been stabilized into a reasonably acceptable formula.

# 9. A SUMMARY

## The Public Domain

The public domain consists of lands which belong to the federal government but which have not been withdrawn for a specific purpose, a commons awaiting transfer to a more specific owner or to a specific federal purpose.

All of the land in the first forty-eight states was once public domain except the original thirteen colonies and the state of Texas. This land was acquired by cession from some of the colonial states; by the purchase of Louisiana from France; by the purchase of Florida from Spain; by conquest and purchase of the Southwest from Mexico; by purchase of lands from Texas; by annexation of the Oregon Territory through agreement with Great Britain; and by the purchase of a small area in southern New Mexico and Arizona from Mexico.

The total extent of these acquisitions was approximately 1, 400, 000, 000 acres. The total cost to the government was about $78, 000, 000 or about five and one-half cents an acre.

The states formed from these acquisitions did not acquire title to the public domain. Until disposed of, the public lands belonged to the federal government with Congress alone responsible for their administration or disposal.

Transfer of land to private ownership passed through three general stages: sales for revenue, grants to states and corporations for internal improvements and to individuals for services to the government, and alienation through the various homestead acts. Most of the western range region which passed into private ownership was transferred via the homestead laws and state and railroad grants.

Altogether the government has transferred over one billion acres to private ownership. About one third of this total was sold and the balance was given away in the form of grants and homesteads. About one fourth of the original public domain still remains in the hands of the government. In the eleven western states (the range region) the government owns about half of the total acreage. Of the total acreage remaining in the hands of the government, about 142,000,000 acres are administered by the Bureau of Land Management as grazing districts. Other categories of federal lands include national forests, Indian reservations, parks and monuments, wildlife refuges, military and other reservations.

The land disposal policies of the federal government were not the results of any long-range program of settlement, distribution or land utilization. Lands were first offered for sale to provide revenue and to discourage movement of people from the industrial centers of the East. Lands were granted to states and corporations for internal improvements. In the first instance the need for additional revenue was the motivating force; in the second, the improvements and the investment opportunities were the important factor. In neither case was the land itself or the mode of settlement considered in making the political decision.

The pre-emption acts and the homestead acts were primarily the results of political pressures from the frontier. But they were passed by a Congress which considered stock raising to be only the advance guard of farming. As a consequence, the various homestead acts provided too little land at too late a period to be successful either as farms or as ranches in the lands west of the hundredth meridian. The result was unnecessary human hardship and failure, deterioration of the range, and an accelerated rate of erosion.

The rectangular survey system, coupled with the grant and homestead systems, resulted in crazy-quilt landownership patterns in uneconomic units, which encouraged and invited conflict and economic instability, overgrazing, and futile attempts at cultivation of submarginal lands.

This incalculable waste of resources and human life was not a consequence of the forces of nature; nor was it a consequence of the operation of economic forces through the market and the price system. It was basically and fundamentally a result of political decisions which ordered social forces in such a manner as to disturb the balance of nature.

## The Taylor Grazing Act

After half a century of range wars and a rapidly deteriorating public range the stockmen themselves came to the realization that some regulation of the public lands was necessary. After several unsuccessful attempts at federal legislation, the Taylor Grazing Act of 1934 was adopted.

The Taylor Grazing Act sought to rectify some of the errors of past public land policies and provided a basis for control and rehabilitation of the public range. The purposes of the act, as set forth in the preamble, are: "To stop injury to the public grazing lands by preventing overgrazing and soil deterioration, to provide for their orderly use, improvement, and development, to stabilize the livestock industry dependent upon the public range, and for other purposes."

To accomplish these purposes, the Secretary of Interior was authorized to establish grazing districts on lands which were in his opinion valuable chiefly for grazing. Lands which were considered more valuable for other purposes could be reclassified and withdrawn from grazing districts.

The act provided for the issuance of grazing permits, not to exceed the carrying capacity of the range, to qualified persons on payment of a reasonable fee, and during such seasons of use as should be specified by the Secretary of Interior.

Shortly after the passage of the act 142,000,000 acres of federal range land plus several million acres of state, county, and private holdings were organized into grazing districts. These grazing districts were scattered throughout all the western states except Washington. In this tremendous area there existed wide diversities in topography, climate, soils, and vegetation. Probably the only significant uniformity was that almost all the grazing districts were located in areas of less than fifteen inches of annual rainfall.

## The Federal Range

For purposes of description the federal range may be divided into three general areas: the eastern plains, the southwest and the intermountain. The plains region includes eastern Montana, Wyoming, Colorado, and New Mexico. This region is a flat, treeless, shortgrass prairie with high wind velocities and a precipitation rate of twelve to twenty inches per year. The southwest region includes southern California, southern Nevada, and Arizona. Much of this area is desert with rainfall averaging less than ten inches annually. The forage consists primarily of desert shrubs with pockets of short grass and curly mesquite. Livestock graze all year round and move to California markets. The intermountain region contains the bulk of the federal range. This area contains great variations in elevation and forage plants. Probably desert shrubs, desert grass, and bunch grass predominate. Cattle and sheep are about equal in importance, with cattle moving to west coast markets and lambs to eastern markets.

In 1955 the federal range supported over 2,000,000 cattle, 6,000,000 sheep, 53,000 horses and 20,000 goats. The range also supported about 120,000 antelope, 770,000 deer, 17,000 elk and other big game.

In addition to its forage production, the range has recreational values, considerable marketable timber, and, in some areas, watershed values which are many times more valuable to the public than grazing or timber production.

## The Western Stockmen

To many of the stockmen of this area, the federal range is an integral part of their ranching operation. Their private holdings may be of little value without continued access to the range. The range is not usually an extra or bonus piece of pasture; it is more likely to be a necessary part of the ranching unit. Grazing permits are ordinarily capitalized into the value of the ranch so that if permits are stabilized a ranch buyer actually pays for both the private and public lands contained in the ranch unit.

The western range industry is one of the most rigid of agricultural pursuits because the ranges are ordinarily of value for pasturage only. The western rancher in the arid region ordinarily can produce only one crop: cattle or sheep. Often he has no real choice even between these two. This dependence on a single crop, coupled with the vagaries of the livestock market and the unpredictable climate of the range region, makes ranching a precarious business.

In spite of these rigidities and uncertainties, western stockmen have traditionally been one of the most individualistic and independent groups in the nation. All these factors have conspired to create a resentment of bureaucratic controls and a strong desire to safeguard the continued use of the public range with a minimum of governmental "interference."

As compared with the total population, western stockmen are few in number, but in the range states they rank high in wealth, prestige, and influence. Not only are they influential in state politics but they also carry considerable weight in Congress, especially in the Senate. There are few groups of comparable size, if any, which are as politically powerful as are the western stockmen.

## Grazing Policy on the Public Range

The major policy objectives followed by the decision-makers of the federal grazing subsystem fall into two major categories: (1) the maintenance of the status quo on the federal range and (2) the maintenance of a minimum rate grazing fee.

The system for allocating range "rights," as discussed in chapter 3, acted to maintain the status quo. The requirements that permittees be "landowners," that they be "in or near" a district, that they possess commensurate properties, and that preference be given to those who had customarily used the range during the priority-period—all work to reserve the range for those who had previously used it and in approximately the same proportion as their previous use. The leaders of the subsystem have not only attempted to maintain the status quo in relation to allocation of range privileges but also with reference to authority to make decisions affecting all phases of range administration.

We have seen that over the years grazing fees have been held down to a minimum rate. The five cents per A.U.M. fee, which was designed to be used as an interim fee during the organizational period only, was retained until 1947. The fee was then raised to eight cents, which was supposed to defray the cost of administration under the Nicholson plan. By 1950 it became apparent that the eight-cent fee was not providing enough revenue to pay the cost of the minimal organization planned by Nicholson. So the fee was raised to twelve cents per A.U.M., but stockmen still considered that they were paying only for the cost of administering the range. In 1954, the "cost of administration" concept was abandoned and fees were raised to fifteen cents per A.U.M. Since 1958, grazing fees have been assessed at the combined per-pound average price of beef and mutton in western markets. This is a more flexible and realistic basis for setting fees than the old "cost of administration" concept, but it still avoids the question of the value of the forage and it is still lower than the fees charged by the Forest Service and by private owners of range lands.

## The Decision-Makers of the Federal Grazing Activity

The principal decision-makers of the federal grazing activity include the advisory board members, leaders of the stockmen's associations, a small number of congressmen, and some members of the federal grazing bureaucracy.

The advisory board system was initiated by the first director of grazing, F. R. Carpenter. Carpenter needed a mass of knowledge about local conditions in order to establish and operate the grazing districts. Probably no other system could have furnished this information so quickly. Some local representation or participation may also have been necessary to sell the program to the users. The advisory boards quickly assumed or were given more than an advisory role. They were most influential in drafting a code of rules and regulations; with some exceptions, they determined the allocation of permits; they supervised the expenditure of range improvement funds; they were probably the real decision-makers in setting grazing fees; they were influential in the selection and tenure of personnel; and they have played an active role in routine managerial decisions.

In theory, the boards carry out an advisory function only. In actuality, they formulate the broad policy, make the rules which spell out that policy and superintend the execution of these rules and policies.

District advisory boards are elected by the permittees in secret elections. Two members of each district board are elected to a state advisory board and each state advisory board, in turn, selects two of its members to the National Advisory Board Council. Voting participation by the permittees is very low and the rate of turnover on the boards is very slow. While the advisory board system may appear to be "democratized administration" or "home rule on the range," there are indications that it may be the formalization and legal recognition of the upper strata of a rural caste system.

The leaders of the stockmen's associations are especially powerful in the legislatures of the range states, in the advisory boards, and in the United States Senate. The range states were settled by stockmen, or miners turned stockmen, and their descendants rate high in prestige and wealth. While many of the descendants of the early stockmen are no longer in the ranching business, they are likely to be especially sympathetic to the problems of the stockmen. Rural areas are commonly overrepresented (proportionately) in state legislatures and in the United States Senate.

The congressional committee system tends to create a series of small, specialized legislatures. The committees may be further specialized into subcommittees which become still more specialized little legislatures. Because of this system of division of labor, not many congressmen have much knowledge of, or interest in, the problems of the federal range. Those congressmen who are most informed and interested naturally come from the range states, with the possible exception of some members of the appropriations committees. In reality, then, the Congress which makes decisions with reference to the public range is ordinarily composed of a very small group of congressmen from the range states. These congressmen commonly are influential both in legislation and in the administration of the range.

The administrators of the federal grazing activity are, of course, participants in the formulation of policy. In some instances administrators have been in general agreement with their stockmen clientele group and have acted as the spokesmen and chief lobbyists for their clientele. When administrators have acted contrary to the objectives of the stockmen they have ordinarily been unsuccessful and occasionally have been subjected to rather severe punitive sanctions.

The decision-makers described above comprise a governmental subsystem which has specialized objectives and which, in many ways, functions as a private, commercial organization. This subsystem might be called a special private government as opposed to a general public government. The special private government attaches to itself most of the trappings and authority of the general public government and very likely the public assumes that it is in fact an integral part of the general public government.

While the private special government has specialized objectives and operates generally for the benefit of a restricted clientele, it does not function in complete isolation. It interacts with other subsystems and it operates within a complex of behavioral patterns which have a high order of consistency. These consistencies may be explained by law, tradition, folklore, custom, habit, "rules of the game" and other such decriptive terms.

While this particular subsystem is concerned with a clientele and a function which may appear to be somewhat unique and "off the beaten path," it seems likely that our government may be composed in large part of an agglomeration of these "unique" subsystems.

### The Process of Policy Formation

Some of the most effective methods used by the decision-makers of the grazing subsystem to advance their policy objectives have been: (1) The formulation of a rather elaborate code of regulations governing the issuance of permits. Every part of the permit system acts to perpetuate the status quo. The permit system also acts to keep grazing fees low by eliminating competition and competitive bidding. (2) The forma-

tion of the advisory board system and the legal recognition of
the boards in the statute. In large measure the boards supply the information on which administrative decisions are
based. The boards themselves make many of these administrative decisions. The Federal Range Code, which inter-
prets the Taylor Grazing Act, is largely the work of the advisory boards. The boards have been mainly responsible for
the maintenance of a low grazing fee. Western congressmen
have relied upon the boards for advice on matters relating to
federal range policy. (3) The tactics of congressional committees. The McCarran Committee for seven years attacked;
stalled for time by investigations, hearings, and "studies";
and generally functioned in such a manner as to weaken bureaucratic control, strengthen stockmen control, and hold down
grazing fees. The appropriation committees, especially in the
House, unwittingly or otherwise played into the hands of the
stockmen by refusing to appropriate more than token sums
for the operation of the grazing activity. (4) The numerous
reorganizations and decentralization moves have acted to further the stockmen's basic policy objectives. The reorganizations have weakened the power of the bureaucracy generally
and have eliminated intransigent key personnel or placed them
in relatively "harmless" positions. A high degree of organizational decentralization coupled with a powerful advisory board
system and low appropriations has acted to minimize the possibility of real federal control and has buttressed the old system of local control of the range by rural elites. (5) The "cost
of administration" basis for setting grazing fees and its even-
tual formalization in the Nicholson plan resulted in low grazing
fees. Low grazing fees caused low congressional appropriations. Low congressional appropriations, in turn, resulted
in minimal regulation and control. (6) Court actions contest-
ing the legality of various grazing fees and methods of assess-
ment, while unsuccessful, have undoubtedly had psychological
effects and may have resulted in less stringent enforcement
of the grazing code. (7) The close collaboration and agreement between the stockmen's associations, the advisory boards,
certain western congressmen, and some administrators has
at times been an invincible combination. (8) The stockmen's

two basic policy objectives—the maintenance of the status quo
and low grazing fees—complement each other. The maintenance
of the status quo involves a minimum of regulation and regulatory personnel. The cost of such minimal regulation will
be relatively low. If the cost of regulation is low, and especially if fees are based on cost of regulation (administration),
there will be less pressure for increases in grazing fees. Conversely, if fees are kept low it will be more difficult to secure
congressional appropriations. Low appropriations can finance
only a minimum amount of regulation and only minor changes
in the status quo.

### Stockmen's Policy Objectives and the Taylor Grazing Act

How have the two major policy objectives of the grazing subsystem affected the attainment of the stated objectives of the
Taylor Grazing Act?

The objectives of the act, as stated in the preamble, are:
"To stop injury to the public grazing lands by preventing overgrazing and soil deterioration, to provide for their orderly
use, improvement, and development, to stabilize the livestock
industry dependent upon the public range, and for other purposes."

The maintenance of the status quo has meant a minimum of
supervision and control over (or "interference" with) the activities of the stockmen on the range. As a result "injury to
the public grazing lands" has not been stopped. The rate of
injury, however, has undoubtedly diminished. "Overgrazing
and soil deterioration" has not been prevented, but it has been
lessened.

Partly because of the insistence on low grazing fees, appropriations for range improvements have been meager. Consequently, there has been little "improvement and development" of the public range. Probably most improvement and
development was accomplished by the Civilian Conservation
Corps. Stockmen are desirous of improving the range, but if
such improvement comes at the cost of closer regulation and
increased fees they seem willing to forego it. The stockmen
seem to hope that by improved public relations methods they

may be able to secure additional appropriations for range improvement without losing their present autonomy in the grazing districts and without raising their grazing fees.

Probably the objective most successfully carried out has been the stabilization of the "livestock industry dependent upon the public range." The phrase "stabilize the livestock industry dependent upon the public range" is almost synonymous with "maintain the status quo on the public range." The range wars have stopped and competition for the range has been practically eliminated.

A further stabilizing factor and one of the signal contributions of the act was the withdrawal of the public lands from the possibility of further unsuccessful homesteading and the resultant destruction of the range.

# APPENDIX

## SOLDIER CREEK UNIT AGREEMENT
### 1-12-56

WHEREAS it is the desire of all those claiming grazing privileges in the Soldier Creek Unit of Oregon Grazing District No. 3 to define the respective grazing privileges to be exercised by each one claiming such privileges for the purpose of definitely establishing such privileges for priority purposes and stabilization of the live stock industry in such Unit,

NOW THEREFORE, it is agreed as follows:

1. That the persons named in the attached schedule shall for priority purposes be recognized as being entitled to grazing privileges in the amounts named therein.

2. It is further understood and agreed that in order to reduce the demand on the range to carrying capacity the parties hereto have agreed to accept a reduction which approximates 10% in time plus 4% in AUM's of their grazing privileges and such reduction is reflected in the attached schedule. In addition to the above reductions, certain persons have agreed to have taken additional reductions in AUM's which reductions are reflected as follows, and which reductions will be the first restored as soon as range conditions will permit:

| | |
|---|---|
| Barrick and Shannon | 200 AUM's |
| James Eiguren | 30 " |

| Pascual Eiguren and Son | 70 | AUM's |
| Orville Fretwall | 68 | " |
| Raymond Gluch | 113 | " |
| Jaca Brothers | 140 | " |
| Ed Maher | 27 | " |
| Don McKay (Myher Ranch) | 50 | " |
| W. J. Pollock | 18 | " |
| George Potts | 68 | " |
| Oran Raburn | 70 | " |
| Dale Sinclair | 75 | " |
| S. K. Skinner | 250 | " |
| T. L. Skinner | 68 | " |
| Dick Staples | 27 | " |
| John Swisher | 120 | " |
| Domingo Urquiaga | 45 | " |
| Vernon Warn | 102 | " |
| John Yturriondobeitia | 91 | " |
| M. F. Hanley | 23 | " |
| Loveland Brothers | 23 | " |
| Dallas Payne | 23 | " |

The United States also agrees that the percentage reduction referred to in the fore part of this paragraph will be restored to each licensee or his successor in interest in the same proportion as the reduction taken when range conditions are such that all or any part of the restoration can be made.

3. It is further understood that if and when those operators who operate partially in Oregon and partially in Idaho are separated from the rest of the operators in the Soldier Creek Unit by means of a drift fence, those licensees who operate on either side of the fence will benefit from their participation with the Bureau of Land Management in any range improvement program in their respective areas. It is further understood that the Government will participate with those licensees in both areas in equal proportion.

4. The signatures affixed hereto in the attached Schedule A which is by reference made a part of this agreement, shall

be considered as approval of this agreement by the signatories.

SCHEDULE A

| Name | AUM's | Date |
|------|-------|------|
| /s/ Barrick & Shannon by | | |
| Roy A. Shannon | 2400 | 1/12/56 |
| /s/ S. K. Skinner | 3216 | 1/12/56 |
| /s/ Jack Swisher | 1725 | 1/12/56 |
| /s/ Ed M. Maher | 605 | 1/12/56 |
| /s/ L. R. Falen | 356 | 1/12/56 |
| /s/ M. F. Hanley | 1187 | 1/12/56 |
| /s/ Donald J. McKay | 816 | 1/12/56 |
| /s/ T. L. Skinner | 790 | 1/12/56 |
| /s/ E. C. Fenwick | | |
| /s/ Loveland Bros. | 432 | 1/12/56 |
| /s/ D. E. Sinclair | 576 | 1/12/56 |
| /s/ Oran Raburn | 365 | 1/12/56 |
| /s/ Blanche S. Miller-Everett | | |
| E. Miller | 605 | 1/12/56 |
| /s/ Larrusea Bros. by Julio | | |
| Larrusea | 613 | 1/12/56 |
| /s/ Andres Yturriondobeitia | 700 | 1/12/56 |
| by Juan Yturriondobeitia | | |
| /s/ Marion F. Wroten | 2562 | 1/12/56 |
| /s/ Domingo Urquiaga | 389 | 1/12/56 |
| /s/ Vernon Warn | 780 | 1/12/56 |
| /s/ Floyd Robison | 230 | 1/12/56 |
| /s/ Pascual Eiguren & Son | 840 | 1/12/56 |
| by Fred Eiguren | | |
| /s/ Orville Fretwell | 752 | 1/12/56 |
| /s/ Geo. Potts | 1231 | 1/12/56 |
| /s/ Raymond E. Gluch | 1836 | 1/12/56 |
| /s/ Tex Payne | 472 | 1/12/56 |
| /s/ W. J. Pollock (Class I) | 173 | 1/12/56 |
| /s/ Ethel Raburn by John R. | | |
| Dentel | 186 | 1/12/56 |
| /s/ Jaca Bros. by Felix Jaca | 2592 | 1/12/56 |

| /s/ Dick Staples | 734 | 1/12/56 |
|---|---|---|
| /s/ William C. Brunel | 207 | 1/12/56 |
| /s/ Thomas & Arthur Whitby | 281 | 1/13/56 |
| /s/ Robert J. Gluch | 1305 | 1/13/56 |
| /s/ Charles G. Dougal | 497 | 1/13/56 |
| /s/ Child Ranches, Inc. | 1279 | 1/17/56 |
| by Arval L. Child | | |
| /s/ John Timmerman Son | 1430 | 1/18/56 |
| /s/ John Archabal Jr. | 288 | 1/19/56 |
| /s/ Maria Corta | 160 | 1/19/56 |
| by Joe Corta | | |
| */s/ Russell Lynde | 260 | 1/19/56 |
| */s/ Frank L. Stearns | 50 | 1/20/56 |

*Note: Russell Lynde and Frank Stearns operate entirely within individual allotments and did not share in the reductions taken by the other users. Therefore, they will not share in any future increase in forage as may become available on the outside range.

RECOMMENDED: /s/ Lloyd Edmunson
_____
LLOYD EDMUNSON, ADVISORY BOARD CHAIRMAN

APPROVED:          /s/ Derrel S. Fulwider
_____
DERREL S. FULWIDER, DISTRICT RANGE MANAGER

# NOTES

Chapter 1

1. Norman Wengert, "How Agricultural Policy is Made," *Farm Policy Forum*, VII (Winter, 1955), 30.

Chapter 2

1. New York, Virginia, North Carolina, South Carolina, Georgia, Massachusetts, Connecticut.

2. Marion Clawson, *Uncle Sam's Acres* (New York: Dodd, Mead and Co., 1951), p. 19.

3. Maryland, Delaware, Pennsylvania, New Jersey, Rhode Island, New Hampshire.

4. Roy M. Robbins, *Our Landed Heritage* (Princeton: Princeton University Press, 1942), p. 5.

5. Clawson, *Uncle Sam's Acres*, pp. 30-31.

6. For a discussion of state claims to public domain lands see Arthur W. Sampson, *Range Management Principles and Practices* (New York: John Wiley and Sons, 1952), p. 119.

7. Clawson, *Uncle Sam's Acres*, p. 45.

8. James Truslow Adams (ed.), *Hamiltonian Principles: Extracts from the Writings of Alexander Hamilton* (Boston: Little, Brown and Co., 1928), pp. 40, 142, 155-61.

9. Clawson, *Uncle Sam's Acres*, p. 58.

10. Robbins, *Our Landed Heritage*, p. 18.

11. Clawson, *Uncle Sam's Acres*, p. 58.

12. *Ibid.*, p. 59.

13. Benjamin Horace Hibbard, *A History of the Public Land Policies* (New York: Macmillan Co., 1924), pp. 103, 106.

14. *Ibid.*, pp. 118, 120, 126.

15. Sampson, *Range Management Principles and Practices*, p. 119.

16. *Congressional Globe*, 40th Cong., 2nd sess. Appendix, p. 424.

17. Hibbard, *A History of the Public Land Policies*, p. 343.

18. General Land Office, Reports of the Commissioner, 1907, p. 84.

19. Hibbard, *A History of the Public Land Policies*, p. 267.

20. *Ibid.*, p. 264.

21. Texas General Land Office, Report of the Commissioner, 1932.

22. Marion Clawson, *The Western Range Livestock Industry* (New York: McGraw-Hill Book Co., 1950), p. 93.

23. Hibbard, *A History of the Public Land Policies*, p. 269.

24. *Ibid.*, p. 288.

25. *U. S. Statutes at Large*, XXVIII, 422.

26. Extracted from U.S. Congress, Senate, *The Western Range*, 74th Cong., 2nd sess., Senate Document 199 (Washington: Government Printing Office, 1936), p. 232.

27. *The Western Range*, p. 234.

28. Thomas Jefferson to Edmund Pendleton, August 13, 1776. Paul Ford (ed.), *The Works of Thomas Jefferson* (New York: G. P. Putnam's Sons, 1904), II, 239-40.

29. Robbins, *Our Landed Heritage*, p. 49.

30. Thomas Jefferson to James Madison, October 28, 1785. Saul K. Padover (ed.), *A Jefferson Profile* (New York: John Day Co., 1956), p. 37.

31. Walter Prescott Webb, *The Great Plains* (Boston: Ginn and Co., 1931), p. 404.

32. Congressional Debates, 19th Cong., 1st sess. (1826), p. 742.

33. Congressional Debates, 19th Cong., 1st sess. (1826), p. 727-28.

34. *Congressional Globe*, 28th Cong., 2nd sess., XIV, 52.

35. Hibbard, *A History of the Public Land Policies*, p. 357.

36. June 27, 1860, quoted in George M. Stephenson, *The Political History of the Public Lands* (Boston: Richard D. Badger, 1917), p. 217.

37. Stephenson, *The Political History of the Public Lands*, p. 242.

38. *U. S. Statutes at Large*, XII, 392.

39. Clawson, *Western Range*, p. 89.

40. E. Louise Peffer, *The Closing of the Public Domain*, (Stanford: Stanford University Press, 1951), p. 137.

41. Hibbard, *A History of the Public Land Policies*, p. 396.

42. Clawson, *Western Range*, p. 91.

43. Hibbard, *A History of the Public Land Policies*, p. 386.

44. *Ibid.*, p. 409.

45. *U. S. Statutes at Large*, XVII, 605.

46. General Land Office, Reports of the Commissioner, 1921, p. 65. Kansas: 2, 005, 831; Nebraska: 2, 546, 696; North Dakota: 1, 226, 606; South Dakota: 2, 124, 754; all other states: 1,952, 377.

47. Hibbard, *A History of the Public Land Policies*, p. 422.

48. General Land Office, Reports of the Commissioner, 1887, p. 506.

49. General Land Office, Reports of the Commissioner, 1923, p. 35.

50. Sampson, *Range Management Principles and Practices,* p. 120.

51. Hibbard, *A History of the Public Land Policies,* p. 392.

52. U.S. Department of Interior, Annual Report of the Secretary, 1915 (Washington: Government Printing Office, 1915), pp. 1, 7.

53. *U.S. Statutes at Large,* XXXVII, 123.

54. Webb, *The Great Plains,* p. 423. Webb is quoted by Peffer, *The Closing of the Public Domain,* p. 154, and in turn quotes Hibbard, *A History of the Public Land Policies,* p. 395.

55. See Peffer, *The Closing of the Public Domain,* p. 157.

56. Webb, *The Great Plains,* p. 424.

57. J. W. Powell, *Report on the Lands of the Arid Region of the United States* (Washington: Government Printing Office, 1879), p. 22.

58. Clawson, *Western Range,* p. 260.

59. For a more detailed description of this practice see Ernest S. Osgood, *The Day of the Cattleman* (Minneapolis: University of Minnesota Press, 1929), pp. 208-15.

60. *Ibid.,* p. 190.

61. Hibbard, *A History of the Public Land Policies,* pp. 476-77.

62. 23 *Stat.* 321.

63. U.S. Department of Interior, *Annual Reports,* I (1886), 40-41.

64. General Land Office, Annual Report of the Commissioner, 1891, p. 53.

65. Gen: 46:34.

66. U.S. Congress, House, Committee on the Public Lands, "To Provide for the Orderly Use, Improvement, and Development of the Public Range," *Hearings,* 73rd Cong., 1st sess. (1933), on H.R. 2835, p. 29.

67. *Ibid.,* p. 70.

68. John C. Frémont, *Memoirs of My Life* (Chicago: Belford, Clarke & Co., 1886), pp. 90 and 385.

69. Bernard DeVoto (ed.), *The Journals of Lewis and Clark* (Boston: Houghton Mifflin Co., 1953), p. 175.

70. George P. Winship (translator), *The Journey of Francisco Vazquez de Coronado* (San Francisco: Grabhorn Press, 1933), p. 75.

71. *Ibid.,* p. 89.

72. Francis Parkman, *The Oregon Trail* (Boston: Little, Brown & Co., 1920), pp. 76-77.

73. Senate Document 199, *The Western Range,* pp. 3, 4, 5.

74. *Ibid.,* p. 7.

75. U.S. Congress, House, Committee on the Public Lands, "To Provide for the Orderly Use, Improvement, and Development of the Public Range," *Hearings,* 73rd Cong., 1st sess. (1933), on H.R. 2835, p. 43.

76. *The Western Range,* p. 13.

77. Ezekiel: 34:18.

78. Sampson, *Range Management Principles and Practices,* p. 509.

Chapter 3

1. General Land Office, Report of the Commissioner, 1875, pp. 6-9.

2. *Congressional Record,* 44th Cong., 2nd sess., V, 32.

3. James D. Richardson, *Messages and Papers of the Presidents* (New York: Bureau of National Literature and Art, 1903), VII, 476.

4. J. W. Powell, *Report on the Lands of the Arid Region of the United States* (Washington: Government Printing Office, 1879), p. 24.

5. *Ibid.,* pp. 33-36.

6. E. Louise Peffer, *The Closing of the Public Domain* (Stanford: Stanford University Press, 1951), p. 75.

7. Will C. Barnes, *The Story of the Range* (Washington: Government Printing Office, 1926), p. 51.

8. Peffer, *The Closing of the Public Domain,* p. 76.

9. *Ibid.,* p. 84.

10. Ora Brooks Peake, *The Colorado Range Cattle Industry* (Glendale, California: Arthur H. Clark Co., 1937), p. 82.

11. American National Livestock Association. Resolution adopted at 10th annual convention, January 23, 1907.

12. General Land Office, Report of the Commissioner, 1907, pp. 79-80.

13. U.S. Congress, Senate, Senate Document 310, 59th Cong., 2nd sess., (Washington: Government Printing Office, 1907), p. 5.

14. Peffer, *The Closing of the Public Domain,* p. 183.

15. *American Sheep Breeder and Wool Grower,* XXXVI (January, 1916), p. 25.

16. *American Sheep Breeder and Wool Grower,* XXXVIII (January, 1917), p. 19.

17. *Ibid.*

18. Remarks of Secretary of Agriculture Houston delivered at a meeting of the United Stockmen's Association for Federal Control of Public Grazing Land, Salt Lake City, Utah, July, 1919.

19. Quoted by Barnes, *The Story of the Range,* p. 57.

20. Peffer, *The Closing of the Public Domain,* p. 182.

21. *Congressional Record,* 68th Cong., 2nd sess., S. Res. 347, LXVI (1924-25), 5505.

22. U.S. Congress, Senate, 69th Cong., 1st sess., *Hearings* on S. 2584 (1925-26).

23. *Congressional Record,* 71st Cong., 1st sess., LXXI (1929), 3570-71.

24. *Ibid.*

25. Peffer, *The Closing of the Public Domain,* p. 208.

26. 45 *Stat.* 380.

27. Harold Ickes, "The National Domain and the New Deal," *Saturday Evening Post* (December 23, 1933), p. 11.

28. U.S. Congress, House, *House Report 1719 on H. R. 11816*, 72nd Cong., 1st sess., (Washington: Government Printing Office, 1932), p. 7.

29. *Ibid.*, p. 6.

30. *Ibid.*

31. *Ibid.*, p. 1. Details of the Colton Bill are not discussed here because essentially the same provisions are embodied in the Taylor Grazing Act, which will be considered in some detail.

32. U.S. Congress, House, Committee on the Public Lands, "To Provide for the Orderly Use, Improvement, and Development of the Public Range," *Hearings*, 73rd Cong., 1st sess. (1933), on H.R. 2835, p. 26.

33. *Hearings*, 73rd Cong., on H.R. 2835, p. 3.

34. Letter of May 22, 1933 to Hon. René L. DeRouen, chairman, Committee on the Public Lands, House of Representatives, quoted in *Hearings*, 73rd Cong., on H.R. 2835.

35. *Hearings*, 73rd Cong., on H.R. 2835, p. 9.

36. *Ibid.*, p. 173.

37. F. R. Carpenter later became the first director of the Division of Grazing.

38. *Hearings*, 73rd Cong., on H.R. 2835, pp. 144-45.

39. *Ibid.*, p. 17.

40. *Ibid.*, p. 34-35.

41. *Ibid.*, p. 72.

42. *Congressional Record*, 73rd Cong., 2nd sess., LXXVIII (1934), 11146.

43. *Hearings*, 73rd Cong., on H.R. 2835, pp. 171-72.

44. *Ibid.*, pp. 101-2.

45. *Ibid.*, p. 189.

46. *Ibid.*, p. 101.

47. U.S. Congress, *Senate Hearings on H. R. 6462*, 73rd Cong., 2nd sess. (Washington: Government Printing Office, 1934), p. 41.

48. *Hearings*, 73rd Cong., on H.R. 2835, p. 188.

49. *Ibid.*, p. 179.

50. *Ibid.*, p. 141.

51. *Ibid.*, p. 42.

52. *Ibid.*, pp. 111, 192.

53. *Ibid.*, pp. 201-2.

54. *Ibid.*, p. 94.

55. *Ibid.*, p. 8.

56. *Ibid.*, pp. 10-11.

57. *Ibid.*, p. 6.

58. *Ibid.*

59. *Ibid.*, p. 7.

60. *Ibid.*, p. 77.

61. Peffer, *The Closing of the Public Domain,* p. 220.

62. *Congressional Record,* 73rd Cong., 2nd sess., LXXVIII (1934), 11162.

63. 48 *Stat.* 1269.

64. *Congressional Record,* 76th Cong., 3rd sess., LXXXVI (1940-41), 4198 (Appendix).

65. U.S. Department of Interior, Annual Report of the Secretary, 1935 (Washington: Government Printing Office, 1935), p. 13.

66. By amendment of June 26, 1936, 49 *Stat.* 1976.

67. U.S. Department of Interior, *The Taylor Grazing Act of June 28, 1934* (Washington: Government Printing Office, 1955), sec. 1, pp. 1-2.

68. *Ibid.,* sec. 2, pp. 2-3. 43 U.S.C., sec. 315a.

69. *Ibid.,* sec. 8, pp. 5-6. 43 U.S.C., sec. 315g.

70. *Ibid.,* sec. 9, pp. 6-7. 43 U.S.C., sec. 315h.

71. *Ibid.,* sec. 14, pp. 8-9. 43 U.S.C., sec. 1171.

72. *Ibid.,* sec. 15, p. 9. 43 U.S.C., sec. 315m.

73. *Ibid.,* sec. 10, p. 7. 43 U.S.C., sec. 315i.

74. 52 *Stat.* 1033.

75. *The Taylor Grazing Act,* sec. 18, pp. 9-10. 43 U.S.C., sec. 315o.

76. Russell Penny and Marion Clawson, "Administration of Grazing Districts," *Land Economics* (February, 1953), p. 26.

77. The *The Taylor Grazing Act,* 7, pp. 4-5. 43 U.S.C., sec. 315f.

78. *Ibid.,* sec. 3, p. 3. 43 U.S.C., sec. 315b.

79. This principle, usually called "commensurate property rights," is by no means a new concept. The earliest recorded Norwegian laws (probably about 1100) contain the following passage, "If two neighbors till the same farm, having rented the land from the same man, their farm is undivided land . . . neither one shall keep more live stock in the summer than he can feed through the winter. . . ." Laurence M. Larson (translator) *The Earliest Norwegian Laws* (New York: Columbia University Press, 1935) sec. 81, pp. 93-94.

80. Farrington R. Carpenter, "The Law of the Range," an address delivered at the 43rd annual meeting of the Colorado State Bar Association held at Colorado Springs, Colorado, September, 1940.

81. For a more detailed examination of this concept see John D. McGowen, "The Development of Political Institutions on the Public Domain," *University of Wyoming Publications,* XI (September 15, 1944), 49-64.

82. *The Taylor Grazing Act,* Sec. 3, p. 4. 43 U.S.C., sec. 315b.

83. U.S. Department of the Interior, *The Federal Range Code for Grazing Districts* (Washington: Government Printing Office, 1956), Sec. 161.1.

84. Transcript of remarks of F. R. Carpenter, director, Division of Grazing, Vale, Oregon, December 15, 1934, pp. 32, 39-40.

85. *The Federal Range Code for Grazing Districts*, Sec. 161. 7.

86. Rad Hall, assistant to the executive secretary, American National Livestock Association, "Only Grazing Can Convert the Great Grass Resources," *American Cattle Producer*, January, 1948, p. 36.

87. *The Federal Range Code for Grazing Districts*, sec. 161. 9.

88. *Ibid.*, sec. 161. 10.

89. Administrative Procedure Act of 1946. 5 U.S.C. 1010.

90. *Sellas* v. *Kirk*, 101 Fed. Supp. 237, (1951); affirmed 200 Fed. 2nd 217 (1953).

91. "Report of Study, Grazing District Offices, " Department of Interior, BLM, Washington, D.C., 1955, p. 19.

92. Adapted from Dent D. Dalby, hearing examiner, letter March 29, 1956 and report of the director, BLM, 1955, statistical appendix, p. 92.

93. Minutes of National Advisory Board Council Meeting, Salt Lake City, Utah, January 17-18, 1949.

94. *The Federal Range Code for Grazing Districts*, sec. 161. 10.

95. Letter from Dent D. Dalby, March 29, 1956.

96. *The Federal Range Code for Grazing Districts*, sec. 161. 6.

97. *Ibid.*, secs. 161. 9, 161. 6.

98. *The Taylor Grazing Act*, sec. 3, p. 3. 43 U.S.C., sec. 315b.

99. Letter from Lee Metcalf, Congressman from Montana, March 24, 1946: "If the permittee has complied with all the rules and regulations there would probably be no reason to deny renewal of his permit unless the available forage of the district was reduced by withdrawal of some of the grazing lands for other purposes or by extreme drought or other natural causes."

100. Memorandum August 5, 1953, Director Woozley to regional administrators: "Most grazing districts have been under administration for 16 or 17 years, but grazing privileges have not been properly adjudicated in many of them, and the present stocking of the Federal ranges under licenses and permits is materially greater than the grazing capacity of the range in many units."

Chapter 4

1. For a more detailed analysis of this concept see David B. Truman, *Administrative Decentralization* (Chicago: University of Chicago Press, 1940), p. 1.

2. 49 *Stat.*, 1976.

3. Farrington R. Carpenter, "The Law of the Range, " an address delivered at the 43rd annual meeting of the Colorado State Bar Association held at Colorado Springs, Colorado, September, 1940.

4. Report of the Director of the Bureau of Land Management. 1955 Statistical Appendix. Washington, D.C., p. 10.

5. Carpenter, *"The Law of the Range."*

6. Report of the Director of the Bureau of Land Management. 1955 Statistical Appendix. Washington, D.C., p. 93.

7. *Ibid.*

8. *Ibid.*, p. 97.

9. Letter from E. N. Kavanaugh, March 18, 1956.

10. Letter from F. R. Carpenter, February 18, 1956.

11. Letter from F. R. Carpenter, December 16, 1955.

12. Leon R. Nadeau, area range assistant, Bureau of Land Management. "Grazing Districts," memorandum of May 3, 1955.

13. U.S. Department of Interior, Annual Report of the Secretary, 1935 (Washington: Government Printing Office, 1935), p. 15.

14. Transcript of remarks of F. R. Carpenter, director, Division of Grazing, Vale, Oregon, December 15, 1934, p. 47.

15. Letter from E. N. Kavanaugh, March 18, 1956.

16. Letter from F. R. Carpenter, February 18, 1956.

17. U.S. Department of Interior, Annual Report of the Secretary, 1935 (Washington: Government Printing Office, 1935), p. 16.

18. *Ibid.*

19. *Ibid.*

20. U.S. Department of Interior, Annual Report of the Secretary, 1935 (Washington: Government Printing Office, 1935), pp. 16-17.

21. U.S. Department of Interior, Annual Report of the Secretary, 1940, p. 332; Annual Report of the Secretary, 1943, p. 188.

22. U.S. Department of Interior, Annual Report of the Secretary, 1936, pp. 15, 16.

23. *Ibid.*

24. U.S. Department of Interior, Annual Report of the Secretary, 1936, p. 17.

25. *Ibid.*, p. 18.

26. U.S. Department of Interior, Annual Report of the Secretary, 1940, p. 334.

27. *Ibid.*, p. 335.

28. *Ibid.*, pp. 332, 336, 338, 344.

29. U.S. Department of Interior, Annual Report of the Secretary, 1942, p. 143.

30. U.S. Department of Interior, Annual Report of the Secretary, 1945, p. 172.

31. *Ibid.*, p. 179.

32. U.S. Department of Interior, Annual Report of the Secretary, 1946, p. 263.

33. *Ibid.*, p. 270.

34. U.S. Department of Interior, Annual Report of the Secretary, 1947, p. 277.

35. *Ibid.*, pp. 278, 288.

36. Marion Clawson, *The Western Range Livestock Industry* (New

York: McGraw-Hill Book Co., 1950), p. 111.

37. U.S. Department of Interior, Annual Report of the Secretary, 1947, p. 283.

38. Transcript of remarks of F. R. Carpenter, director, Division of Grazing, Vale, Oregon, December 15, 1934, p. 4: "We expect them [advisory boards] to set the rules." R. K. Pierson, range officer, Bureau of Land Management, "Evolution of the Range Code," *Our Public Lands*, V (October, November, December, 1955), 3: "Proposed changes or additions to the Code are first submitted to the grazing district advisory boards authorized by the act for review as to their effect upon range operations. Following such study and recommendations by district and State advisory boards and the National Advisory Board Council acting in an advisory capacity to the Director, the Code is then revised and submitted to the Secretary for approval."

39. U.S. Department of Interior, Annual Report of the Secretary, 1947, p. 284.

40. *American Cattle Producer*, September, 1946, p. 13.

41. *Ibid.*

42. U.S. Department of Interior, Annual Report of the Secretary, 1948, p. 268.

43. *Ibid.*

44. Transcript of remarks of F. R. Carpenter, director, Division of Grazing, Vale, Oregon, December 15, 1934, p. 16.

45. U.S. Department of Interior, Annual Report of the Secretary, 1948, p. 263.

46. U.S. Department of Interior, Annual Report of the Secretary, 1952, p. 283.

47. Floyd Hart *et al.*, memorandum of December 18, 1953 to Assistant Secretary Lewis.

48. Memorandum to the director, Bureau of Land Management, from Assistant Secretary Lewis, January 26, 1954.

49. U.S. Department of Interior, Bureau of Land Management, *Managing the Federal Range* (Washington: Government Printing Office, 1954), p. 10.

50. U.S. Department of Interior, Bureau of Land Management, delegation order 541 dated April 21, 1954. Federal Register, April 28, 1954, pp. 2473-77.

51. Floyd Hart *et al.*, memorandum of December 18, 1953 to Assistant Secretary Lewis, p. 3.

52. Minutes of National Advisory Board Council Meeting, Washington, D.C., April 6-8, 1955.

53. Minutes of National Advisory Board Council Meeting, Salt Lake City, Utah, January 17-18, 1949.

54. See Brooks Adams, *The Theory of Social Revolutions*, (New York: Macmillan, 1913), chapter 6.

55. Truman, *Administrative Decentralization*, p. 15.

56. 43 U.S.C., sec. 315o.

57. Truman, *Administrative Decentralization,* p. 15.

Chapter 5

1. "Report of Study, Grazing District Offices, " U.S. Department of Interior, BLM, Washington, D.C., 1955, pp. 3, 4.

2. 43 CFR 161.12 (e).


Chapter 6

1. Farrington R. Carpenter, "The Law of the Range, " an address delivered at the 43rd annual meeting of the Colorado State Bar Association held at Colorado Springs, Colorado, September, 1940.

2. U.S. Department of Interior, Annual Report of the Secretary, 1935 (Washington: Government Printing Office, 1935), p. 16.

3. Letter from F. R. Carpenter to author, December 16, 1955.

4. U.S. Department of Interior, Bureau of Land Management, *The Taylor Grazing Act of June 28, 1934* (Washington: Government Printing Office, 1955), sec. 18. 43 U.S.C., sec., 315c-1.

5. U.S. Congress, Senate, 76th Cong., 1st sess., *Senate Report 505,* 1939.

6. Minutes of National Advisory Board Council Meeting, Denver, Colorado, July 20, 1940.

7. *Ibid.*

8. Letter of August 20, 1940, Director R. H. Rutledge to all regional graziers.

9. J. Russell Penny and Marion Clawson, "Administration of Grazing Districts, " *Land Economics,* February, 1953, p. 26.

10. *Ibid.*

11. U.S. Department of Interior, Bureau of Land Management, *The Federal Range Code for Grazing Districts* (Washington: Department of Interior, 1956), sec. 161.13.

12. *Ibid.*

13. Minutes, Oregon state advisory board meeting, Burns, Oregon, December 15, 1952.

14. *Ibid.*

15. *Ibid.*

16. U.S. Department of Interior, *The Federal Range Code for Grazing Districts,* sec. 161.13 (b).

17. Minutes, Oregon state advisory board meeting, Burns, Oregon, December 15, 1952.

18. Henry Gerber, Floyd C. Vaughn, Gaylord Madison.

19. Minutes of National Advisory Board Council, 1940-59.

20. *Ibid.*

21. See Grant McConnell, *The Decline of Agrarian Democracy* (Berkeley: University of California Press, 1953) for a detailed discussion of this question.

22. U.S. Department of Interior, *The Federal Range Code for Grazing Districts*, sec. 161.13 (e).

23. U.S. Department of Interior, *The Taylor Grazing Act*, sec. 18. 43 U.S.C., sec. 315o-1.

24. U.S. Congress, Senate, *Hearings*, Committee on Public Land and Surveys, Pursuant to Senate Res. 241, 77th Cong., I, 187.

25. Minutes of National Advisory Board Council meeting, December 2, 1951.

26. Transcript of remarks of F. R. Carpenter, director, Division of Grazing, Vale, Oregon, December 15, 1934.

27. U.S. Department of Interior, Annual Report of the Secretary, 1945 (Washington: Government Printing Office, 1945), p. 173.

28. U.S. Department of Interior, Annual Report of the Secretary, 1948 (Washington: Government Printing Office, 1948), p. 266.

29. U.S. Congress, Senate, *Hearings*, Committee on Public Lands and Surveys, Pursuant to Senate Res. 241, 77th Cong., V, 1851.

30. *Ibid.*, I, 190.

31. *Ibid.*, II, 375.

32. Personal letter. Writer's name withheld.

33. U.S. Congress, House, 80th Cong., 1st sess., *Hearings* on the Interior Appropriation Bill for 1948, p. 1234.

34. Minutes National Advisory Board Council meeting, February 25, 1954.

35. Transcript of remarks of F. R. Carpenter, Director, Division of Grazing, Vale, Oregon, December 15, 1934, p. 93.

36. Letter from F. R. Carpenter, December 16, 1955.

37. Minutes National Advisory Board Council Meetings, 1940-55.

38. Minutes National Advisory Board Council Meetings, 1951, 1953.

39. Stockmen's Grazing Committee, "The Federal Grazing Problem and the Stockman's Solution," Denver, Colorado, 1952.

40. See Samuel Phillips Huntington, Clientelism: A Study in Administrative Politics (Ph.D. dissertation, Harvard University, 1950), for a detailed consideration of this topic.

Chapter 7

1. Minutes, Oregon grazing district 4, February 17, 1936.

2. Letter of March 17, 1936, from Soldier Creek cattlemen to district advisory board.

3. Minutes, Soldier Creek grazing unit held September 18, 1936, in Jordan Valley, Oregon.

4. Letter from Marvin Klemme, April 23, 1957.

5. *Ibid.*

6. Minutes, Oregon grazing district 4, January 22-23, 1937.

7. Minutes, Oregon grazing district 4, November 16, 1940.

8. Letter of December 31, 1940, S. R. Bennett to Nick W. Monte, regional grazier.

9. Minutes, Oregon grazing district 4, December 20, 1940.

10. *Ibid.*

11. Minutes, Oregon grazing district 4, January 29, 1941.

12. Ross was elected to the state advisory board in 1940 and served until 1954.

13. Personal letter. Writer's name withheld.

14. Minutes, Oregon grazing district 4, March 25, 1943.

15. Letter from Sam Ross to author, February 2, 1956.

16. Minutes, Oregon grazing district 4, June 26, 1943.

17. Minutes, Oregon grazing district 4, June 26, 1943, December 18, 1943.

18. Data from Bureau of Land Management file, Oregon 1-RM-1.

19. Undated notes of district range manager Campbell.

20. Minutes, Oregon grazing district 4, February 22, 1946.

21. These are funds that are returned to the states by the federal government for range improvement. Ordinarily the expenditure of these funds is supervised by the district advisory boards.

22. Minutes, Oregon grazing district 4, January 25, 1946.

23. Undated notes of district range manager Campbell.

24. Member of Oregon grazing district 3 advisory board, state advisory board, National Advisory Board Council, one-time president of the Oregon Woolgrowers Association and brother of former United States Senator Stanfield of Oregon.

25. Letter, Gerald E. Stanfield to author, January 14, 1956.

26. Minutes, Oregon grazing district 3, February 18, 1947.

27. Letter of May 10, 1948, district range manager M. H. Galt to regional grazier Kelso P. Newman.

28. Memorandum of May 14, 1948, regional grazier Kelso P. Newman to district range manager M. H. Galt.

29. Letter, Donald J. McKay, advisory board member, Jordan Valley, Oregon, to author, January 1, 1956.

30. Minutes, Oregon grazing district 3, January 22, 1948.

31. Minutes, Oregon grazing district 3, February 1, 1949.

32. Minutes, Oregon grazing district 3, November 8, 1949.

33. Letter, Marion Clawson to author, February 10, 1956.

34. Letter, Gerald E. Stanfield to author, January 14, 1956.

35. Letter, Sam Ross to author, February 2, 1956.

36. Undated notes of district range manager A. K. Hansen.

37. Jones is also a former president of the Oregon Woolgrowers Association.

38. Letter, David T. Jones to author, January 2, 1956.

39. *Ibid.*

40. Minutes, Oregon grazing district 3, February 4-8, 1952.

41. *Ibid.*

42. Minutes, National Advisory Board Council, December 2, 1951.

43. Letter of February 27, 1952, M. A. Easterday to Secretary of Agriculture (in error).

44. Letter of August 14, 1952, Stewart Elsner to Senator Herman Welker.

45. Minutes, Oregon grazing district 3, October 20, 21, 22, 1952.

46. Technically, the district range manager already had that responsibility.

47. Minutes, Oregon grazing district 3, October 20, 21, 22, 1952.

48. *Ibid.*

49. Personal letter. Writer's name withheld.

50. U.S. Department of Interior, Bureau of Land Management, *The Federal Range Code for Grazing Districts* (Washington: Department of Interior, 1956), sec. 161.6.

51. Minutes, Oregon grazing district 3, December 17-20, 1952.

52. Minutes, Oregon grazing district 3, January 19-24, 1953.

53. Letter of January 13, 1953, Tex Payne to district range manager, Oregon grazing district 3.

54. Minutes, Oregon grazing district 3, January 19-24, 1953. We should note that this was the statement of the Chairman of the Oregon state advisory board and a member of the National Advisory Board Council.

55. *Ibid.*

56. Telegram of January 24, 1953, to Sam Coon, U.S. Representative, from David T. Jones, Burns, Oregon.

57. Letter of January 26, 1953, Sam Coon to Douglas McKay, Secretary of the Interior, Washington, D.C.

58. Memorandum of January 28, 1953, Director Clawson to Secretary McKay.

59. Letter of February 14, 1953, M. F. Hanley to Secretary McKay.

60. Letter of February 15, 1953, Mr. and Mrs. Richard Staples to Secretary McKay.

61. The Jaca Brothers ranch was supposedly mortgaged to Sam Ross.

62. Letter of February 2, 1953, Jaca Brothers, Jordan Valley, Oregon, to Secretary McKay.

63. Letter of February 24, 1953, Fred Morton to Secretary McKay. On April 3, Morton was found to have cattle on the federal range in trespass and paid charges of $150.00.

64. It will be recalled that Elsner was cited for trespass in 1952.

65. Letter of November 2, 1953, Stewart Elsner to Secretary of Agriculture.

66. Letter of November 16, 1953, Dr. A. D. Woodmansee to Secretary McKay.

67. Letter, Gerald E. Stanfield to author, January 14, 1956.

68. Memorandum of December 23, 1953, regional chief to district range manager, Vale, Oregon.

69. Letter of February 9, 1954, Malheur County Court, Vale, Oregon to Secretary McKay, Senator Cordon, Representatives Walter Norblad, Homer Angell, Harris Ellsworth, and Sam Coon.

70. Letter of February 24, 1954, Director Edward Woozley to Senator Guy Cordon.

71. U.S. General Accounting Office, Division of Audits, Report on Audit of Region I, Portland, Oregon, Bureau of Land Management, Department of Interior. For the fiscal year ending June 30, 1954.

72. Memorandum of December 23, 1954, acting director W. G. Guernsey to area administrator, area I.

73. Dent D. Dalby, hearing examiner, decision of February 4, 1955 on appeals of Raymond E. Gluch, M. F. Hanley, Loveland Brothers, Frank Maher, and Dallas Payne.

74. Skinner is a member of one of the oldest and most influential families in southeastern Oregon. He apparently made his offer entirely on his own volition, to be a "good neighbor" and because he was weary of years of squabbling. Skinner. is also the largest operator in the Soldier Creek unit and may have felt some moral compulsion to make a concession.

75. See appendix.

76. *Malheur Enterprise,* January 19, 1956.

Chapter 8

1. See A. Leiper Freeman, *The Political Process* (New York: Doubleday, 1955), pp. 1-15, for a discussion of the concept of subsystems and subunits. A similar concept called "whirlpools of activity focusing on particular problems" is considered by Ernest S. Griffith, *Congress: Its Contemporary Role* (New York: New York University Press, 1951), pp. 37-38.

2. See Paul H. Appleby, *Policy and Administration* (University: University of Alabama Press, 1949), pp. 10-15.

3. U.S. Congress, House, Committee on Public Lands, *Hearings,* 73rd Cong., 1st sess., (1933), on H. R. 2835, p. 16.

4. U.S. Congress, Senate, Committee on Public Lands and Surveys, *Hearings,* 73rd Cong., 2nd sess., (1934), on H. R. 6462, p. 7.

5. U.S. Congress, House, Committee on Public Lands, *Hearings,* 73rd Cong., 1st sess., (1933), on H. R. 2835, p. 68.

6. U.S. Department of Interior, Bureau of Land Management, *The Taylor Grazing Act of June 28, 1934* (Washington: Government Printing Office, 1955), sec. 3, p. 3.

7. Transcript of remarks of F. R. Carpenter, director, Division of Grazing, Vale, Oregon, December 14, 1934, p. 82.

8. U.S. Department of Interior, Annual Report of the Secretary, 1939 (Washington: Government Printing Office, 1939), p. xi. The Grazing Service, in the person of grazier Brooks, demurred and assigned as reasons, among others, that the complaint failed to state facts suf-

ficient to constitute a case against him and that the District Court was without jurisdiction. The District Court overruled the demurrer with leave to answer. Brooks elected to stand upon his demurrer and the court thereupon entered a decree in favor of the plaintiffs, Dewar and Others.

9. *Dewar* v. *Brooks*, 60 Nev. 219; 106 P 2d 755.

10. *Dewar* v. *Brooks*, 313 U.S. 354. Justice Roberts also held that, since the judgment of the Nevada court was erroneous on the merits of the case, the Supreme Court would "abstain from inquiring" as to whether or not it was acting outside its jurisdiction.

11. U.S. Congress, House, subcommittee of the Committee on Appropriations, *Hearings*, 79th Cong., 1st sess., (1945) on Interior Department, Appropriations Bill for 1946, part 1, p. 469.

12. Report of the director of the Bureau of Land Management, 1955 Statistical Appendix, Washington, D.C., p. 93.

13. U.S. Congress, House subcommittee of the Committee on Appropriations, *Hearings,* 79th Cong., 1st sess., (1945) on Interior Department, Appropriations Bill for 1946, part 1, p. 470.

14. *Congressional Record,* 76th Congress, 3rd sess., LXXXVI (1940-41), 2593.

15. Senate Res. 241, 76th Cong., extended by Senate Res. 147, 77th Cong., Senate Res. 39, 78th Cong., and Senate Res. 139, 79th Cong.

16. Bureau of Land Management, A Comparison of Grazing Fees on National Forests and Grazing Districts. Unpublished paper prepared for National Advisory Board Council meeting, September 6, 1950.

17. Senator Pat McCarran, "A Report on Public Land Grazing Fees, " *American Cattle Producer,* June, 1946, p. 8.

18. Bureau of Land Management, "A Comparison of Grazing Fees on National Forests and Grazing Districts, " 1950.

19. Minutes, National Advisory Board Council meeting, January 5, 1942.

20. Letter of April 2, 1942, Secretary Ickes to Senator Hatch of New Mexico.

21. U.S. Congress, Senate, 78th Cong., 1st sess., *Senate Report 404,* (1943), Appendix B, p. 83.

22. U.S. Congress, Senate, 79th Cong., 2nd sess., *Senate Report 808,* part 2, (1946), p. 20-21.

23. U.S. Congress, House, subcommittee of the Committee on Appropriations, *Hearings,* 77th Cong., 2nd sess., on the Interior Department Appropriations Bill for 1943, part 1, p. 133.

24. U.S. Congress, House, subcommittee of the Committee on Appropriations, *Hearings,* 78th Cong., 2nd sess., on the Interior Department Appropriations Bill for 1945, p. 127.

25. *Ibid.,* p. 129.

26. *Ibid.,* p. 131.

27. *Ibid.,* p. 133.

28. The NABC passed this resolution late in 1944.

29. *Congressional Record,* 78th Cong., 2nd sess., XC, (1944), 9558-59.

30. B. L. Bunker, "The Taylor Grazing Act," *Congressional Record*, 79th Cong., 1st sess., XCI, (1945), 665-66, appendix.

31. Letter of December 15, 1944, Secretary Ickes to Senator McCarran.

32. Letter of January 5, 1945, Senator McCarran to Secretary Ickes.

33. Letter of February 9, 1945, Senator McCarran to Secretary Ickes.

34. U.S. Congress, House, *Hearings* before a subcommittee of the Committee on Appropriations, 79th Cong., 1st sess., on the Interior Department Appropriations Bill for 1946, p. 463.

35. Senator Pat McCarran, "A Report on Public Land Grazing Fees," *American Cattle Producer,* June, 1946, p. 15.

36. Letter of January 25, 1946, Secretary Ickes to Senator Carl A. Hatch.

37. U.S. Congress, House, *Hearings* before a subcommittee of the Committee on Appropriations, 79th Cong., 2nd sess., on the Interior Department Appropriations Bill for 1947, p. 147.

38. *Ibid.,* p. 148.

39. *Ibid.,* p. 161.

40. *Ibid.,* p. 156.

41. U.S. Congress, House, *Hearings* before a subcommittee of the Committee on Appropriations, 79th Cong., 2nd sess., on the Interior Department Appropriations Bill for 1947, p. 148.

42. *Ibid.,* pp. 174, 177.

43. *Ibid.,* pp. 1252-54.

44. *Congressional Record,* 79th Cong., 2nd sess., XCII, (1946), 4634.

45. *Ibid.,* pp. 4690-94.

46. U.S. Department of Interior, Annual Report of the Secretary, 1947 (Washington: Government Printing Office, 1947), p. 277.

47. *Ibid.,* p. 283.

48. *Ibid.,* p. 284.

49. *61 Stat.* 630, July 30, 1947.

50. Tabulation prepared by Bureau of Land Management.

51. F. E. Mollin, "Mollin Clarifies," *American Cattle Producer*, August, 1947, p. 22.

52. William B. Wright, "President Wright Testifies on Grazing Appropriations," *American Cattle Producer,* June, 1947, p. 8.

53. U.S. Department of Interior, Annual Report of the Secretary, 1948 (Washington: Government Printing Office, 1948), p. 268.

54. Bureau of Land Management, "A Comparison of Grazing Fees on National Forests and Grazing Districts," 1950.

55. *Ibid.*

56. Minutes, National Advisory Board Council meeting, September 6, 1950.

57. Minutes, National Advisory Board Council meeting, February 16-19, 1953.

58. G. M. Kerr, A Basis for Determining Grazing Fees in Grazing Districts, November, 1954.

59. U.S. District Court for the District of Nevada, Order No. 1213, August 8, 1955.

60. Letter E. R. Greenslet, Nevada State Supervisor, Bureau of Land Management, to author February 11, 1958.

61. *Federal Register*, January 28, 1958, p. 546.

# BIBLIOGRAPHY

*Books*

Adams, Brooks. *The Theory of Social Revolutions.* New York: Macmillan Co., 1913.

Adams, James Truslow (ed.). *Hamiltonian Principles: Extracts from the Writings of Alexander Hamilton.* Boston: Little, Brown and Co., 1928.

Appleby, Paul H. *Policy and Administration.* University: University of Alabama Press, 1949.

Bales, Robert F. *Interaction Process Analysis.* Cambridge, Mass.: Addison-Wesley Press, 1950.

Barnes, Will C. *The Story of the Range.* Washington: Government Printing Office, 1926.

Clawson, Marion. *Uncle Sam's Acres.* New York: Dodd, Mead and Co., 1951.

-------. *The Western Range Livestock Industry.* New York: McGraw-Hill Book Co., 1950.

DeVoto, Bernard (ed.). *The Journals of Lewis and Clark.* Boston: Houghton Mifflin Co., 1953.

Dicken, Samuel N. *Oregon Geography.* Ann Arbor, Michigan: Edwards Bros., 1950.

Fenneman, Nevin M. *Physiography of the Western United States.* New York: McGraw-Hill Book Co., 1931.

Freeman, A. Lieper. *The Political Process.* New York: Doubleday and Co., 1955.

Frémont, John C. *Memoirs of My Life.* Chicago: Belford, Clarke and Co., 1886.

Griffith, Ernest S. *Congress: Its Contemporary Role.* New York: New York University Press, 1951.

Hibbard, Benjamin H. *A History of the Public Land Policies.* New York: Macmillan Co., 1924.

McConnell, Grant. *The Decline of Agrarian Democracy*. Berkeley: University of California Press, 1953.

McKinley, Charles. *Uncle Sam in the Pacific Northwest.* Berkeley: University of California Press, 1952.

Osgood, Ernest S. *The Day of the Cattleman*. Minneapolis: University of Minnesota Press, 1929.

Parkman, Francis. *The Oregon Trail*. Boston: Little, Brown and Co., 1920.

Peake, Ora B. *The Colorado Range Cattle Industry*. Glendale, Calif.: Arthur H. Clark Co., 1937.

Peffer, E. Louise. *The Closing of the Public Domain*. Stanford: Stanford University Press, 1951.

Richardson, James D. *Messages and Papers of the Presidents*. Vol. VII. New York: Bureau of National Literature and Art, 1903.

Robbins, Roy M. *Our Landed Heritage*. Princeton: Princeton University Press, 1942.

Sampson, Arthur W. *Range Management Principles and Practices*. New York: John Wiley and Sons, 1952.

Saunderson, Mont H. *Western Land and Water Use*. Norman: University of Oklahoma Press, 1950.

Selznick, Philip. *TVA and the Grass Roots*. Berkeley and Los Angeles: University of California Press, 1949.

Stephenson, George M. *The Political History of the Public Lands*. Boston: Richard D. Badger, 1917.

Truman, David B. *Administrative Decentralization.* Chicago: University of Chicago Press, 1940.

Webb, Walter P. *The Great Plains*. Boston: Ginn and Co., 1931.

Winship, George P. (trans.) *The Journey of Francisco Vazquez de Coronado*. San Francisco: Grabhorn Press, 1953.

## Public Documents

Dalby, Dent D., hearing examiner, BLM. Decision of February 4, 1955 on Appeals of Raymond Gluch, M. F. Hanley, Loveland Brothers, Frank Maher, and Dallas Payne.

*Dewar v. Brooks*, 313 U.S. 354.

Donaldson, Thomas C. *The Public Domain*. 46th Cong., 3rd sess., H.R. Ex. Doc. 47. 1881.

National Advisory Board Council. Minutes of Meeting, July 20, 1940.

-------. Minutes of Meeting, January 5, 1942.

-------. Minutes of Meeting, February 15, 1944.

-------. Minutes of Meeting, April 27, 1945.

-------. Minutes of Meeting, August 17, 1946.

-------. Minutes of Meeting, May 4-7, 1948.

-------. Minutes of Meeting, January 17-18, 1949.

-------. Minutes of Meeting, September 6, 1950.

‒‒‒‒‒‒‒. Minutes of Meeting, December 2, 1951.
‒‒‒‒‒‒‒. Minutes of Meeting, February 16-19, 1953.
‒‒‒‒‒‒‒. Minutes of Meeting, February 25-27, 1954.
‒‒‒‒‒‒‒. Minutes of Meeting, August 2-3, 1954.
‒‒‒‒‒‒‒. Minutes of Meeting, April 6-8, 1955.
Oregon Grazing District No. 4. Minutes of Meeting, July 13, 1935.
‒‒‒‒‒‒‒. Minutes of Meeting, August 17, 1935.
‒‒‒‒‒‒‒. Minutes of Meeting, February 17, 1936.
‒‒‒‒‒‒‒. Minutes of Meeting, January 22-23, 1937.
‒‒‒‒‒‒‒. Minutes of Meeting, November 16, 1940.
‒‒‒‒‒‒‒. Minutes of Meeting, December 20, 1940.
‒‒‒‒‒‒‒. Minutes of Meeting, January 29, 1941.
‒‒‒‒‒‒‒. Minutes of Meeting, March 25, 1943.
‒‒‒‒‒‒‒. Minutes of Meeting, June 26, 1943.
‒‒‒‒‒‒‒. Minutes of Meeting, December 18, 1943.
‒‒‒‒‒‒‒. Minutes of Meeting, January 5, 1946.
‒‒‒‒‒‒‒. Minutes of Meeting, January 25, 1946.
‒‒‒‒‒‒‒. Minutes of Meeting, February 22, 1946.
‒‒‒‒‒‒‒. Minutes of Meeting, May 13, 1946.
Oregon Grazing District No. 3. Minutes of Meeting, February 18, 1947.
‒‒‒‒‒‒‒. Minutes of Meeting, January 22, 1948.
‒‒‒‒‒‒‒. Minutes of Meeting, February 1, 1949.
‒‒‒‒‒‒‒. Minutes of Meeting, November 8, 1949.
‒‒‒‒‒‒‒. Minutes of Meeting, February 4-8, 1952.
‒‒‒‒‒‒‒. Minutes of Meeting, October 20-22, 1952.
‒‒‒‒‒‒‒. Minutes of Meeting, December 17-20, 1952.
‒‒‒‒‒‒‒. Minutes of Meeting, January 19-24, 1953.
Oregon State Advisory Board. Minutes of Meeting, February 7-9, 1940.
‒‒‒‒‒‒‒. Minutes of Meeting, March 2, 1946.
‒‒‒‒‒‒‒. Minutes of Meeting, November 22, 1949.
‒‒‒‒‒‒‒. Minutes of Meeting, November 17, 1950.
‒‒‒‒‒‒‒. Minutes of Meeting, November 14, 1951.
‒‒‒‒‒‒‒. Minutes of Meeting, December 15, 1952.
‒‒‒‒‒‒‒. Minutes of Meeting, November 3, 1953.
‒‒‒‒‒‒‒. Minutes of Meeting, December 10, 1954.
‒‒‒‒‒‒‒. Minutes of Meeting, February 2, 1956.
*Sellas* v. *Kirk*. 101 Fed. Supp. 237, (1951); Affirmed 200 Fed. 2nd 217 (1953).
Soldier Creek Grazing Unit. Minutes of Meeting, September 18, 1936. Jordan Valley, Oregon.
U.S. Department of Interior, BLM. Accomplishments—Soil and Moisture Conservation Operations in Grazing Districts 1935-1948. (Mimeographed).
‒‒‒‒‒‒‒. Delegation Order 541 dated April 21, 1954. *Federal Register,* April 28, 1954.
U.S. Department of Interior, Division of Grazing. Transcript of Pro-

ceedings, Meeting of December 15, 1934. Vale, Oregon.

---------. *The Taylor Grazing Act of June 28, 1934.* Washington: Government Printing Office, 1955.

---------. *The Federal Range Code for Grazing Districts.* Washington: Government Printing Office, 1956.

U.S. Congress. *Congressional Debates,* 19th Cong., 1st sess.

---------. *Congressional Globe,* 28th Cong., 2nd sess., Vol. XIV.

---------. *Congressional Globe,* 40th Cong., 2nd sess., Appendix.

---------. *Congressional Record,* 44th Cong., 2nd sess., Vol. V.

---------. *Congressional Record,* 60th Cong., 1st sess., Vol. XLII, (1907-8).

---------. *Congressional Record,* 62nd Cong., 2nd sess., Vol. XLVIII, (1911-12).

---------. *Congressional Record,* 68th Cong., 2nd sess., S. Res. 347, LXVI, (1925-26).

---------. *Congressional Record,* 71st Cong., 1st sess., Vol. LXXI, (1929).

---------. *Congressional Record,* 73rd Cong., 2nd sess., Vol. LXXVIII, (1934).

---------. *Congressional Record,* 76th Cong., 3rd sess., Vol. LXXXVI, (1940-41).

---------. *Congressional Record,* 78th Cong., 2nd sess., Vol. XC, (1944).

---------. *Congressional Record,* 79th Cong., 1st sess., Vol. XCI, (1945). Appendix.

---------. *Congressional Record,* 79th Cong., 2nd sess., Vol. XCII, (1946).

---------. House, *House Report 1719 on H.R. 11816,* 72nd Cong., 1st sess., (1932).

---------. House, Committee on the Public Lands. *Hearings on H.R. 2835.* 73rd Cong., 1st sess. (1933).

---------. House, Committee on the Public Lands. *Hearings on H.R. 6462.* 73rd Cong., 2nd sess. (1934).

---------. House, subcommittee of the Committee on Appropriations. *Hearings* on the Interior Department Appropriations Bill for 1943. Part 1. 77th Cong., 2nd sess.

---------. House, subcommittee of the Committee on Appropriations. *Hearings* on the Interior Department Appropriations Bill for 1945. 78th Cong., 2nd sess.

---------. House, subcommittee of the Committee on Appropriations. *Hearings* on the Interior Department Appropriations Bill for 1946. Part 1. 79th Cong., 1st sess.

---------. House, subcommittee of the Committee on Appropriations. *Hearings* on the Interior Department Appropriations Bill for 1947. 79th Cong., 2nd sess.

---------. House, subcommittee of the Committee on Appropriations.

*Hearings* on the Interior Department Appropriations Bill for 1948. 80th Cong., 1st sess.
-------. Senate, *Hearings* on S. 2584. 69th Cong., 1st sess. (1925-26).
-------. Senate, *Hearings* on H.R. 6462. 73rd Cong., 2nd sess. (1934).
-------. Senate, Committee on Public Lands and Surveys. *Hearings* Pursuant to Senate Res. 241, 77th Cong.,.Vols. I, II, V.
-------. Senate, *The Western Range*. Senate Document 199, 74th Cong., 2nd sess. (1936).
-------. Senate, *Senate Report 505*, 76th Cong., 1st sess. (1939).
-------. Senate, *Senate Report 404*, Appendix B. 78th Cong., 1st sess. (1943).
-------. Senate, *Senate Report 808*, Part 2. 79th Cong., 2nd sess. (1946).

### Reports

Bureau of Land Management, *Managing the Federal Range*. Washington, 1954.
-------. Report of the Director, Statistical Appendix. Washington, 1955.
-------. *The Public Domain in 1953*. Washington, 1953.
-------. Report of Study, Grazing District Offices. Washington, 1955.
General Land Office. Reports of the Commissioner. Washington, 1877.
Powell, J. W. *Report on the Lands of the Arid Region of the United States*. Washington, 1879.
Texas General Land Office. *Report of the Commissioner*. 1932.
U.S. Department of Interior. Annual Report of the Secretary. 1886.
-------. Annual Report of the Secretary. 1915.
-------. Annual Reports of the Secretary. 1935-52.
U.S. General Accounting Office, Division of Audits. Report on Audit of Region I, Portland, Oregon, Bureau of Land Management, Department of Interior. For the Fiscal Year ended June 30, 1954.

### Articles

*American Sheep Breeder and Wool Grower*, XXXVI (January, 1916), 25; XXXVIII (January, 1917), 19.
Foss, Phillip O. "The Determination of Grazing Fees on Federally-Owned Range Lands," *Journal of Farm Economics*, August, 1959, pp. 535-47.
Hall, Rad. "Only Grazing Can Convert the Great Grass Resources," *American Cattle Producer*, January, 1948, p. 36.
Ickes, Harold. "The National Domain and the New Deal," *Saturday Evening Post*, December 23, 1933, p. 11.
*Malheur Enterprise*, January 19, 1956.
McCarran, Pat. "A Report on Public Land Grazing Fees," *American*

*Cattle Producer*, June, 1946, pp. 8, 15.

Mollin, F. E. "Mollin Clarifies," *American Cattle Producer*, August, 1947, p. 22.

McGowen, John D. "The Development of Political Institutions on the Public Domain," *University of Wyoming Publications*, XI (September 15, 1944), 49-64.

Penny, J. Russell, and Marion Clawson. "Administration of Grazing Districts," *Land Economics*, February, 1953, pp. 23-24.

Pierson, R. K. "Evolution of the Range Code," *Our Public Lands*, October-November-December, 1955, p. 3.

Wengert, Norman, "How Agricultural Policy is Made," *Farm Policy Forum*, VII (Winter, 1955), 30.

Woozley, Edward. "New Grazing Fee Explained," *Our Public Lands*, April-May-June, 1955, p. 10.

Wright, William B. "President Wright Testifies on Grazing Appropriations," *American Cattle Producer*, June, 1947, p. 8.